"Tim Teeman's biography of Gore Vidal is the perfect combination of racy gossip—from steamy celebrity liaisons to hustlers in Rome—and penetrating analysis. It shows how a complicated attitude to sex and sexuality shaped an author's life and work. An original, intriguing, and necessary portrait of an American icon."

—Edmund White, author of *City Boy*

"Sex with hustlers and Hollywood stars—for all his insistence that sexuality did not define him, Gore Vidal sure got around. And while he didn't hit the streets with placards, he was still, in many ways, a gay rights revolutionary. Tim Teeman's biography, full of new material and interviews, reveals how Vidal's sexuality and sex life influenced his life and his work—and tells, for the first time, the moving story of his painful last years. With deftness, wit, intelligence, and a journalist's nose for a good story, Teeman pulls back the curtain on an American icon. It seems Gore Vidal can still surprise us. What a page-turner!"

—William J. Mann, author of *Kate: The Woman Who Was Hepburn* and *Hello, Gorgeous: Becoming Barbra Streisand*

"Gore Vidal was a good friend for over sixty years. If you want to know who Gore really was, read *In Bed with Gore Vidal*, which uncovers, and evokes, his complicated private life and how that influenced and shaped his wider life, politics, and work. Lost loves, sex with hustlers, a life with Howard Austen, his relationships with women and the truth about his sexuality: this is a juicy, intelligent and honest portrait of a dear friend and exceptional writer and man."

—Scotty Bowers, author of *Full Service: My Adventures in Hollywood and the Secret Sex Lives of the Stars*

In Bed with Gore Vidal

In Bed with Gore Vidal

*Hustlers, Hollywood, and the Private
World of an American Master*

Tim Teeman

MAGNUS
BOOKS

Magnus Books
An Imprint of Riverdale Avenue Books
5676 Riverdale Ave., Suite 101
Bronx, NY 10471

Printed in the United States of America

First Edition

Cover by: Nick Vogelson, Townhouse Creative
Cover photo used by permission of the Granger Collection, New York

Print ISBN: 978-1-62601-041-3
Digital ISBN: 978-1-62601-040-6

www.riverdaleavebooks.com

For David, Neil, Anna, Leonie and John

Table of Contents

Acknowledgments

Thanks to Burr Steers and Nina Straight for talking about their uncle and brother so openly and for all their help. Thanks to Matt Tyrnauer for his invaluable advice, generosity and guidance, and to Juan Bastos for his many introductions in Los Angeles, his driving—which was beyond the call of duty—and for the wonderful pictures. Thanks to Claire Bloom, Susan Sarandon and Scotty Bowers for not only talking about Gore, but so candidly; the same to Jean Stein, Boaty Boatwright, Fred Kaplan, Jason Epstein and Jay Parini; also to Steven Abbott, Sean Strub, Jack Larson, Fabian Bouthillette, Grace Millar, Patrick Merla, Richard Harrison, Felice Picano, Edmund White, Michael Childers, David Schweizer, Nicholas Wrathall, Judith Harris, Tom Powers, Barbara Howar, Elinor Pruder and her son Hubert, Norberto Nierras, Kenneth M. Walsh, Jeremy Coleman, and Christopher Murray and to the many others who spoke on and off the record. Thanks to Bernie Woolf for guiding me to Walter Clemons's unseen manuscript.

My dear friend, the journalist Liza Foreman, carried out essential research and interviews in Italy, adding immeasurably to the book. Christopher Bram and William J. Mann kindly read the manuscript and their wise suggestions and guidance greatly enhanced and improved it. Nick Vogelson designed a beautiful book-jacket.

Thanks to the staff at the Houghton Library at Harvard University, where Vidal's archive is held, for their patience and professionalism. Emilie L. Hardman was particularly sterling, sourcing and holding material and was understanding when various complications impeded my journeys there. Thanks for similar accommodation, efficiency and expertise to John C. Johnson, Manager of Digital Archival Resources in the Gotlieb

Center of the Mugar Library at Boston University, and to Janet Lorenz at the National Film Information Service/Margaret Herrick Library at the Academy of Motion Picture Arts and Sciences in Los Angeles.

Thanks also to friends and colleagues: to Bruce Shenitz and Richard Canning for setting me off on my journey, Michael Zam, Bob Smith, Richard Schneider, Eric Price, Philip Sherwell, Paul Schindler, Erica Wagner, Paul Clements, Debra Craine, Brian Sills, Jeffrey Trachtenberg, Mark Lasswell, Robbie Millen, Nancy Durrant, Michael Carroll, Nicola Jeal, Alex Frean, Eric Gutierrez, Alex O'Connell, James Harding, Neil Fisher, Catherine Nixey, Neil McKenna, Will Pavia, David Robertson, Tom Gatti, Tom Farina, Paul Burston, Matthew Todd, Celia Duncan, Abigail Radnor, Richard Chapman, Stephen Foley and William Candia. And to Don Weise, my editor and publisher, thank you for your expertise, guidance and for such an unexpected adventure.

Prologue

Outpost Drive: Los Angeles, December 2012

Nearly five months after Gore Vidal's death, colorful Christmas baubles hung on the wall outside the author's Spanish Revival home on Outpost Drive in the Hollywood hills. Inside, the Master no longer home, there was still a fierce, irascible presence to contend with: Baby Rat, his seven-year-old King Charles spaniel now under the care of Vidal's major domo Norberto Nierras, was primed to snarl and yap at any stranger's feet and "pisses all over the house," Burr Steers, Vidal's nephew, said.

Vidal died, aged eighty-six, of complications from pneumonia on July 31, 2012 in the early evening in a bed set up in his downstairs living room so he could look out to his garden, including the tall fir trees that so reminded him of his years living in Rome in the 1960s: his very own *Dolce Vita* featuring a lot of sex with beautiful young men. He enjoyed looking at a fountain pool filled with koi, erected by Muzius Gordon Dietzmann, his unofficial godson and for many years a devoted caregiver. But Vidal's death had been anything but peaceful, marked by heavy drinking, dementia, painful feuding with family and friends, and a "miserable, drawn-out" decline, according to Burr Steers. "I really loved him," he says, sitting in the living room. "I stuck with him in those last few days. He was like a pretzel, all twisted up. You could hear him dying from the inside out, it really fucking affected me. It was really sad how it all ended up."

Other rooms showed the Vidal legacy in transition: a collection of family pictures in random groupings and books being boxed up. The eighty-six-year-old author left everything, all his possessions and fortune (an estimated 37 million dollars, according to Nina Straight, his half-sister; "a not inconsiderable chunk of change" Steers said with a smile), to Harvard University with "a few paintings" going to the Huntington Library in San Marino,

California, Steers told me. Vidal left nothing to his family, even though Steers had been promised, verbally, the Outpost Drive house. His mother, Nina Straight, revealed this to me rather than Steers; he seemed relaxed or resigned at his uncle's will provisions, having already endured, very painfully and upsettingly, the reverberations of his mental and physical decline.

In death as in life, Vidal continues to unsettle, cause trouble, ruffle feathers, confound. Nina and three other half-siblings were, at the time of this writing in June 2013, challenging the will on the grounds of Vidal's "mental competence" in the spring of 2011 when the late codicil, awarding Harvard everything, was drafted. They would like Vidal's verbal wish, that Steers get the Outpost Drive property, to be respected and a sum of money to be made available to the devoted Nierras. According to Nina, there is an unpaid debt "of close to a million dollars" Vidal owed to her, arising from the sequence of legal tussles he had with his conservative adversary William F. Buckley, who famously called Vidal a "queer" in a television confrontation in 1968. A Harvard University spokesman told me the university was not "involved" with the legal challenge "and awaits resolution of all issues" before it would comment on the bequest and how its proceeds would be spent. Those overseeing Vidal's estate would not cooperate with this book, or give me access to whatever papers and documents of Vidal's the Estate holds.

The Outpost Drive house felt as if it was entering a period of uncertain hibernation. In a raised part of the garden, a full-length swimming pool was full of water but was a brackish mess of dirt and cracks. "You could see William Holden floating face down in this, couldn't you?" Steers said drily to me. "Norma Desmond was kind of what Gore was becoming."

The house contained its own encapsulating version of the Vidal story: the author's twenty-five novels, twenty-six non-fictional works, including books of essays, fourteen screenplays and eight stage plays were neatly ordered on shelves. When I interviewed him in 2009 for the *Times of London*, I said to Vidal that he had crossed every boundary. "Crashed many barriers," he cor-rected me. "It's a museum of a house," noted Steers as he took me around. The walls of Vidal's bedroom were lined, in a concise echo of Vidal's super-sized ego, with magazine covers—from *Time* to gay literary magazine *Christopher Street*—featuring the author.

Steers revealed that his uncle had moved to the room down the hall of his longtime partner, Howard Austen, who died in 2004, when, getting sicker, he started having hallucinations of raccoons in his own room. "Poor Norberto would have to pretend to pursue the raccoons out with a broom," Steers said as we looked at Vidal's now empty bed. Later Vidal moved downstairs to the living room to die. A television, on which he watched CNN, still faced his bed. Above his bed hung a small portrait of Theodosia Burr, the daughter of Aaron Burr, US Vice President between 1801 and 1805, and the subject of one of Vidal's historical novels.

Vidal was so thrifty, "perhaps a Depression-era thing," says Steers, he wouldn't install air conditioning so his nephew bought him a special unit. A jumbled treasure trove of pictures stood against a wall: of Vidal's good friend, the actress Susan Sarandon with her son Miles (Vidal's godson), his friend the musician and writer John Latouche, Raquel Welch from the critically panned 1970 film of his celebrated novel *Myra Breckinridge*, and the artist Don Bachardy's beautifully detailed pencil drawing of Austen, dated February 4, 1977. There was a poster for Vidal's 1982 campaign running in the California primary for the Democratic nomination for the US Senate, proclaiming him "the serious alternative" (to Jerry Brown who went on to win). Vidal also ran for office in 1960 as the Democratic Congressional candidate for the 29th District in upstate New York, where he also lost.

A photograph of the writer as a young man, handsome with bee-stung lips and an air of hauteur, was propped alongside first editions of Henry James, Nadine Gordimer and Caleb Carr, a full-length cutout of Abraham Lincoln to advertise a talk Vidal, who wrote a historical novel and TV mini-series about Lincoln, was giving. An office adjoining the bedroom was piled with boxes of books, there were pictures of his good friends Joanne Woodward and Paul Newman, and Vidal's Olivetti typewriter on which Steers remembered his uncle "hammering out" his works. Austen's room made Steers recall how Vidal, who always maintained their relationship was based on no sex and that they were only friends, rather than romantic partners, would sleep next to Austen when Austen was dying of cancer "to comfort him."

Inveterate gossip about other people's sexual peccadilloes as he was, Vidal would have hated this exploration of his private life, taking in new interviews with family, friends and associates, including Susan Sarandon and Claire Bloom, material from Vidal's archive at Harvard University, as well as the diaries and memoirs of others, including Christopher Isherwood and Tennessee Williams, and the detail-rich 1999 biography written by Fred Kaplan, who he complained to, "I don't like talking about myself and certainly not about private matters, so I don't know how you're going to do this because there isn't anything there." To a friend he once wrote: "I'm fairly candid, in principle; as a memoirist, though, I don't go in for naming names other than those who have outed me." He was "dimly aware" of Susan Sontag's private life (her lesbianism, her relationship with Annie Leibovitz), but he had no interest in it or anyone else's, "unless it was comical." It often was, and his interest was often piqued.

In his memoir *Palimpsest*, Vidal seeks to head off at the pass any enquiry into his sex life with a vintage passage of withering sarcasm about not being like other contemporary autobiographers with their "tempestuous love affairs, bitter marriages, autistic children, breakdowns, drugs, therapy standard literary life. But I was to have no love affairs or marriages [how easily he dismissed his deep, fifty-three-year relationship with Austen], while casual sex, is by its very nature, not memorable. I have never 'broken down,' as opposed to slowly crumbling, and I've steered clear of psychoanalysts, nutritionists and contract bridge-players." In fact Vidal did break down, about love, about Austen, both in their past and certainly after his partner's death, although he would never admit to it.

They always had separate bedrooms and "separate interests" sexually, Steers said as we stood in Austen's room, but they were affectionate with one another, even if "Italy was all about the guys," the hustlers and young men both Vidal and Austen enjoyed on their own and in orgies. In his wallet Vidal did not keep a picture of "an adult Howard," but "Howard as a teenager." At the top of the house's back stairs, where a chairlift had been assembled to transport the wheelchair-bound Vidal between floors, hung a portrait of a blond teenage boy holding a model sailboat. It was Jimmie Trimble, the painting a reproduction of the original painted by Trimble and owned by his mother. It embodies the most intriguing, possibly most telling mystery of Vidal's personal life, a former classmate from prep school who Vidal claimed to have had an intimate relationship with before Trimble was killed at the Battle of Iwo Jima in 1945. In previous years it hung above Vidal's bed in Ravello, recalls his good friend, the director and writer Matt Tyrnauer, who edited Vidal's essays for *Vanity Fair* and Vidal's former literary executor. In later years, Vidal would "meditate" in front of the picture before going to bed in Outpost Drive.

In an assistant's office, another surprise sprang out: the only book not neatly shelved was Randy Shilts's *The Mayor of Castro Street*, Shilts's much-acclaimed 1982 biography of Harvey Milk, the crusading, properly lionized and inspirational gay San Francisco city supervisor assassinated in 1978. Its presence was jolting because, while Shilts and his subject were openly gay and pursuing vocal public lives in rougher times, Vidal's own sexuality occupied a more vexed, hidden, undeclared, un-trumpeted place. He said he was bisexual, but few of his friends who generally believe he was gay, believe he was. Vidal thought "gay" referred to a sexual act, rather than a sexual identity.

Politically, he did little overt gay rights campaigning, and remained silent during the AIDS epidemic. He also had a personal animus against Shilts, who also wrote *And the Band Played On*, the complex, moving, fury-inducing history of the early years of the pandemic, though maybe that was resolved. A Christmas card from Shilts to Vidal in 1991, stored in Vidal's Harvard University archive, carries a famous quote from Ecclesiastes: "To everything there is a season…A time to mourn, and a time to dance…."

"He would be aware of Shilts and Milk and very supportive of all they did," insisted Steers. "He had Larry Kramer's books too, and other people who were in the fight, yet he never really connected with it." Steers's brother Hugh, an artist who died of AIDS, beseeched Vidal to use his fame and speak up for those with AIDS. Vidal didn't. "I don't think he ever worried about HIV and AIDS. I think he was quite confident it was something that wouldn't happen to him." Because he thought he was at less risk of infection as he liked fucking men rather than being fucked? Steers laughed. "No. Because he was Gore Vidal."

That Vidal had sex with hustlers and not much, if any, with Austen, his partner of fifty-three years, he was open about. But what was the truth of that and of his and Austen's relationship? The details of his sex life, his attitude toward love, his supposed bisexuality, relationships with women, the true terrain of his relationship with Austen, how he felt about his own sexuality, the reality of that sexuality and where it intersected with his writing, ambition and politics are the foundation of this book. Indeed the darker, unknown shores of his sexuality lie at the heart of the challenge to his own will, in that unpaid debt to his sister and what belied Vidal and Buckley's interminable legal tussle. One of my interviewees asked if examining Vidal's sex life and sexuality "reduced" him "when he was the great writer he was." I replied that all the contradictions and mysteries around his sex life and sexuality were of Vidal's own making: understanding them would expand an understanding of him and his work. This is a book with sexuality at its heart; it is neither a general biography, nor evaluation of Vidal's writing career.

A reminder of one of Vidal's very public gay moments was there on the shelf above the Shilts book: a group of first editions included one of *The City and the Pillar*, Vidal's novel published in 1948, the first American novel to feature explicit gay sex and characters in a gay milieu; alongside it were other titles like *Live from Golgotha* and Vidal's 2006 memoir *Point to Point Navigation*. A copy of *Up Above the World* by Vidal's friend Paul Bowles was signed by another famous friend, Tennessee Williams ("I wish I had written it, Love Tennessee"). There was even a wry encomium from one of Vidal's great rivals: in his novel *Harlot's Ghost*, Norman Mailer inscribed: "This pertains my debt, since your competitive heart will now produce at least two more novels than you had intended. Cheers, Norman, Sept 91." From old enemies to growling, grand old men, the two had gone from punches thrown to, at the end of their lives, a rapprochement and performing together in Provincetown in a production of *Don Juan in Hell*. In a note to Muriel Spark, Vidal wrote: "Mailer and I were grousing over our shrunken estates and M said, sighed, 'At least Gore, in the future, you and I will be cults.' My cold response: 'A cult may be good enough for you but I expected to be a major religion.'"

Downstairs in a small study was a cross-section of Vidal's cultural tastes: a poster of a magazine cover proclaiming his "wit and wisdom," a *Simpsons* "ultimate episode guide, seasons 1-20" (Gore had appeared on the show; Lisa had once spoken yearningly that she would never kiss as many men as he had), a biography of Kenneth Tynan (an old friend) and Bill Clinton's autobiography *My Life*. In his dining room were chairs from the set of *Ben-Hur*, the 1959 film that Vidal co-wrote, inserting a notorious scene implying a teenage relationship between Ben-Hur (Charlton Heston) and Messala (Stephen Boyd).

In the living room were pictures of Edgewater, his former house in Dutchess County, upstate New York, and on the ceiling paintings by Paolo de Matteis, an eighteenth-century Baroque painter, Vidal had hung in La Rondinaia, his home in Ravello, Italy, which was originally built in the 1920s overlooking the Bay of Amalfi and which Vidal sold when his own health made living there too difficult. One louche-looking, barely clothed maiden, arms wantonly outstretched in the de Matteis painting, was described by Vidal in the image of one of his most famous house-guests: "Princess Margaret asking for another gin and tonic."

Steers warned me not to sit in Vidal's cushioned red chair: "He lost control of his bladder, so that chair's been through a lot of ugly things." A walking stick perched against a lamp. Steers remembered how a fire burned in the grate "even when it was 110 degrees outside": Vidal was always cold; he suffered hypothermia in the war and his left knee was made of titanium. "You still feel him here. He was such a presence," said Steers as we stared at the empty chair. "This house is so full of memories, I can't imagine ever being able to come in here and not be overcome by them. There are so many ghosts here and nothing's changed since the 1970s: you expect to come around a corner and see someone who's been dead for years."

Steers knows that friends and family are outraged on his behalf about the verbal bequeathal of Outpost Drive to him not being enshrined in black and white in Vidal's will but says he feels "in an awkward position. It's a depressing house, there is very little light. Would I turn it down if it was left to me? No, of course not, but I'm not going to passionately pursue it. I don't want to deal with the people and his Estate. I am repulsed by the whole situation." Steers, though he wouldn't name names, said "the only thing I wanted after Gore's death was to see those people who exploited his illness punished. They were on his payroll in different ways."

Whatever the results of the challenge to the will, Burr Steers said he wanted his separation from the house to be clean-cut: "It was unsettling, dealing with Gore at the end with dementia, rather than dealing with the person you had once known. It was like having him replaced, and someone very different take his place." But even in good health, there were many Gore Vidals—all the author's own inventions, first evident when he renamed himself "Gore Vidal" after being christened Eugene Luther Gore Vidal Jr. "Then I got to Exeter [the Phillips Exeter Academy, in New Hampshire, an American private school] and dropped the Eugene Luther and re-invented myself as Gore Vidal," he told his first biographer Walter Clemons. "I didn't like my nickname, Deenie. I wasn't too wild about Gene either, as Gene was clearly my father. I thought I was going to be a politician and then suddenly realized I was a writer, and Gore Vidal was better for both."

Vidal may have wanted "a sharp, distinctive name, appropriate for an aspiring author or national political leader," as his biographer Fred Kaplan writes, but the changing of his name was also the first signal Vidal would craft his own identity, not least an intriguing sexual identity in bed and on the page. Friends say his mother's homophobia and their fractious relationship were the root of a deep loneliness he felt. He enshrined a first love, Trimble, as his true love; he made his name by writing *The City and the Pillar*, one of the first explicitly gay novels of modern times, yet spent a lifetime in, if not retreat then a complicated tango, around his own sexuality.

Vidal was in a relationship with another man for fifty three years, yet only after his death did he reveal the depth of his feelings for Howard Austen in a searing chapter of *Point to Point Navigation*. Why did Vidal like sex and orgies with prostitutes and young men? How young were those men? Why he did never write about AIDS? Was his keenly felt desire for a political career, to be president, ultimately thwarted by his homosexuality? How heavy a shadow to live up to did his grandfather cast, the political legacy of another familial generation that Vidal never felt he properly fulfilled after losing two races to win public office?

It was absolutely in keeping with the subject's own confusing shadow play on the subject that one of the corrections the New York Times published after running Vidal's obituary was around sex. The author of the obituary had originally repeated what Vidal himself used to say: that he and Austen had never had sex. Yet in *Palimpsest*, his memoir, Vidal wrote they had had sex the night they met, but not after they began living together. Many of his friends think that's an implausible underestimation in itself, and it certainly doesn't convey the truth and depth of the men's relationship.

The *New York Times*'s correction ran thus: "According to Mr. Vidal's memoir *Palimpsest*, they had sex the night they met, but did not sleep together after they began living together. It was not true that they never had sex." But it was Vidal's own deliberate ambiguities around what he did sexually that led to the confusion. He would have loved and hated the correction, just as he would have balked at this examination of his personal life and its impudent central question: what *did* Gore Vidal do in bed, how did it shape, or not, his life and work? Was he a closet case, a product of his generation? Was he "post-gay" before his time, refusing to be boxed in to any category? How does his refusal to define his own sexual identity help us understand him, his passions and personality? In essence—and here imagine the most withering of curled lips from the Master himself—how *gay* was Gore Vidal?

Chapter One

Terms of Engagement

He may not have fought on the barricades for gay equality or come out in a conventional way, but Vidal was "upfront" about sex, Burr Steers says. Vidal and Austen took Steers to Studio 54 "when I was eleven. It didn't catch me by surprise." Vidal told Steers he had also successfully pursued and had sex with Fred Astaire when he first moved to Hollywood. "He also loved listening to his albums in Ravello," Steers says with a laugh. "He also told me Dennis Hopper had a lovely tuft of hair above his ass. He never told me how he knew that." Another close friend of Vidal's revealed Vidal had asked, when hearing the friend was staying at the legendarily rock-starry, scandal-drenched Chateau Marmont, "How is the Chateau?" He then added: "Brad Davis [star of *Midnight Express* and *Querelle*] was a beautiful boy and I fucked him on the bathroom floor of the Chateau Marmont." Davis, who was bisexual and HIV-positive, died of a drug overdose in 1991.

Vidal was determined to craft his own biography, sexual and otherwise. Vidal wrote of rumors linking him sexually with Marlon Brando, without confirming them but joking about a "secret committee" linking celebrities in new sexual combinations. "There is a strange compulsion for journalists to reveal that stars of every sort and every field are either homosexual or anti-Semitic or both." Yet Vidal gossiped and reveled in gossip.

"Gore didn't think of himself as a gay guy," says Vidal's close friend, the author and academic Jay Parini. "It makes him self-hating. How could he despise gays as much as he did? In my company he always used the term 'fags'—'Oh god, this fag magazine wants to interview me.' Why when you're gay would you make such remarks? He was uncomfortable with being gay. Then again he was wildly courageous, when he published *The City and the Pillar* in the 1940s. He was proud of it. Howard was to-tally comfortable with being gay and that relaxed Gore, and that is why it was so sad when Howard died. Howard brought him into the world. Gore can thank his lucky stars for Howard Austen. Without Howard he would have been a sad, drunken bastard with no friends."

"Gore didn't feel there was any such thing as being gay," Fred Kaplan says. "He may have been a heroic figure in the gay world but for much of his life he was not part of the gay rights move-ment. He was not interested in making a difference for gay peo-ple, or being an advocate for gay rights. One of the ironies is he became such a heroic figure. There was no such thing as straight or gay for him, just the body and sex." David Schweizer, a former lover of Tennessee Williams who met Vidal in Rome, recalls him saying how "silly" the term "gay" was. That summer Fellini was shooting his movie *Satyricon*, and Vidal talked about "how you can't define sexuality in a ridiculously formulaic way. Everyone is everything. Everyone was naturally bisexual to him. I don't think he lived it out so much, but his sense of it was authentic. He was a provocateur. He put out theorems."

In his own writing Vidal deliberately clouded or fudged per-sonal and sexual issues; he doesn't make clear if affairs, with Anaïs Nin for example, happened. It suited Vidal—keen to put the reader or biographer off the scent—to tease us, ramp up the mystery and blur the boundaries and categories he was so op-posed to. All of it helped us know Vidal less, never exposing the parts of his inner self or his desires that he wanted to keep off-limits. In not defining himself, and being so emphatic about that, he gave himself freedom and also avoided accusations of lying or covering up. "People ask, 'When did you come out?'" Vidal told Donald Weise in an unpublished interview from 1999. "I was never *in*."

In *Palimpsest*, Vidal wrote that his tendency to lie was "seldom indulged in except when picking up a stranger. Then, with real delight, I invent a new character for myself, one that I think will appeal to my quarry." For Vidal, "obviously sexual buccaneers who want to succeed in American politics must lie all the time," neatly explaining his priapic pals John and Jacqueline Kennedy, as well as himself. "Most young men, particularly attractive ones, have sexual relationships with their own kind," Vidal wrote. "I suppose this is still news to those who believe in two teams: straight, which is good and unalterable" and "queer, which is bad and unalterable unless it proves to be only a Preference, which must then, somehow, be reversed, if necessary by force."

Vidal insisted *Palimpsest* would not be a tell-all autobiography. He would adjudicate the stories worth telling and character worth revealing. The lack of control conferred by having a biographer like Walter Clemons, and later Fred Kaplan, unsettled Vidal, especially when it came to what they were going to say about him and sex. Yet sex and love, the closet and sexual identity—just as much as analyses and reveries on the end of American empire and the failings of corrupt government—are at the heart of Vidal's story. Of course, he professed to think differently to put off snooping noses. "There is nothing more to be done about it," Vidal wrote about sex. "Sex builds no road, writes no novels, and sex certainly finds no meaning to anything in life by itself." Talking about one's sex life "is one way of saying nothing about oneself."

Such protestations come with a large dollop of irony. "He talked about sex a lot," says his lifelong friend, the agent Boaty Boatwright. "He loved telling stories with sex in them," recalls his bibliographer Steven Abbott, who remembers a particular story told during lunch in the dining room at Ravello "with an expatriate English aristocrat at the table about someone walking in on an English Lord having sex with his butler." Vidal told Michael Childers, a photographer who was also film director John Schlesinger's partner for thirty-one years, "What good is gossip when you can't repeat it?" He loved divulging morsels. Donald Gislason, Vidal's house-sitter in Ravello, recalls Vidal telling him that George Bush Sr. had come to play baseball at Exeter, his school, as the pitcher for the other school. "He was seventeen and considered rather fetching by everyone looking at him."

Vidal was a superior joker and gossip, but did not like to be the subject of either: he told Childers he was "shocked" by what he saw as the betrayal of Christopher Isherwood, who wrote unsparingly of his feelings about Vidal in his diaries. There was much for Vidal to take offense to, not least knowing Isherwood saw him as a literary subordinate, not a peer as Vidal imagined. An entry from Isherwood's diaries, on September 29, 1955, reads: "Being with Gore depresses me, unless I'm feeling absolutely up to the mark, because Gore really exudes despair and cynical misery and a grudge against society which is really based on his own lack of talent and creative joy."

Vain enough to be upset by what others said and wrote about him, Vidal was also fame-hungry, attention-bathing and wanted to be talked about, and to, as much as possible. *Williwaw*, his first novel, published in 1946 when he was nineteen, made him famous, then *The City and the Pillar* and *Myra Breckinridge* infamous. Hollywood, where he decamped to write for TV in 1954, gave him what his friend Paul Newman called "fuck-you money." Movies and Broadway plays (*Visit to a Small Planet* in 1957 and most successfully the pointed political drama *The Best Man*, first performed in 1960) would follow, then historical fiction like *Burr* and *Lincoln* (earning him the right to be known as the nation's biographer, he thought) and essay-writing, which many critics deem to be his most impressive area of his literary output.

Vidal's wit, intelligence and quickness of thought and wicked, withering turn of phrase made him a well-known TV face, especially on *The Tonight Show Starring Johnny Carson*. One of the most absurd attempts at lofty self-deprecation on his part erupts in a letter to Muriel Spark in which he places himself "in an older tradition, along with Byron, whom I resemble in a number of ways neither of us would boast of—gin and overweight (sic) BUT a sense that one's writing is for itself, not for others particularly and certainly not for fame much less money." Vidal loved all three: fame, money, and writing for itself and like

Byron he was quite the sexual swordsman. If his most famous sexual boast was that he had slept with over a thousand men by the time he was twenty five, the rest of his life wasn't spent in chaste seclusion. What remained consistent was his refusal to define himself as "gay" and his insistence that there was no such thing as gay people, only gay sexual acts.

Jason Epstein, Vidal's longtime editor until they fell out in the 1980s, strongly supports Vidal at his word: "He wasn't unhappy about being gay," Epstein says. "He was unhappy about being wrongly classified, pigeonholed. I think his main interest was men, but of course he slept with women—why wouldn't he? He'd sleep with anything. He was horny. For him, sex was like having lunch. He was certainly quick about it. He didn't linger." Once, at the American Embassy in Rome, Vidal's eye was caught by a young Marine. Marines had sex "for pin money," Vidal told Epstein. Vidal told Epstein to wait for him. Epstein began reading a magazine article, when Vidal very suddenly appeared in front of him. "When is he coming?" Epstein asked Vidal of his hookup. "He's been," Vidal replied.

Epstein puts the number of men Vidal had sex with down to his desire for dominance. "He talked about sex like you talked about a golf game, and he bought sex because it was the easiest way to do it." Vidal's "life's obsession," says Epstein, was the idea of the continuum of sexuality "with its roots in classical civilization. Everything wrong in the world could be put down to how narrowly sexuality was seen, he thought. For Gore it was ridiculous, and I agree, that people were being forced to live in these little prisons of definition invented by stupid people. Gore's so-called radicalism has a lot to do with that. He felt he was being forced to accept a sexual definition by a culture that wasn't worthy to make such a definition. He wouldn't make a sacrifice like that, around sexual identity, for the corrupt culture he lived within if he could help it. No one wants to be defined in a way that doesn't feel right to them: it's annoying, and if it's about your sexuality it's extremely annoying."

When asked in a 2007 interview with the Canadian broadcaster Allan Gregg how he felt about being seen as a "gay icon," Vidal replied, "Mild discomfort. Anybody who's dumb enough to think anyone else's personality is governed entirely by his sexual tastes is insane. There's no such thing as a gay person, there's a gay act. We know what that is or can be, that's it. Once you allow yourself to be categorized, you know, Adolf Hitler is going to come along and say, 'We don't like your category, I think we'd better remove you types.'" Vidal didn't consider those who were attracted to their own sex as linked by a collective identity, even in political terms when grouping together to counter homophobia and fight for social and legal equality; "gay pride" meant nothing to him.

For Jason Epstein, Vidal "didn't trust women after what his mother, who was drunk all the time, did to him, although that oversimplifies it. And he didn't have that gene problem that accounts for some kinds of homosexuality." I ask Epstein what he means. "He was totally male, there was nothing feminine about him at all: he wasn't Liberace, he was more like Oscar Wilde." If people ask why Vidal didn't just declare himself as gay, Epstein says: "He couldn't declare himself, he honestly felt he lived on a sexual continuum. He preferred men to women, yes, but that was also a way to protect himself against relationships with women. He was attracted to women if they were bright and funny. He liked women. You can't partition attraction."

"I have never allowed actively in my life the word 'gay' to pass my lips. I don't know why I hate that word," Vidal told *Fag Rag* magazine in 1974. "I could have been, from 1948 on, the Official Spokesman. But I have no plans to be so limited. I'm a generalist, and I'm interested in a great many other things. Knowing the mania of the media, they want everybody to be in a pigeonhole. Oh, yes. He's the Official Fag. Oh, yes, He's the Official Marxist. And I have never allowed myself to be pigeonholed like that. Also I don't regard myself as one thing over another. The point is why not discard all the words? Say that all sexual acts have parity. Which is my line."

Vidal may have declared he was anti-category, but his snobbery conferred categories on others. "The working class, god knows, they're filled with terrible passion and prejudice," he told *Fag Rag*, "but give them a sexual act to perform that seems amusing...In Texas, that relentless Bible belt, there's nobody who's not available. It's like Italy...the Italians are naturally sensual and opportunistic about sex. They don't fuss. That's one of the reasons why there are really no queer bars."

Vidal railed against people putting him in a gay context, says his nephew Burr Steers, "but also anybody getting underneath the way he wanted to be portrayed. This is the guy who chose his own name and created his persona. He really wasn't about to let anybody else change that." Friends remember his lethal wit and his proudly worn loftiness warmly. "He was a real intellectual and delightfully arrogant," says his friend Barbara Howar. "Gore was incredibly vain: after completing a book he'd prepare for his TV appearances with extreme visitations to La Costa, the fat farm, as he called it, to lose weight," his close friend Jean Stein says. Kenneth Tynan recalled it as the place where Vidal "spent a thousand dollars a week to lose thirty pounds." In later years Muriel Spark wrote to him asking for diet advice: "I know you and Howard have some experience in this field."

"Vidal insists he never gave anyone a blow job, which I find...well gee, did he really miss out on one of the greatest pleasures of sex between men?" says Christopher Bram, author of *Eminent Outlaws*, a study of the writers—Vidal being a significant fulcrum—who shaped modern American gay-themed fiction. "He also said he never kissed, he never went down on anybody, and never took it up the ass. He just fucked, allowed himself to be blown and maybe mutual masturbation and the 'Princeton rub,' or frottage—what Auden called 'plain sewing.'" Bram takes Vidal at his word when he claimed, as Bram puts it, "Of course I pay for sex, I'm such a bad lay, I should pay for it." "There's no reason not to believe Vidal," Bram says with a smile. "It's not the kind of thing someone lies about."

Control mattered to Vidal more than anything, Fred Kaplan tells me. "One of the great paradoxes of Gore was that he portrayed himself as the great truth-teller, but he didn't always tell the truth. He said he never read my biography but surely he would have been incapable of that, or at least glancing at it. Howard loved it." Vidal signed a statement agreeing not to see or seek to influence the manuscript before it was published. Then he demanded to see it. "He was very much into power-play. That fit into his notion of sex: paying hustlers to do what he wants. He always wanted to be in control. Defy him at your peril." When *Fag Rag* magazine asked him in 1974 whether he liked being seduced, Vidal was clear: "I hate being seduced, I like seducing." He also said he didn't flatter the young sexually: "That doesn't mean I don't like them."

When Leonard Bernstein visited L.A., Vidal arranged for two would-be actors to join them for sex, he relates in *Palimpsest*. Both men adjourned with their partners; Vidal's departed while neither Bernstein nor his young man reappeared. Vidal opened his door to discover Bernstein lecturing a "mesmerized" youth "on his career, character, future—and the act of performing." Vidal had to stay in control in front of everyone, from sexual partners to powerful friends and enemies: he had seen the loss of control and its price early in life. The swirling emotions around love and sex would never master him.

Chapter Two

Vidal Family Values

If Vidal's personal life was complicated, and its intersection with his public life fraught, his understanding of love and sexuality was grounded in a scrambled childhood. Vidal once described himself as a "third generation celebrity," telling Walter Clemons, his first biographer whose previously unseen material I unearthed for this book, "My father was on the cover of *Time*, a West Point football hero and Roosevelt's director of aeronautics. I adored him. My mother was another story. Alcoholic mothers are never easy. I kept away from her during the last twenty years of her life."

Eugene Vidal founded three airline companies, including one that went on to become TWA. Jean Stein recalls Vidal as inordinately proud of his ancestry. "He talked about it *ad infinitum*. He was very proud of his family, the aristocratic side. He once took me to a cemetery in Venice where some of his relations were buried. For somebody supposed to be a man of people he talked more about breeding, ancestors and background than anything else."

Never one to miss out on an important moment, Vidal even remembered being born, telling Fred Kaplan, his second biographer, "I am in a narrow tunnel. I cannot move forward or backward. I wake up in a sweat. Nina's pelvis was narrow and I was delivered clumsily, with a forceps." His earliest memory was getting his head stuck in the slats of a playpen, fuelling what became an adult claustrophobia. His mother was absent and he was freed by his beloved grandmother.

Vidal's father moved his family into his wife's father's house in Washington when Vidal was three. The blind Senator Thomas Gore was a superb orator and a hero to the young Vidal: "He was an absolute star," Vidal told Clemons. "It was like having Helen

Keller for a grandfather." Vidal went on to deploy the same kind of ruthless wit his grandfather had. Clemons points out that when the hero of Vidal's 1960 play, *The Best Man*, says of his reptilian opponent, "He has every characteristic of a dog except loyalty," he is quoting Senator Gore. Vidal's grandmother taught him to read with *The Duck and the Kangaroo*, which Vidal recalled later as "a tale of unnatural affection." Later Vidal, then around six, would read to his grandfather and lead him to the Senate floor to speak. Once because it was so hot he did this attired just in his bathing suit.

It was his upbringing that endowed Vidal with an unapologetically lofty sense of entitlement. In an until-now undiscovered, intimate interview in 1999 with Donald Weise, who published his essay collection *Sexually Speaking*, Vidal said, "There wasn't anything I didn't know about American politics. I knew how the country was run. I was bought up in the middle of it. When you are born at the top, you get to look at the world from a senator's position." The young Vidal saw "how everyone was getting away with murder"; if one was "totally relaxed about that you're quite prepared for a lot of things in life, including a quite unorthodox sex life which might have some risk involved. But as I said to [actor, Sir] Ian McKellen, 'I've never had a moment of sexual guilt,' and he said, 'I bet you haven't.' If you're bought up in the house of a senator you're not going to be very concerned about what a postal worker thinks of your private life."

Early in the 1930s his parents' marriage began to disintegrate: his mother loved to argue, Vidal claimed, while his father was gentle. Both had affairs, his mother a long off-and-on one with Clark Gable. When they divorced, Vidal said later, "I was delighted. Everybody else was too." Was he really so unperturbed at nine, Clemons wonders. Vidal told Clemons that his mother had married stockbroker Hugh Auchincloss, who owned Merrywood, a thirty-acre estate on the Virginia bank of the Potomac, "on the understanding that there would be no sex between them...she was disagreeably surprised when he imposed himself on her after the ceremony." Vidal's mother was constantly aggrieved at others' perceived infractions while acting monstrously towards her own children: it was a "wild world of tooth and claw," he writes in *Palimpsest*.

Many of his friends think whatever complexities underpinned Vidal's sexuality can be traced back to his poisonous and destructive relationship with his mother; that his formidable carapace, the parts of him that were rude, rancorous, withering, his outright rejection of love and intimacy, his coldness, were all sourced in his emotionally difficult childhood in which he was the victim of her drunken neglect and viciousness. Vidal was once asked at an audience event what, if anything, would he have changed in his life. He replied, "My mother." The audience laughed: after all, there is nothing like Vidal at his quickest, most cutting and caustic. But many friends saw it as a macho, repelling cover for raw, unresolved sadness.

Jason Epstein, his longtime editor, says Vidal reminded him of the questioning character in Eugene O'Neill's *The Great God Brown*: "Why was I born without a skin? Oh God, that I must wear armor in order to touch or be touched?" That lack of skin in Vidal "was down to his complicated relationship with his mother. She was a monster and not something you get over but have to pretend it didn't matter. There was great pain there." Vidal was "very fragile. His whole manner was a defense not to be wounded, to strike first and walk away with a victory—the tough guy, the 'I slept with a thousand people before I was twenty-five but don't care about any of them.'" For Epstein, Vidal's epic drinking later in life was another aspect of his defense: "Wanting to dull feelings in that way suggests an inner turbulence you can't handle. I'm sure the inner Gore was tortured. Having a crazy mother does you damage, but at some point you have to cut off your feelings to deal with it."

Hilton Als, in a *New Yorker* article after Vidal's death, expanded on a similar theme: "Like many ambitious gay male children born to alcoholic or self-dramatizing mothers—Edward Albee, Stephen Sondheim—Vidal's own youthful romanticism was eviscerated by his perforce gimlet eye: he could not afford to trust. Life has taught him otherwise. This cost him a career of first-rate fiction; he could not expose himself to empathy, which is trust's kissing cousin, and fiction's necessity. (Albee and Sondheim are very great artists indeed, but they do not write prose; their characters impersonate the hatred and high drama they had at home.)"

When he was a young boy, Vidal told the producers of *The Celluloid Closet*, the first time he went to the movies, aged four, his father and mother took him to a cinema in St Louis. "Ann Dvorak was on the screen," he related in the full transcript of the interview. "As we walked down the aisle, Ann Dvorak in her character said something on the screen and I answered her...I've always talked back to the movies and to the text." Vidal remembered (also in his book *Screening History*) when he first saw *The Prince and the Pauper* released in 1937 "with the Mauch twins [Billy and Robert J.], two twelve-year-olds, and I was twelve years old, and one was the prince in Mark Twain's story, son of King Henry the Eighth, and the other was a pauper and they meet. They change places. Well, that was ravishing. One person could be two, two people could be one. One could be the other. The other could be one. It opened up such mirrors to my mind...What would it be like to have a twin? To have another? Another self."

In *Screening History*, Vidal writes on seeing the film, "I wanted to be not one but two...I wanted to be myself twice." Vidal imagines a similar theme of doubleness and completion around himself and childhood friend Jimmie Trimble: "What I was not, he was, and the other way around," Vidal writes in *Palimpsest*. "I was never lonely," he says of growing up. "I was solitary, and wanted no company at all other than books and movies, and my own imagination." As no one had found "perfect wholeness in another human being...the twin is the closest that one can ever come toward human wholeness with another."

Vidal was the favored child, his half-sister Nina tells me. She was persecuted by their mother "for being a girl. She'd beat me, say, 'Gore could read this when he was four, why can't you?' She just tortured me, beat me silly with coat-hangers, brushes, saying, 'Your brother could do better than this.' It didn't make me hate Gore. I recognized he was superior. I worked really hard to be vaguely adequate. I had to run away twice before anyone noticed." Ruth Goodman, Vidal's nanny when he was a baby, told Walter Clemons that she could "never quite forgive" Nina for how she treated her daughter. "She hated her."

Vidal lived indoors in a tent, dressing up as a sheikh or the Wizard of Oz, "living inside his head and fantasies." His mother was vocally disapproving of his locking himself away to write, rather than motivated by the things that meant so much to her: money and social standing. She didn't realize her son was too: he wanted to write as well. In 2009, Vidal told me of his mother, "Give her a glass of vodka and she was as tame as could be. Growing up is going to be difficult if the one person you hate is your mother. I felt trapped. I was close to my grandparents and my father was a saint." His parents' many remarriages meant that he never met all his step-siblings. He remembered his mother telling him that rage made her orgasmic ("I forgot to ask her if sex ever did"). She also said, en route to their honeymoon, Vidal's father told her he had three balls. How could you fail to originate your own skewed view of sex and sexuality with parents like that?

A family friend, Vidal revealed to Fred Kaplan, told his mother that his love of theatrics could signal gay "tendencies." Nina "took that to heart" and sent her ten-year-old son to some kind of doctor, "probably" a psychiatrist, "who asked me sex questions and so on. I gave perfectly polite answers. And that was the end of it. She then loses interest. Never again does the subject come up." It resurfaces in 1948 when, after publication of *The City and the Pillar,* Vidal's mother sent him a letter suggesting he seek psychoanalytic correction for his sexual proclivities: "Sweetie, you have too much ability to permit letting the ropes be fouled," she wrote.

Nina Straight says Vidal's relationship with his mother was "extra-close. My mother wasn't a generic thinker. Gore said she was anti-gay and anti-Jewish, but my mother didn't get that far above sea level. She was not that way, she loved the arts, she taught Howard (who was Jewish) how to cook. But Howard was competition. She was going to be seen out with her famous literary son. She was his calling card, his class act."

Vidal was already a precocious, self-made star at twelve, when he gave a signed picture of himself to his friend, Doris O'Donnell, signed "Eugene," his given name. Ruth Goodman, Vidal's nanny, began a conversation about him with Walter Clemons, stating breezily: "Well, Deenie [Vidal] is a homosexual, I guess you know, and I think his mother was mainly responsible for that. They were very close. She loved Deenie in a very possessive way. He was about eleven when I first met him at Merrywood. A sweet boy, very beautiful and well-mannered. I distinctly remember going to her bedroom one night and finding Deenie on the floor, holding his face. She had slapped him down to the floor. And the next night she had him in her bed with her."

Goodman recalls Vidal's mother's drinking, which echoed her son's later addiction. "She got so she would drink a bottle of sherry in the afternoon, switch to Scotch before dinner, and by the time she got up from the dinner table she could barely make it to her room." She was hospitalized and went to a drying out facility: "When she came back she was okay for about three months, and then it started again." She had "terrible" affairs, one with John Hay [Jock] Whitney as Gene had one with Whitney's wife, Elizabeth. Vidal said one of her partners, John Galliher, had said to him, "Gore, I've gone to bed with your mother, and I'd like to go to bed with you." In *Palimpsest*, Vidal unearthed the writing of Robert McAlmon, an author who alluded to having an affair with his father, Eugene, in passages that mirror in tone and structure the romance passages of *The City and the Pillar*.

Vidal was, Goodman recalled, a lonely boy who read all the time and played with model soldiers with his half-brother Hugh; the models given to him by his father. "In the time I knew him, Deenie didn't hear much from his father...and I think he felt deserted by him. I remember he was terribly upset when his father got married again, to a much younger woman. I sat with

Deenie for a whole morning and tried to comfort him when he got that news." Vidal later said relations with his father were friendly.

"Mr. Vidal only came to see his son once in the whole time I knew the family, and I'm afraid I kind of held that against him," said Goodman. "I thought he neglected Deenie. Instead of his father, Deenie only had his grandfather, but the senator was too old to be much help and Deenie, I think, felt that his father didn't do right by him. I felt very sad for him. It was a very sad family, to my way of thinking." Nina's marriage to Hugh lasted five years; he went on to marry Janet Bouvier, becoming the stepfather of Jacqueline Kennedy. Nina went to marry General Robert Olds. Vidal's father had a relationship with Amelia Earhart, who Vidal wanted to have as a stepmother. "If you went down Fifth Avenue with Amelia Earhart you would have 500 people following you," Vidal told a newspaper in 2008. "Even at ten I was impressed."

His father, Vidal told Nicholas Wrathall in his 2013 documentary *Gore Vidal: The United States of Amnesia*, dreamed of "being the Henry Ford of aviation" and invented many prototype aircraft; Vidal flew one at ten. "It's easier than learning to ride a bicycle," he said to cameramen in front of the craft with predictable precociousness.

Growing up, Vidal would have been aware of, his half-sister tells me, the Sumner Welles case: one of Franklin D. Roosevelt's brightest foreign policy advisers, Welles was forced to resign after it was revealed he solicited Pullman car porters for sex while travelling back from the funeral of William Bankhead, Alabama congressman, Speaker of the House, and father of actress Tallulah. "A scandal, all hell broke loose," says Nina Straight. She agrees with Gay Talese and other of Vidal's friends who say he was a victim of hostile times. After Vidal's death, Talese wrote in *Time* magazine, "I do believe his reputation, such as it was, on television—argumentative and supercilious and sometimes downright nasty—I think it had to do with the fact that he couldn't be relaxed in public as he would have been with small groups of people." Vidal knew he was gay but his parents' public status meant he "built kind of a wall within which to defend himself."

Nina Straight denies her mother and family were "remotely homophobic" and would have been "very relaxed" if Vidal had been open about his sexuality. They were not conservative or "cared about those things—he did, but it was him not them." Their mother was friends with gay men about town like John Latouche, later a good friend of Vidal's, and Patrick Dennis, author of the *Auntie Mame* series of books. "The most ferocious designers and whoopie-doo actors were her friends," says Nina. "It was Gore who had the problem, he could never get into it. His line that there was no such thing as gay, only gay sexual acts was characteristic of his critique of many things. He would just scratch against the accepted."

His friends judge the impact of Vidal's mother variously. For Jean Stein, one of Vidal's oldest friends, "he was a desperately lonely human being. He was one of the loneliest people I've ever met. I think some of his alcoholism was due to his intense feelings of abandonment going all the way back to his early relationship with his mother. I always thought, in regards to his mother, that as much as Gore hated her, he loved her. A friend of mine who visited him one time in Ravello noticed he had his mother in a framed photograph on the table. She asked him about it and the next day it had vanished. Gore said his mother was monstrous about his homosexuality and Howard. I don't know if she was, but alcoholics, as I believe she was, often have a vicious streak. He claimed he hated her, but I knew underneath that he probably loved her passionately."

The photographer Michael Childers also once noticed a picture of Vidal's mother; Vidal told him, "That was my mother, the most vile woman who ever lived. I loathed her, loathed her." Vidal was particularly furious when she snubbed Howard, an occasion that led mother and son to never see each other again. Vidal was enormously protective of Austen, who would leave the room when mother and son would argue. "She didn't make an issue of his sexuality head on, and if she did, I would have been out of the room long before," Austen told Fred Kaplan. Austen said she would go to bars in New York asking for pity that her son was homosexual.

In 1957 when his mother, staying with them in London, denounced "her son the fairy and his Jew boy," Vidal ordered her from the house. She sent him a letter saying her life had been ruined by him; he sent her one back saying "I'll never see you again as long as you live." They didn't see each other again, although she asked for money, Vidal told Judy Balaban, a friend who wrote about his friendships with women for *Vanity Fair*, and he sent "seven or eight thousand dollars." When Vidal's picture appeared on the cover of *Time*, she sent a letter to the magazine saying he was unworthy of its attention.

"Gore would set people straight if they treated Howard in a patronizing way," says Burr Steers. "He said that his mother didn't want Howard around and that was totally unacceptable to Gore. Perhaps he was over-compensating for earlier in the relationship when Howard was kept out of the glare. It was an intense relationship that swung in different directions. He never let go of it." She denounced him in a letter to *Time* magazine. "He never had a nice word to say about her," says Richard Harrison, a former 1950s beefcake model, actor and friend of Vidal's. "Gore hated his mother: he would say she was a complete and utter drunk," says Elinor Pruder, a friend of Vidal's since the 1950s.

"Isn't she beautiful?" Vidal said with genuine warmth, observing a picture of his mother with his friend, the actress Nancy Olson Livingston. "He was agonized by the lack of real caring and love from his mother," she tells me. "He was born fifty years too soon: to be homosexual in a very conservative family who cared so much about image. So even with his gifts, being gay was a problem for him, as it was for anyone growing up eighty years ago surrounded by a society, schools, family and churches and community that didn't know how to accept it. Look at how long progress has taken. He was always in conflict about his sexuality. He never acknowledged it. Gore was enormously intelligent, but had a deeply wounded heart."

Later in life, Vidal wrote to his friend Judy Halfpenny scornfully of his childhood home that it had raised his blood pressure to return later in life to Merrywood, "the gilded trap out of which came three of the most selfish professional hookers that I have ever met—Jackie [Kennedy], Lee [Radziwill] and Nini. The first two have—had—a few mitigating good qualities but all three, moneyless in a moneyed world, spent their lives on the commodities exchange market, selling ass as did our mothers before them." Vidal told Halfpenny that it was not a healthy atmosphere to grow up in. He had been the first to make his own fortune, he wrote. "I think the family regards me as a white sheep."

In a hitherto unpublished 1999 interview, Vidal said that the Army had paid for him "from seventeen to twenty" after which he earned his own money becoming "much better off than my father was. I think he regarded me as a miracle. The sons of his friends were having divorces and troubles or going bankrupt. Here I was, sailing along. He was very proud. We never quarreled. He was one of the greatest charmers that ever lived. To counterbalance my monstrous mother I had a charming father." But the scars of Vidal's childhood would leave intense, indelible marks, vivid right up until his death.

Chapter Three

Jimmie Trimble: His True Love?

"He was the unfinished business of my life," Vidal said. He met Jimmie Trimble as a boarder, from 1937 to 1939, in the lower form dormitory of St. Albans School, "along with other Washington sons whose parents didn't want them underfoot," as Walter Clemons put it. Vidal was unself-conscious about his own early sexual feelings, he told Fred Kaplan, reassuring one of his friends that it was alright to masturbate. Trimble was an idol to all the boys: a star athlete at fifteen who was offered a contract with a professional baseball team. "Romantic jargon was out of the question for these two very masculine young men," writes Kaplan. "For both, it was prelapsarian, a combination of adolescent sex and friendship."

In 1999, Vidal spoke to Donald Weise about "longing for the unattainable" being common for boys and girls. "But when you get it at twelve or thirteen [when he met Trimble] you've made a very good start." Trimble is the sexual archangel of Vidal's story: a love and lust-object whose potency was never equaled in Vidal's bed or mind, long after he physically left Vidal's life. John David, a teacher, recalled to Kaplan that his memories of Trimble "were those of unrequited libidinousness. At seventeen he moved through the halls "briskly, but when he idled along he had a generous roll of the hips—the flexible hips of the athlete—that promised, like the Anglican definition of faith—'the substance of things hoped for, the evidence of things unseen.'" Trimble's mother, Ruth Sewell, later told Vidal that Jimmie had asked her once, "Did you ever tell a man he was beautiful?" A girl had just said it to him; for Vidal he "overflowed with animal energy, not to mention magnetism for both sexes."

In the showers Trimble belonged to Vidal's "elite" group— boys with pubic hair—the "aristocrats" of the group, rather than the "plebes" who did not, Vidal wrote in *Palimpsest*. "I was part of the aristocracy," he affirms—well, of course he was. When Trimble arrived Vidal went for a shower with him. "As I looked at him, he gave me a big grin and so it began, likeness drawn to likeness, soon to be made whole by desire minus the obligatory pursuit." In *Palimpsest*, Vidal claimed Trimble embodied his fascination with twins and mirroring was his "other half." Vidal writes, "We were friends immediately. I was one week older than he. We were the same height and weight. He had pale blue eyes; mine were pale brown. He had the hunter-athlete's farsightedness; I had the writer-reader's myopic vision. I was blond, with straight hair. He was blond, with curly hair. His sweat smelled of honey, like that of Alexander the Great."

In Vidal's youth, he said in 1974, "if the handsomest athlete was queer every boy was going to bed with every other boy; but if he wasn't, they'd all imitate him and go to bed with girls. Quite extraordinary how one or two idols always set the tone." Straight men could be turned. "An erection has no conscience as they used to say in the army many years ago." His blooming sexuality was a great adventure, Vidal said. "Things were not always as open as they are now. But we all, hetero, homo or bi, were just obsessed. If you were in town and did not get laid every day, I mean, the spirit died. I can remember when I'd miss two days in a row, and I'd think life was over, that something terrible had happened." He once wrote to the British equality campaigner Lord Longford, "If you don't love people sexually, you cannot love them at all."

Vidal was always extremely pro-sex, for its psychological benefits as much as physical pleasure. "If you always inhibit your sexual response, you will have a terrible time dealing with others in other respects," he once said. He liked athletes like Trimble because they were "at home" with their bodies. The intellectual, on the other hand, "is the last person you could or would want to get into bed. Or a fag. The uptight queen." Of course, Vidal, a gay man himself, was different from all those inferior "fags" and "uptight queens." There was no way he could be like them. He was of a higher, distinct order.

Trimble would spend weekends at Merrywood, swimming and playing tennis and belly-rubbing to orgasm with Vidal, said Vidal. They had this kind of sex on the white tile floor of the bathroom, somewhere else in the house the butler was on the prowl. "But there we were, belly to belly, in the act of becoming one. As it turned out, Jimmie had been involved with another boy, while I, despite wet dreams, had never even masturbated." Mutual masturbation was impossible, Vidal said, because Trimble had callused hands that "gripped the cock like a baseball bat. So we simply came together, reconstituting the original male that Zeus had split in two...There was no guilt, no sense of taboo. But then we were in Arcadia, not diabolic Eden." Trimble's mother later told Vidal that her son became a boarder to escape his step-father who may have sexually abused him.

In 1939, Vidal told Kaplan, he and Trimble made love "in the woods above the roaring [Potomac] river...his almost mature body with the squared bony shoulders and rosy skin against bright green." After sex they swam and lay side by side on a rock. "We're going to go on doing this for the rest of our lives, I remember thinking, tempting—no, driving, fate to break us in two." He imagines snatches of conversation about jazz, writing, political ambition, becoming a pro-ball player. Years later a teacher of Vidal's told Vidal that he and Trimble had been involved sexually and had once driven past Merrywood and Jimmie had seemed sad.

But the two boys were not entirely alike. Trimble was an athlete, Vidal played "erratic" tennis. "I tried to read everything I could," Vidal writes in *Palimpsest*, "he read as little as possible." Vidal was therefore fascinated by Trimble asking his mother later to send Walt Whitman's *Leaves of Grass* to him when he was serving abroad: "This set off a tremor. He and I certainly lived out the Calamus idyll." The boys would go to Benny Goodman jazz concerts. But the boys had wildly divergent family lives. Trimble loved his mother, Vidal "detested" his.

They did not see each other much after 1939 when Vidal left to attend the Los Alamos Ranch School in New Mexico, presided over by A.J. Connell, who fondled the students. "He always made overtures, I kept out of reach," Vidal told Kaplan. With an ambition to be a senator like his grandfather, Vidal next went to the Philips Exeter Academy, his father's alma mater; Trimble had stayed at St. Albans. Vidal saw him for the last time in 1943 at the Sulgrave Club in Washington. "We met awkwardly in the ballroom," Vidal writes, between dancing with girls to songs like "The Lambeth Walk" and "The Big Apple." Vidal said that he and Trimble orgasmed over each other while talking about girls and marriage in a toilet cubicle.

Vidal returned to Exeter, where he encountered gay men in the fiction of Somerset Maugham; a friend told Kaplan that Vidal had told him Maugham used to pay for sex. "I got the distinct feeling that he was talking about a role model." At seventeen, Vidal broke off from writing a gay-themed novel inspired by *Cakes and Ale*. Much later in his life, reviewing a biography of Maugham, Vidal wrote—and again, the echoes with himself are, at minimum, ironic—"I suspect that Maugham's experiences with women were not only few but essentially hydraulic. Writers, whether same-sexers or other-sexers, tend to have obsessive natures; in consequence, they cross the sexual borders rather less often than the less imaginative who want, simply, to get laid or even loved. But whereas a same-sexer like Noël Coward never in his life committed an other-sexual act ('Not even with Gertrude Lawrence?' I asked. 'Particularly not with Miss Lawrence' was the staccato response), Dr. Maugham had no fear of vaginal teeth—he simply shut his eyes and thought of Capri." Note Vidal could not bring himself to say "gay" or "homosexual," but rather "same-sexer" and "homosexualist."

After graduation, Vidal enlisted in the army. Stationed in Colorado Springs in 1943, a handsome, red-haired Southern lad played with himself while Vidal, now eighteen, told him stories. "There was a great deal of [same-sex] sex going on...there were many men eager to know us," Vidal writes in *Palimpsest*, "and once, as I was blown by an old man of, perhaps, thirty—my absolute cutoff age—he offered me ten dollars, which I took. As a result I, alone in the family, did not condemn Jackie's marriage to Onassis, since I, too, had once been a small player in the world of commodities' exchange market."

The excitement was in "anonymity, transgression, the almost infinite opportunity for pleasure without the tedium of establishing a relationship or the danger of entanglements," writes Kaplan in what could sum up Vidal's sexual *modus operandi* for the rest of his life. A friend recalls Vidal telling him that during his military service, a group of gay men had been expelled from the army after being caught having sex: Vidal was "outraged that something like that had happened."

Thirteen million Americans were engaged in wartime service, Vidal said in 2000. "They moved away from home, many overseas. People got out of the military to see what the world was like. They certainly tried same-sexuality with each other and god knows other sexualities were going on." Those that went to college "liberalized if not educated them." For Vidal, a real moment of revelation—as for many other gay men who were aware of it—was the publication of Alfred Kinsey's *Sexual Behavior in the Human Male* in 1948, the same year as the publication of *The City and the Pillar*, and Vidal knew Kinsey. "Two or three years later there was the pill that liberated women from fear of pregnancy." Penicillin was made available in the Army. "I was one of the first people to have a penicillin shot...So we had a sort of circus."

Vidal told Sean Strub, founder of *Poz* magazine who became friends with Vidal in 1995, that he believed that the "modern gay rights movement" really began in the late 1940s (rather than with the Stonewall Riots), with the publication of his book and the Kinsey reports and "Bachelors for Wallace," the political group set up by Harry Hay to support Henry Agard Wallace's campaign to become President. The group became the foundation of the Mattachine Society in 1950. To Vidal, Strub quoted an explanation of urban gay ghettos arising from soldiers returning from the war, settling in the ports of New York, Boston, Washington, San Diego, Los Angeles, San Francisco, Portland and Seattle, "creating what ultimately became the 'gayborhoods.'" This "interested" Vidal, says Strub. In 1990 Strub ran for Congress in the same lower Hudson

River Valley region where Vidal had run thirty years before. Vidal lost his race by about the same margin as Strub later lost his.

The 1960s "had nothing to do with anything apart from drugs and not getting killed in Vietnam," Vidal said in 1999. It was in the 1940s and early 1950s that the true sexual revolution took place, "a generation released from its superstitions." In the full transcript of his interview with the makers of the documentary *The Celluloid Closet*, Vidal said, "All sorts of things started to happen which would not have happened if a boy remained in his small town, so vistas were opened for him as well...It was those of us who had come out of the war and had seen a good deal of the world, not to mention of the human psyche, and we knew that to be attracted to a member of the same sex was a perfectly natural business. We also knew it was a natural business to be attracted to the other sex. Some people went in for both, some went in for one, the other...there was a mixture."

In Seattle before the end of the War, in a smoky dive—smelling of "beer, cheap Ivory soap, fog-damp wool uniforms...we were a lean, sinewy, sweaty race, energized by sex and fear of death, the ultimate aphrodisiac"—Vidal picked up a merchant marine of twenty-five, weighing around 170 pounds. He was shorter than Vidal, "but seemed a fair fit." In a cot in a samples room in a hotel, Vidal had no plan, an "error" he soon realized as the marine climbed on him. Vidal tried to push him off. The marine "used an expert half nelson in order to shove partway in. I bucked like a horse from the pain, and threw us both off the bed. We rolled across the floor, slugging at each other. Then, exhausted, we separated. He cursed; dressed; left. That was my first and last experience of being nearly fucked." Later he saw the man again in New York's Astor Bar; Vidal was heavier and wryly contemplated suggesting "a return match," but when he said hello, the man frowned, said, "Oh" and turned away.

After he had returned from service in the Aleutians in 1945, Vidal discovered that Trimble had been killed, having heard nothing of him, through an offhand remark from someone else.

"We went off to war, and he was shot in the head at Iwo Jima. So popular was he that his fellow soldiers named a baseball field there for him, Trimble Field," Vidal later told Walter Clemons (in *Palimpsest* Vidal says Trimble "got a grenade in the face"). Fred Kaplan says he put Jimmie's death "on emotional hold" after hearing about it, as he prepared for a new literary life in New York. "I was stoic since, forever after, I was to be the surviving half of what had once been whole," Vidal writes in *Palimpsest*.

The City and the Pillar, which Vidal wrote in Guatemala City, is dedicated "For the memory of JT" and Trimble is also thought to be the inspiration for the novel's "Bob," who is killed by "Jim" when the men meet again, years after a passionate affair in their youth; in a later edition of the novel, Jim doesn't murder Bob at the end but rapes him, then leaves him. In the novel *Washington, D.C.*, Walter Clemons notes in his unfinished Vidal biography, the character Peter Sanford has great sex with a handsome straight athlete called Scotty, who teaches him how to masturbate in a bathroom in the fictional Sanford mansion, based on the real-life Merrywood. Vidal, writes Clemons, "is careful to point out that both figures represent not autobiography but imaginative projections of 'what might have happened.'"

When I met Vidal in 2009 I asked if Trimble really had been the love of his life, as he once said. "That was a slight exaggeration. I said it because there wasn't any other." He told me that in the book he was then completing, *Snapshots in History's Glare*, there were "wonderful pictures" of Trimble from their schooldays. "He was a great athlete." His voice softened from its cutting imperiousness and he looked emotional, briefly. "We were both abandoned in our dormitory at St. Alban's. He was killed at the Battle of Iwo Jima because of bad G2 [intelligence]," he said in a mournful, absent growl. Did Trimble's death affect him, I asked. "No, I was in danger of dying too. A dead man can't grieve a dead man." I asked Vidal if love had been important to him, and he was back to withering form. "Don't make the error that schoolteacher idiots make by thinking that gay men's relationships are like heterosexual ones. They're not." He "wouldn't begin to comment" on how they are different.

Friends and intimates question the Vidal retelling of the Trimble story and its overall significance. E. Barrett Prettyman, a classmate of Gore and Trimble's "and the third member of their school trio" at St. Albans, told Jay Parini, Vidal's good friend and soon-to-be biographer, that nothing happened between the two boys. Parini said: "Prettyman told me that if Gore had tried anything, Jimmie would have either been shocked or tried to deck him. Barrett said it was only in Gore's dreams. Jimmie Trimble was a fantasy. Gore only really liked heterosexual, unattainable men. He liked athletic, a little butch, men without a grain of stereotypical gayness."

Vidal felt more comfortable with heterosexual men, says Parini. "It helped him feel comfortable with me, it helped him feel comfortable with Paul Newman. He didn't like effeminate men, he could barely tolerate them. He could barely bear to talk about gay liberation. He thought everybody was bisexual. He came to believe his fantasy about Jimmie Trimble. I think he needed an objective correlative for his sense of longing and loss. Jimmie stands for all of Gore's longings. If anything had happened or was there, Jimmie wouldn't have noticed it: we're talking maybe about a look in the eye, the brushing of a hand. Jimmie would have taken those for what they were. Every time Gore talked about Jimmie with me the story came out slightly differently. He was like the ghost of Christmas Past."

Austen, says Parini, would "jerk off" behind Vidal's head if he talked about Jimmie. "Gore's talking and writing about Jimmie came comparatively late in their relationship. I think Howard would have disliked it. He understood Gore, and rolled his eyes. 'Oh Gore, basta basta with the Jimmie Trimble, here we go again.' 'Stop it now, put it to bed.' There was an awful lot of that."

"Jimmie Trimble becomes the consistent pattern for the kind of hustler he liked," Fred Kaplan tells me. "Gore didn't want relationships. None of those young men ever became part of his life: they were fifteen minutes of sex. As for professing eternal love for Jimmie, Gore's capacity for love struck me as quite limited. Gore's interest was substantially in himself. He was as narcissistic a personality as you can imagine. I don't think Gore was ever in love with anyone, male or female, or any of the people he had sex with."

For Matt Tyrnauer, Vidal was a "great weaver of narratives," and the Trimble narrative was "elaborate and brilliantly incorporated into the sublime *Palimpsest*. When he wrote about Jimmie himself, these stories flourished for him. *The City and the Pillar* was dedicated to it. His later novel, *The Smithsonian Institution*, is about it in a certain way. There was a little of Jimmie in [Vidal's 1970 autobiographical novel] *Two Sisters*."

"Seventh grade is pretty young," says Burr Steers. I don't know when it would have happened. Howard was sick of hearing it. 'Oh my gaaaad, that fucking Jimmie Trimble again,' he'd say in that Bronx accent. It came up a lot. Trimble was Gore's ideal. But maybe he was a confabulation." As for loving Jimmie Trimble in the all-consuming way he claimed to, Kaplan and many others doubt it. "His 'I lost my one true love forever' about Jimmie is credible but ridiculous. Any ordinary person would have to say, 'What are you going on about, you schmuck? You loved once, you'll love again.' It's a miscreation, a self-myth, the grand love affair, 'I'll never love again' fits a certain kind of expression of his personality. It gives him credibility as a feeling human being—'I too was in love'—with the license never to love again. Really: how could he not have loved Howard?"

"Jimmie came up a lot in conversation and in front of Howard too," says Bernie Woolf, an old friend of Vidal's from his Rome days and close friend of Walter Clemons. "It seemed very immature to me, though for Howard it seemed water off a duck's back. That's not to say he may have been hurt by it, but it was too late to do anything about it—and anyway, he and Gore had been together for so long."

Some of Vidal's friends and intimates take his deification of Trimble at face value. "He fell in love madly when he was young which can happen," says Boston bookstore owner John Mitzel, who interviewed Vidal for *Fag Rag* in 1974. "Then he was obsessed with this lost love affair all his life. That can either inspire you or inhibit you, and I think in his case it inspired him. Jimmie clearly wasn't homosexual. He was having fun with Gore, and had Jimmie come back from the war there would have been no future to that relationship." Vidal "always" talked about Jimmie Trimble, says Vidal's longtime friend, the author and famed Hollywood pimp Scotty Bowers. "I was on Iwo Jima and had a brother who was killed there," says Bowers. He mentioned him so often. He would say how fond he was of Jimmie and how much he liked him. I got the feeling he was one of Gore's first loves."

The theater director David Schweizer, who first met Vidal in Rome when Schweizer was having a relationship with Tennessee Williams, found the Trimble story "the least compelling of Gore's legends. That makes me sad, the infatuation. I would like to think there were more complex social and intellectual reasons for his sealing himself off from full-blooded relationships than a school-boy crush that he had for his entire life. I think it's a writing trick. I don't think it's nothing. I do think there was boy he was wildly infatuated with, then it became a trope, then he bought his own literary trope, kind of because he was a cold fish. It suited him to live this other way. It seems very literary to me."

"How can a fifteen-minute encounter in 1938 be *the* gay memory you take with you?" wonders Vidal's bibliographer Steven Abbott. "In 1948, Gore dedicated *The City and the Pillar* "to the memory of J.T." In 1956, he dedicated *A Thirsty Evil*, a much lesser-known book of short stories, to Austen. "Why, after forty-plus years spent with Howard, did Gore in *Palimpsest* focus more on Jimmie Trimble, a person who's been dead for decades, than Howard? I did not understand why he didn't dedicate *Palimpsest* to Howard." Richard Harrison says, "I think he only liked Jimmie because he died. Once somebody dies they are a god forever. Gore told me the maximum they did together was lie down and masturbate. That's not a hell of an interesting thing to me. I didn't find it so impressive, do you?"

Vidal wrote of having lunch with Trimble's mother in

Washington D.C. in 1992, "aged ninety but like fifty...a wispy Southern woman of considerable beauty" angry about a *Vanity Fair* article exposing Vidal and Trimble's relationship or Vidal's version of it. "'Well we both loved him,' she said at last," Vidal writes. "His letters to her as he approaches extinction on Iwo Jima are wrenching still. He was a Marine scout and knew there was no way that he could survive—as indeed he did not. The night of February 28-March 1, 1945, he got a grenade in the face. That's what I call really unfinished business."

His mother recalled that Trimble had told her that when he stayed with them at Merrywood the Vidals had silk sheets and a butler asked at night what you wanted for breakfast. His letters to her as he is about to die are more like a husband to a wife than son to mother, Vidal writes: "He is plainly in a rage at being killed before he could have his life." In Nicholas Wrathall's *Gore Vidal: The United States of Amnesia*, Vidal says that Trimble had told his mother that the soldiers of Iwo Jima would "never be thanked" for their service, that all that "they" [the powerbrokers, corporate kings] would remember was how much money they made during the war.

In *Palimpsest*, Vidal reconstructed Trimble's years in military service and quotes his final letter to his mother: "I'll never forgive myself for refusing to follow your advice to stay in college. After the war we won't receive any credit for having been out here...Mom, please don't get the blues over what I am about to say, but some insurance should be taken just in case." He asks to make sure his girlfriend Christine White gets a gold ring with diamonds: "Kind of a memorial the other way around." Jimmie had excitedly told his fellow soldiers he and Christine were to be married. In his letter Trimble says he'll write again in a couple of days. "All my love to the swellest mom in the world. Your devoted son, Jimmie."

Vidal holds Trimble's decency up to the reader as a talisman and foundation for all his future beliefs, in mournful memory of the idealism and good natured patriotism of these "real" boys "before the great sullenness spread over the land." Vidal sketches

Trimble's death grimly, his jumper and innards shredded to-gether. In one version Vidal tells, Trimble is shot and bayoneted, in another he is "luckier," killed by a grenade to the face. In a 1992 letter to his friend Judy Halfpenny, Vidal wrote, "One of his platoon remembers he saw him at midnight on March 1, 1945 when Jimmie, a scout, relieved him in Iwo Jima. At 4:15 am the Japanese attacked in force. Of eight scouts, six were killed."

For Vidal, Trimble was a symbol of how far American lead-ership and politics had fallen; in *Point to Point Navigation* he writes that as a soldier he would hear much "fierce grievance for those back home who were decimating our adolescent genera-tion." His grief and anger over how Trimble died informed his keenly felt fury at the end of American empire and the arrogance and folly of the country's political leaders.

Vidal wrote in *Palimpsest* that Trimble was his chance at "wholeness"; he writes that "experience suggests that desire of any kind is brief." In *The City and the Pillar*, the realm of fiction allows him to write about what might have happened if he and Trimble had met years later; the conclusion (love unreciprocated, the erup-tion of violence instead of passion, a life together dashed) may have been too harsh as judged by some readers—but for Vidal "there is no common reality beyond desire, the pursuit, and, in at least one case, the achievement of the whole. It would be greedy—not to say impractical to expect a repetition of a lucky accident. I was very much aware of my once perfect luck, and left it at that." He didn't know if Trimble ever received, as he had asked for, *Leaves of Grass*; if he had read about Whitman's "brotherhoods of lovers."

Vidal revisited Trimble in *Two Sisters*, not as a character, but in its theme of doubling and twins. "Death, summer, youth—this triad contrives to haunt me every day of my life," Vidal writes, "for it was in summer that my generation left school for war, and several dozen that one knew (but strictly did not love, except per-haps for one) were killed, and so never lived to know what I have known...and someone hardly remembered, a youth...so abruptly translated from vivid, well-loved (if briefly) flesh to a few scraps of bone and cartilage scattered among the volcanic rocks of Iwo

Jima. So much was cruelly lost and one still mourns the past, particularly in darkened movie houses, weeping at bad films, or getting drunk while watching the Late Show on television as our summer's war is again refought and one sees sometimes what looks to be a familiar face in the battle scenes—is it Jimmie?"

In 1973, having a "rare" experience with hallucinogens (smoking ganja, he writes in *Palimpsest*) in Kathmandu, Vidal says "Jimmie Trimble arrived in my bed wearing blue pajamas...And I could actually feel his body." It lasted only an instant: "Then he rejoined Achilles and all the shadowy dead in war." Writing to Judy Halfpenny, Vidal reported Trimble's mother to be like "a character in *Driving Miss Daisy*, only sharper, younger." Trimble had left "so many grieving girls" behind, she had no fear of "any taint to his memory and, 'After all' she said sipping her vodka martini over lunch, 'you love him too' and I always loved anyone he did." Christine White, Trimble's girlfriend, was an actress and "nemesis of [his good friend] Joanne Woodward," who got the early parts Woodward wanted.

Vidal emphasized the propriety of his feelings for Trimble to his correspondent Judy Halfpenny. "I was never, in Nixon's delicate parlance, a jock-sniffer," Vidal wrote. "I never saw Jimmie play baseball, or anyone else if I could help it at school, or elsewhere. I'm not a spectator by nature. What we had in common is that, at fourteen, each was a fully developed man in character as well as procreativity and he knew exactly what was going to do with his life (after baseball he was a saxophonist) and I knew then that I was a writer." They were two halves that made a whole, he says.

In *Palimpsest*, Vidal writes of his researcher meeting Christine White, who says she had originally not wanted to meet Jimmie; she was in high school and private schools like St. Albans were considered snobbish. But a friend told her how he liked jazz and had a fantastic personality and smile "that would just knock the birds out of the trees." She invited him to her New Year's Eve party, which took place a week after the boys, if you believe Vidal's story, had ejaculated over each other in the Sulgrave Club's toilet cubicle. White told Vidal they were definitely going to be married, he didn't mind her wanting to become an actress. After hearing she was dating another guy while he was away in the army, he wrote her a stinging letter about stringing him along. She assured him she wasn't. He told her he was going to become a professional baseball player. After Trimble's death, Ruth gave her the diamond ring he wanted her to have. On his dead body were two pictures of White and a couple of letters.

Vidal said of the era of Trimble and him meeting, boys messed around but weren't "queer." They did not kiss each other, "cruel fun" was made of "sissies" and there were dangerous older men, like the one who put his hand on Vidal's crotch in a theater. He and Trimble and boys like them were "up to a perfectly normal homoeroticism" that for many did not lapse "into the physically more complex homosexuality" or "serious heterosexuality." Trimble, wrote Vidal, was "homoerotic and heteroerotic. I suppose I am curious about the balance between the two in his nature. But then when one lover goes into shock at the news of his death and another mourns him to the end of his life, we have moved beyond sex or eroticism and on to the wilder shores of love, and shipwreck." For Vidal, "gay" meant limp wrists and a ghetto he wanted no part of; his mind never allowed that "gay" could mean firm wrists, men of all kinds having sex with, and loving, one another and being open about it; even realizing the potency of its political appropriation, or something to reveal, rather than hide. A theoretical die was cast, which some may see as radical, others as the distillation of sad personal denial and Vidal's stereotype-drenched prejudice. Much seems to have sprung from Vidal's image, memory and idealization of Jimmie Trimble.

Filming a documentary the day after Jacqueline's Kennedy's death in May 1994, Vidal visited Trimble's grave, saying, "I keep my mind fairly blank: find it hard to believe Jimmie has been just bones in a box for half a century." His "current Jimmie" was blue-eyed and grinning. He met Christine White himself the next day, who showed him snapshots of Trimble as well as a photograph of her they found on his body bent into the curve of his body. She said he "cannot" be forgotten; Vidal says he "*will* not be forgotten."

Vidal's claims on Trimble were roundly condemned by White in a 1996 letter to the author Val Holley (who sent it on to Vidal). In a furious letter she first castigated "confirmed homosexuals" reclaiming the dead who "cannot answer or defend themselves" to "give the living deceived Sodomites legitimacy." Vidal "presumes that his riches from Standard Oil, etc, family ties and Hollywood links verify all of his declarations. Gore has a long list of literary credits, but in doing his memoirs, he just had to play Pharaoh 'to the cause' and dig up another talent from the grave, who happened to be an athletic genius, who happened to be my fiancé (she underlines those last two words).

"Do any of you care about the feelings of the living 'straights'? You do not, we are the enemy to you. Oh, that the whole earth would be Sodom and Gomorrah." As an atheist Vidal "can lie and steal and shrug at the mention of 'pay day.' He lied and invented and is so blinded that he can barely tell the difference. It's too bad because he liked me very much and I did want to be friends with him. James Trimble barely knew of [underlined] him, never associated with him, never mentioned him. Jimmie Trimble's MIND & HEART were definitely on me, on baseball, his mother, his friends, fellow athletes & marines and The War...and in that order. I have it in writing. And Gore Vidal has that [underlined] in writing from me."

Vidal was determined to have the last word. In a letter to Holley, he wrote that White "saw Jimmie a half dozen times—she has now, thanks to me?, built this up into a major fantasy. But he was [underlined] crazy [underlined] about her and wrote her letters up until the end." Christine White outlived Vidal, dying on April 14, 2013.

White wasn't alone in rejecting the sexual and romantic link between Trimble and Vidal. Nina Straight states with certainty, "Gore and Jimmie didn't happen. Gore liked famous people and before all the celebrities he knew, Jimmie was already famous: the blond, blue-eyed fantasy, the multi-sports star, the pitcher of the century. He was a knockout hero in the suburbs of Bethesda and Chevy Chase. But he would have been utterly clueless about Gore. He left school in seventh grade. They didn't have sex. Because gay sex and relationships became chic to write about, Gore constructed it. Jimmie was what he hoped he was. All those guys at St. Albans: he could have had romantic moments looking at them in the showers—they never knew it and wouldn't care. I guess Gore was a romantic: romance was a Phantasmagoria of Gore's." Vidal's longtime friend Jean Stein says: "From what I understand, Jimmie Trimble was a complete fantasy. Nothing ever happened between them but Gore memorialized this idealized figure who otherwise would have been completely lost in history. We all have our fantasies. Perhaps Jimmie was Gore's golden boy, or everything that Gore wished he could be."

After Howard Austen's death and near Vidal's own, Trimble again asserted his place in Vidal's heart and mind. Fabian Bouthillette, his caregiver from 2008 to 2010, a former Navy veteran, recalls that "many nights" Vidal would stop in front of Trimble's portrait on the back stairs "for a few minutes and look at the picture. Gore talked about him all the time, about how beautiful he was, how 'my' Navy had killed him. He was still fixated on him. He still loved him. For anybody to be still fixated on their high school love interest at that age might seem odd, but Gore Vidal was, and not just Jimmie but that whole generation of boys who were killed at Iwo Jima."

Richard Harrison agrees, and adds that there must have been something substantial to the fantasy. "I do think something happened. Do I think they fooled around a little bit? A little bit. But Jimmie wasn't interested or grew out of it, and Gore stayed fixated. He always said *The City and the Pillar* wasn't about Jimmie, but gimme a fucking break. I think people underestimated just how serious and genuine Gore was about his anti-imperialism, and how that was personified by all those boys losing their lives at Iwo Jima. Jimmie was the intimate link to that. Gore loved this boy and the person he loved was killed in a horrific way in one of the most horrific battles in history."

In *Palimpsest*, Vidal writes that for years "whenever I was in a numinous place like Delphi or Delos, I would address the night: Jimmie, are you anywhere? And almost always the wind would rise. But I am neither a believer in an afterlife nor a mystic...I cannot begin to imagine what it must be like. Yet I still want Jimmie to *be*, somewhere, if only on this page." At the end of *Palimpsest* he reveals that he and Austen will be interred in Rock Creek Cemetery midway between Trimble and Henry Adams—"midway between heart and mind, to put it grandly"—in "subdivisions 2 and 4 of Lot 29312 in Section E." Adams was a journalist, novelist and historian Vidal admired who like him came from a political family: his paternal grandfather John Quincy Adams and great grandfather John Adams were US presidents.

Whatever romance there might be to the Trimble story Vidal crafted, many people are more circumspect. To the novelist Edmund White, Vidal's loving enshrining of Trimble "sounds like an alibi. 'This is why I haven't had a love affair, because I was so in love with boy who died in the war.' Don't you find something lightly putrid about that, like (William) Faulkner's story 'A Rose for Emily' [in which the dead body of the female protagonist's lover is found in her bed after she has died]. I just think that anyone like Gore would have gotten on with things, met people, especially someone as rich and good-looking as him. It's such a weird fixation you feel he doesn't really believe it himself."

Certainly, Vidal's sex life was only just beginning, Trimble the never-to-be-bettered gateway to a life of unfettered sexual expression. At Exeter school, Vidal wrote to a friend years later in an undated letter, the athletes "were—are—the most sexually (physically) confident and even in that dark age not as easily put upon as the others. If they enjoy sex with one another, no one is going to stop them." There was no sex for Vidal at school, he writes in *Palimpsest*: "On the rare occasions when sex was a possibility, he who made the first move would forever be in the power of the moved upon, no matter what happened. This made for a certain irritability in all relations."

Love and valorize him as he did, Trimble's death didn't lead to Vidal stopping the clocks. Before he met Austen in 1950, Vidal told Michael Childers he'd had "a grand love affair" with a dancer, Harold Lang. Vidal would talk a lot about Lang, recalls his friend Patty Dryden. "He would go on and on about him. He told one story that one time Harold was in a bar and a guy came up to him and called him a faggot or fairy. Harold did a leap from one foot up on to the bar and said, 'Fuck you, Mary, I can dance.' Gore loved to tell that story and laughed himself silly." In itself this is intriguing: Vidal, so long assumed to be disdainful of camp, here laps it up.

Lang and Vidal met in East Hampton in 1947 in a bar; Lang was in town dancing (he would find career success in the stage musicals *Kiss Me, Kate* in 1948 and *Pal Joey* in 1952). Lang had sex with men and women, was both promiscuous and monogamous, whatever felt right with the person, Fred Kaplan writes in his Vidal biography. Vidal found him "just extraordinary to be with...It was really the sexual life force. I've never seen anything like it and never saw anything like it again...It was 'the greatest ass in history,' as Bernstein said, and Lenny was a true authority." The first night, the muscular, dark-haired Lang was the pursuer, writes Kaplan, then argued with Vidal the next day. "I wasn't capable of an affair, he thought," Vidal told Kaplan. "I seemed so much like so many other people he knew." Then they went back to bed. "That was the way the loving started."

In *Palimpsest*, Vidal writes that during his short time with Lang he was "obliged to face the fact that I was never going to make the journey from homoerotic to homosexual and so I was never going to be able to have anything other than one-sided passing sex. Thanks to Harold, this belated revelation was to prove a great time-saver over the years."

Yet that was him being defensive and dismissive; in truth, being with Lang led for the first time to Vidal making love "with the intent to give as well as get pleasure," as Kaplan puts it. Vidal and Lang went to Bermuda, and a rift opened up after Lang went out drinking in a bar one night and Vidal didn't. Then Lang went on sex-strike claiming Vidal didn't satisfy him. Lang wanted to talk and jest about the theater world. "Finally, one morning, I took him against his will and he was angry and hurt," recalls Vidal. "We fought and I was ready to fly back...He asked me to get him an analyst when we got back, he felt he would go to pieces soon." They moved into the Chelsea Hotel in New York, both saw therapists with Vidal leaving his fairly quickly, the therapist saying to him in an "ain't-that-the-truth" observation: "You think your shit is better than other people's shit."

Lang left New York suddenly. In a 1947 letter from Vidal to Lang, notable not just for its contents but also Vidal's unusually emotional tone, Vidal writes he is "quite upset" over not hearing from Lang. "Analysis is quite a frightening experience. I think we've both reached a similar impasse: when our careers don't give the same satisfaction, the same forgetfulness as they once did; it's not a pleasant thing to see oneself but it must be faced sometime. I think this is the right moment for you; I know it is for me. I hope you go on with it." Vidal, at that moment writing an unnamed play, is finding "the theme of elusiveness a little too personal and poignant to write about. I must wait until I'm settled; until I've heard from you. My feelings about you are unchanged; from now on it's up to you preserve this: if you want it. I wish you'd write me." They reconciled, broke up, and Vidal began seeing a new lover, probably dancer Johnny Kriza, who he enjoyed "casually thoughtless" sex with, wrote Kaplan. The composer Ned Rorem, a "solid accomplice rather than good friend" to Vidal, recalls Vidal's boyfriend before Austen was a mutual friend, Chuck Turner, a "naïve innocent," who Rorem bumped into with Vidal strolling through Saint-Germain-du-Prés in Paris in 1950.

Next Vidal would meet Austen, and they would spend their lives together, even if Jimmie Trimble stayed firmly lodged in Vidal's romantic memory and intellectual consciousness. Maybe the experience with Trimble devastated him, maybe his heart ached and never recovered, maybe the memory of Trimble and what they shared—whatever that was—stayed with him. Maybe Vidal parlayed the story of Trimble into a story of ultimate love, a useful fiction of what the love between men could and should be, never to be defined and diminished in Vidal's eyes by being classified as "gay," even though he would live the reality of a long-term relationship with Austen. Intriguingly, acknowledging that life-long relationship's importance was far harder for Vidal than relishing the memory of whatever happened with, and was memorialized by, Jimmie Trimble.

Chapter Four

A Partner in All But Name

For someone who claimed he wasn't gay, Vidal first encountered his male partner of fifty-three years at one of New York's gayest locations of its time. Vidal met Howard Austen, then twenty-one, on Labor Day 1950 at the Everard Baths, where men went for sex. Vidal was twenty-five and the same year had published his fifth novel in five years, *A Search for the King*, a retelling of the thirteenth-century saga following the troubadour Blondel as he attempts to rescue Richard the Lionheart, the English King Richard I, from prison.

How had he and Austen stayed together so many years, Vidal said they were often asked. "No sex" was the answer. "This satisfies no one, of course, but there, as Henry James would say, it is." Austen gave Matt Tyrnauer a different answer about the sex frequency: "Maybe a little bit at the beginning." It took twenty-four years for Vidal to acknowledge Austen's place in his life. In 1974, *Fag Rag* magazine asked, "Concerning your relationship, with Howard Austen. What is the financial arrangement and/or how will you leave your money?" Vidal responded, "I have lived twenty-three years with the same person. Presumably because I am older I will die first and just leave it to him. That's all." It wasn't a hearty endorsement of his partner, of the man who cared for him closely and adoringly, leaving him free to pursue his writing and broadcasting careers. But publicly Vidal disavowed Austen's place in his life and his importance, until finally after Austen's death he redressed the balance in *Point to Point Navigation*.

Of meeting at the baths, Austen told Fred Kaplan, "I saw Gore coming down the corridor, and he was really something. Good-looking. Somehow our eyes struck. In the corridor. Towels here and a *schmatte* there. Then we started talking and ended up in bed. And it was just a total disaster." However, "there was an enormous attraction, but it wasn't physical. It was kind of relief. I felt like I had met a soul mate." Vidal lied that he was a student. Austen said he'd never met a student who read *The New Yorker*. Vidal asked him to lunch the next day.

Austen, a then-recent graduate of New York University, was from a working class Jewish family living in Pelham Park in the Bronx. "In those days it was a nice area, there were gardens, the Bronx Zoo," recalls his sister Arlyne Reingold, now seventy-two. The young Austen was artistic and liked to draw and play the saxophone. Their father, Harry, was a truck driver, and their mother, Hannah, a housewife. At five or six Austen said he was hit by his mother for masturbating. He also liked musicals and singing: he wanted to be a pop star and would later become a stage manager for Broadway shows. Vidal and Austen's many friends remember his voice; Vidal often listened to it after his death on CD. His sister recalls Austen singing "New York, New York" and "Bewitched, Bothered and Bewildered."

Austen wasn't close to his parents, it has been said, although Reingold says the family was close and that they "didn't mind in any way" Austen being gay. By ten Austen was having sex with the super's son, who was around twenty years old, in the park. "I really did the seducing," he told Fred Kaplan. "I was really very aggressive about it as a child." Austen worked in advertising at Lever Brothers before he and Vidal met (Vidal encouraged him to change his surname from the original Auster to Austen to avoid anti-Semitism in the industry), funding his way through New York University by working at a Walgreens store. He had had his first "really serious" sexual experience with a woman; it wasn't good and he began having sex with men, growing to like the baths.

"Howard was a rebel, very bright," says Reingold, who was eleven and a half years his junior. "He took me to classes, like psychology, museums and ballet. He was my savior. My father wanted him to stay in the Bronx, Howard wanted to sow his oats. He wanted a lot more than staying in the Bronx." Reingold laughs as she recalls her and their mother visiting an apartment Austen had moved into at Lexington Avenue at 55th Street. "He'd painted all the walls black, probably to be bohemian. You should have seen her face. She said, 'Why have you done this?' Howard laughed and said, 'Oh, I love it.'"

The party line, repeated by Vidal in withering, homophobic terms to Judy Balaban in her 2013 *Vanity Fair* article about Vidal's friendships with women, was that "all the faggot fan magazines wanted to know how these two famous fags stayed together all these years. They wanted to know what was the basis of our relationship. So I told them. We never had sex. I had sex and he had sex, but it was never together. Of course, they were furious and hated me for that answer...We never had sex, because I'm more intelligent than most people, and that's the way I wanted it. I was smart enough to know that if you wanted to keep a friendship you made sure there was no sex. It was self-preservation." This may be true, but another more basic truth—lived out by many couples, deeply in love and committed to one another—is that sex can tail off, or cease to be so important.

"Sex is very important in one's youth," Vidal told Donald Weise. "If you have no interest in the other person you're not really being heterosexual or homosexual, you're self-gratifying and that's frowned upon in a world where warm, mature human beings are having warm, mature sex, reaching out their hands towards the other. 'I'm heeere, Vernon.' 'I knowww, Millliiee.'"

Nobody seemed to take his "no sex" answer seriously, when it came to explaining his relationship with Austen, Vidal told Weise, who replied, "Because it sounds like a joke. It sounds like you're not being serious." "I've always made a point: never have sex with a friend," Vidal said. But Austen wasn't his friend, he was his partner—at that moment of forty-nine years. "You can always get somebody for sex," Vidal continued. "Nothing is easier. You're not going to make many friends in life in any case, and having sex with them wrecks it. Maybe there are those who triumph at it but I am certainly not one of them and I don't know many people who do triumph at it."

Many of Vidal's friends and family roll their eyes at Vidal's contention his and Austen's relationship worked because they didn't have sex. "I wonder about that no-sex thing, especially in the early part of the relationship," says Dennis Altman, a long-time friend of Vidal's and author of *Gore Vidal's America*. "But adopting that detachment made it easy to separate sex out. It was a Victorian view almost, a high-society relationship: on the surface respectability, then sexual adventure on the side. He was discomfited with gay sexual liberation because it challenged his assumptions: being gay wasn't to be kept quiet or to the side, it was integral to one's identity." Vidal never thought it should be. "He had an absolute distaste for identity politics," says Altman. "Gore was a patrician: he had a very strong sense of himself as needing to play a central role in the affairs of his country. He had a continual bitterness that not everyone agreed with him. Queer theory would have annoyed the shit out of him."

Fred Kaplan writes that both Vidal and Austen were "eager for friendship, for family on their own terms. Both recognized some potential for creating a relationship, for family on their own terms. Both recognized some potential for creating a relationship that might substitute for what they had been denied or had rejected." Vidal had had a lot of sex with working class young men, with Austen "he had an immediate strong feeling of protectiveness, companionability, seniority" whom he referred to as his "child." Austen was in awe. When Vidal asked him to stay at Edgewater one weekend Austen said he might be busy, Vidal told him if he couldn't make it, it was "goodbye." Austen went up for that weekend. Vidal made it clear the relationship wasn't sexual, which might have led to jealousy early on, Austen told Kaplan. "I would have gone on doing it...I would have gone on willingly." He said he supposed he "ended up a permanent playmate, Greek chorus, and Jewish mother."

In 2009, Vidal told me that when people didn't believe him that he and Austen had lived together so long because they didn't have sex, "That was when I realized I was dealing with a public too stupid by half. They can't tell the difference between 'The sun rose in the East' and 'The sun is made of yeast.'" Was sex important to Vidal, I asked. "It must have been, yes." Vidal once wrote, "I'm exactly as I appear. There is no warm, lovable person inside. Beneath my cold exterior, once you break the ice, you find cold water." But, as his relationship with Austen proved, that was a hardened, well-honed public image. The private Vidal was more complex, certainly more loving and some would say very cruel: a hive of paradoxes. In *Palimpsest*, Austen had to read that while Vidal had been with him for over half a century, not only had they not had sex but also "where there is no desire or pursuit, there is no wholeness. But there are satisfying lesser states, fragments." Vidal was telling the world Austen was no Jimmie Trimble, his true love; so what exactly kept them together? What comprised their commitment, their love?

Letters from Austen from the early years of the relationship reveal the flirtation, warmth and sexual intimacy between the men, which throw serious doubt on Vidal's claim that sex was a fleeting aspect of their relationship. The tone of the letters speaks of the passion and tenderness of lovers, not friends. Austen often signs the letters with the affectionate moniker "Tinker" Vidal gave to him. And they had no sex, as Vidal said? In 1950, Austen writes to Vidal, who is away, "I feel terribly restless. All my manhood is going to waste in dirty socks and underwear."

On February 1, 1951, Austen writes to say he is feeling confined living at home: "It's worse since you've been gone. You were such a pleasant escape—so pleasant and influencing that now I feel like caviar in a can of sardines. My parents really are gruesome." When he's with Vidal, "you're Gore—a nice, sweet guy who writes brilliantly and whom I'm very fond of: not Gore Vidal, THE writer...Oh I'm on a diet. It probably won't be very effective tho'." On March 1, 1951, Austen writes of work woes and says Vidal, who is travelling, is lucky. "You're a great writer first, last and always...I miss you so much. A month is so little in a lifetime, but so much in a time of love...Boy, I'll bet you're really going to look like your 'bound slave' when you get home, nice suntanned skin and golden hair. You'll be so handsome."

The letters thrum with horniness, the early stages of falling in love and emotion. On December 3, 1951, Austen writes, "I am missing you so terribly much...I love you, Tinkerbell" and in another note: "Tinker misses you so much...He wishes desperately that he were there with you or you back home. I don't think he trusts you very much either, because he always has this silly suspicions of you being spirited away from him by some bad bogeyman...T is getting sentimental, like a little baby when all his life he fought to be free from sentiments and wanted to be a full-fledged man." The letters are from one boyfriend to another, not two friends.

In 1953, Austen writes to Vidal ("Mr. Me"), chiding him: "A little bird came through the window last night and said, 'Tinkerbell, Mr. Me really wants to write but he is so busy having such a good time while you have nothing to do, that he 's just forgotten all about his Tinker rat'...Is Mr. Me concerned about his Tinker rat? No!...Is Mr. Me nasty? Yes!! Is Mr. Me selfish? Yes yes!! Does Mr. Me care? No! No! No!...Tinker's been trying terribly hard to be good and it's even harder not to be bad, but does Mr. Me appreciate that and write and tell Tinker that he appreciates it and loves him for it? No, course not, thank you very much...I decided I would give Mr. Me one more chance because after all I still love Mr. Me more than anybody else in the world and though I don't see him I still think about him all the time and he seems to be so very far away...But you can believe me too when Mr. Me comes back he's going to be hit so hard for not writing that he'll be blue and black for the rest of his life. I miss you so much. All love, Tink."

A reassuring letter must then have arrived from Vidal. "I take it all back," responds Austen. "You're the best Mr. Me in the whole world." In the early years of the relationship Austen was "rarely seen or heard," says Nina Straight. "Howard was treated like shit. We would go out for dinner with Gore, and Howard would be 'elsewhere.' Gore did not want to admit his homosexuality to himself." Indeed, there are a few letters from Austen reprimanding Vidal for not writing, of "missing him terribly" and, in a 1956 letter, an entreaty for some consideration: "This has been rather a complaint letter, but I consider it part of your responsibility to be interested, in the same way that I am interested in your life and problems. I miss you and I love you—both very much." The letters express not the sexless domesticity of a couple of friends as Vidal presented as an image to the world, but partners. In 1965, Austen writes to Gore, "Please take care. I don't know what I would do without you."

Vidal's good friend Elinor Pruder recalls Vidal's apartment, a walk-up, on East 52nd Street, in the late 1950s, a period of multi-creativity for him: he was still writing novels—like *The Judgment of Paris* (1952) and *Messiah* (1954)—but becoming better known, and getting better-paid, writing TV shows and working on film scripts like *Suddenly, Last Summer* (1959) and *Ben-Hur* (1959). After feeling stung that he felt his talents were not being recognized properly as a novelist, Vidal was also writing mystery novels under the pseudonym Edgar Box, like *Death in the Fifth Position* (1952) and *Death Likes It Hot* (1954).

"Howard was definitely the dominant partner at that point," says Pruder. "They had a fight once at my apartment. Norman Mailer and his girlfriend were there: she got very drunk and could barely walk at the end. Then Howard suddenly left. Gore panicked. 'Where is he? Where did he go? We must find him. We must get him.'" Pruder had "never seen a reaction like it from Gore. He depended on Howard. He told me, crying, that night, 'Elinor, you don't realize, I need Howard.' 'OK, we'll find him, hold on there, darling,' I said. 'I depend so much on Howard,' he said."

Nina Straight remembers that the "only time" she saw her half-brother upset was when, "sometime in the '50s or '60s," they were staying "at a friend's place in some woods" and Vidal lost a tiny picture of Austen he carried in his wallet, "of Howard as a little boy with bangs and Mary Jane shoes. He lost it and we had to look all over for it. He was really upset and saying, 'He's the only good person I've ever known'—'good' meaning simple, guileless—and he loved the image of that little boy, the basic, innocent dedication and purity." Vidal would say to his sister "all

the time" that "the smell of little boys' hair is baked bread."
Straight says: "He talked about homosexuality like that: as something beautiful, like looking in the pond at oneself."

At other New York parties were the kinds of handsome,
younger men Vidal liked, often actors. But no flirtations
advanced into relationships, says Elinor Pruder. "Howard was
his heart-throb. He never took off, he was with Howard," she
says of Vidal's early commitment to Austen. "Howard was so
funny. 'I'm from Queens,' he'd say in his Bronx accent. 'Look
where I am now.' Later on he would handle everything: the
travel, menus. He made anything gray, white. For him a sense
of humor could help with any situation. Gore was always in control, but Howard knew how to manage him. If Gore lost control,
Howard handled the situation." In 1962, Austen went to hospital
with suspected thyroid cancer, which proved to be benign. In
the same hospital Frank Merlo, Tennessee Williams's lover, was
dying of lung cancer. ("The Bird would mourn Frank ever after,"
wrote Vidal, even though they had broken up years before.)

Austen, who moved in with Vidal in 1960, was the practical,
grounding figure in the relationship: he made Vidal take care of
himself, made him go to bed early, made sure before public
appearances he had dried out from his drinking. His great achievement was in running Gore's life smoothly. Yet the first time
Austen's importance in Vidal's life was alluded to publicly was in
an interview in 1974 and even then only in response to a question
of who Vidal was leaving his money to. I asked Austen's sister
whether he was fulfilled as Vidal's full-time caretaker and
protector. "Oh yes," Arlyne Reingold said. "He travelled all over
the world meeting famous people, travelling luxuriously, he did
everything he wanted and was kind, sincere and very honest."

Austen seemed "like a nice guy" to Scotty Bowers. "It seemed
like an equal relationship to me and not lopsided. They got along
like two young businessmen, no petty arguing as to who ate a slice
of bread or drank the Coca-Cola. It was very honest, above board,
cool, everything done nicely, not in a queeny or chintzy manner.
Howard did his own thing between singing and cruising and fuck-

ing around. He was always cruising." Another friend recalls that Austen was "very low-key, a nice guy, not pretentious, from the outer boroughs, sassy, a little rough around the edges."

The actress Susan Sarandon, a good friend of Vidal's for many years, recalls that the men together seemed "like an old married couple. Howard took care of real life, did all the heavy lifting." She, her then-partner Tim Robbins and their children spent a lot of time at La Rondinaia, Vidal and Austen's home on the Amalfi coast that Vidal purchased in 1972. "He spoke better Italian than Gore, took care of the house. When we went out for dinner, after a few drinks, Gore would say, 'Go ahead, Howard, sing.' And he would sing, *a cappella*, something bluesy. Gore would gaze at him proudly and lovingly." Nina Straight disagrees over Austen's singing ability: "It was terrifying if you had to listen to it. The minute he started singing you looked toward the window to see who had thrown the cat out of the window." In 1961, Christopher Isherwood recorded in his diary that he and partner Don Bachardy felt "great warmth" from both Vidal and Austen in Edgewater, though "on different wavelengths...Gore is always cool. Howard is the eager, loyal spaniel who irritates him with his fussing."

He also, by common assent, kept the good-ship-Vidal afloat. Arlyne Reingold tells me her brother kept Vidal "in line," doing "everything" for him. Vidal invited her and Austen's parents to Edgewater, then later to Rome and Ravello. "Gore was fabulous to me," says Reingold. "I felt like his baby sister." On one visit to Hollywood when she was fifteen, Vidal and Austen took her shopping at Saks Fifth Avenue to buy a red lace dress for a party where she remembers dancing with Robert Wagner and meeting Burt Reynolds. "There I was, a poor kid from the Bronx," she says with a laugh. "We're not having an affair," Austen told her when she was young of the men's relationship; Austen shared with Vidal, it seems, a refusal to classify their relationship as anything of the kind. Or perhaps just exhibiting filial embarrassment or sensitivity, or some closet-sourced shame. "Howard came to see all my plays at school," says Reingold. "He wanted to get me out of the Bronx too by exposing me to things."

Austen had wanted to see "more of the world," she says. "My parents were small-minded." But they never said anything derogatory about their son's sexuality or the men's relationship, she insists. Again at a total variance to his public image and pronouncements that he and Austen were just friends, Reingold reveals that Vidal had a very close, loving relationship with his in-laws. Austen's mother would make Gore chicken blintzes and stuffed cabbage "and bring them to him all over the world," she says. "Gore would joke with them putting on an exaggerated Jewish accent and say things like, 'Oy gevalt.'" In Rome, Vidal would take Reingold to exhibitions. "He was hysterical, such good fun." Her parents were not poor, but neither were they "in any way well-off," yet their exposure to Vidal's world didn't "overwhelm" them, says Reingold. "We knew people who were rich, it wasn't a big thing." Vidal in turn was a generous, doting son-in-law, however he defined his relationship with Austen. Of his own family, Vidal once told Reingold, "They're bitches."

Vidal relished being with Austen's family, says Reingold. When her daughter Karen, then sixteen, visited Vidal and Austen in Rome, she excitedly told her mother that Vidal encouraged her to try what he described as "good French fries." She told Reingold, "Mom, he made me eat calamari and it turns out I quite like them." For Reingold, Vidal was "such a special man, kind, funny." He called her, affectionately, "Arlynie" and was "tender and open-hearted" with Austen's wider family. Did she ever see him angry, more withering? "He didn't have much patience," she says. "If you were talking nonsense, he would walk out of the room." Her fondest memories are of sitting around the pool at Ravello, Austen, "a wonderful cook," rustling up his favorite dish, pasta Alfredo. "Gore didn't put on any airs with us, he was a good, nice person, so quick and witty. To me, as a young woman, he was a father figure."

The men's relationship had "built over years," Susan Sarandon tells me. "They would tease each other, snap at each other, and had so much in common. I don't know about the hustlers, but once I was staying there, there was a muscle guy staying too, whose function I was never sure of. He had a girlfriend in the village and seemed more Howard's than Gore's." Austen's role was vital, says Michael Childers. "Gore wouldn't have accomplished half of what he did without Howard. Howard was the engine that made the train run." Vidal told Muriel Spark that Austen's "medium dry wit is always a source of pleasure to me."

"Gore was really cold: a really cold, cold fish, says Matt Tyrnauer, "Howard was much warmer." Austen was adept at puncturing Vidal's pomposity or lightening the mood with well-timed crudity. "He lightened it up," recalls Tyrnauer. "If Gore started to attack he'd say, 'Don't worry, baby, it's the gin talking,' or 'Shut up, Gore, you're wrong' if Gore was crossing a line or getting aggressive. If Gore was banging on about the Bill of Rights, Howard would break in with, 'Gore, how big do you think [Porfirio] Rubirosa's penis was?'" [referring to the 1950s Dominican diplomat and international playboy]. Vidal, recalls Tyrnauer, gave a serious answer: "Probably eight inches I imagine. The mythical nine is barely possible." Tyrnauer laughs. "That was what I loved them for: something treated as social history even if it was sexual, which is what Gore's novels were built on. He takes the stuff that seems dirty and fripperous and makes it considered. That is one thing that was great about Gore. He was like a contemporary Suetonius, giving equal time to the dry political drama and the unspeakable sexual gossip."

Another friend recalls watching with Vidal and Austen President Clinton's Senate impeachment hearings on television, Vidal drinking Scotch after Scotch and noting of one young Republican congressman: "Oh, he's kind of cute." A few Scotches after that, as the same handsome Republican continued to talk, Vidal announced, "Well, that's the mouth of a cocksucker if ever I saw one."

Like any relationship, it had its own subtle power dynamics. Austen "worshipped Gore, and Gore needed to be worshipped full-time, and Gore couldn't live without Howard in a practical sense and I think Howard used that power to keep it together," says Tyrnauer. "I think neither of them was interested in romantic love. They were a perfect pair and Howard complimented Gore perfectly. He was the sorbet course to Gore's mutton." Austen was also the recipient of Vidal's rough drafts. "He would try out a personal attack or essay or passage in a novel and put it to Howard. When Howard died the filter was gone. A lot of people were hit by missiles that Howard would have intercepted." Austen's sister recalls her brother admonishing Vidal "Lay off, stop already" when Vidal became impossible or rude. She noted a "businesslike companionship" about the couple. "Looking after Gore was a full-time job."

Bernie Woolf says he "can certainly imagine living with somebody for a long time and not having sex after a certain period. But to say you hadn't had sex with the man who was your partner was so rude and not a nice thing to do. Howard was a prince to him. And he had a mouth on him. He was very entertaining and if a little bit vulgar, so what? He was very New Yorky: it was 'cawfee.' He wasn't Noël Coward. The impression was he was Gore's servant but Howard didn't think of himself like that. He saw himself as an intricate part of Gore's life."

The couple socialized glamorously: they "loved" Barbra Streisand and were often at her house, recalls Donald Gislason, their Ravello housesitter. They talked about going to a dinner of hers with Helena Bonham Carter, Sidney Poitier and his wife, Joanna Shimkus, and Robert Downey Jr. "They said the vodka martinis came out, which no one had as they were all watching their weight and having water," Gislason recalls. "There were five choices of meal: red meat, fish, chicken and two vegetable meals. There was five of everything so you didn't have to wait for anything." In Rome, the journalist and author Judith Harris remembers suppers with author Italo Calvino, Vidal at his "happiest," but also rounding occasionally on people "viciously" at the table. Occasionally the comments would be anti-Semitic, "even though Howard was Jewish. He would sit there and not say anything."

Burr Steers recalls that Senator Gore, Vidal's beloved grandfather, had a wife, Dot, "who took care of everything, which was what Howard did. They obviously had a deep affection for one another, it was a healthy relationship. They were great friends. But Gore kept Howard in the shadows, in newspaper articles he was known as 'Gore's secretary.'" David Schweizer "only understood" the Vidal-Austen relationship as "love, after Howard died and seeing how bereft Gore was. In Rome in 1971 I thought the terms of the relationship were clear and rewarding to both. There was a little bit of bitchery, Gore would undercut Howard sometimes, lightly humble him in front of people, embarrass him over his accent. It was affectionate too, like an old routine. But the efficiency of the relationship was unmistakable. Howard did all the practical things, Gore had a lot of work to do. They were a team." Hubert de la Bouillerie, a friend of Vidal's since he was a little boy through his mother Elinor Pruder, said, "He always said it was a platonic relationship with Howard. I didn't believe a word."

Diana Phipps Sternberg, a longtime friend of Vidal's, says Austen's organizational skills were wanting. "He was referred to a 'secretary' at an early stage, but never managed to organize anything. Gore organized airplane tickets and all of that. Somehow Howard mixed it up. Gore always referred to Jimmie Trimble being his great love. He and Howard were like a play. Gore scolded Howard all the time, Howard whined and complained, Gore complained about Howard. Howard organized all the orgies." The orgies—and there were many—happened in Ravello and Outpost Drive. Burr Steers recalls one guest at Vidal's memorial service telling him that he had once come to Outpost Drive, then spied "a row of cowboy boots and a sea of bodies in a room beyond."

Phipps Sternberg says of the couple, "They'd lived together for so many years, one can't know what holds a relationship together." For her, what bound Austen and Vidal was "companionship and quarrel. People like Gore need, if you'll excuse my wording, a whipping boy. Gore needed somebody he could scold and cherish, like a child. That was Howard. I never had the feeling Howard was his great love, although after he died Gore was desperate. Gore cherished him a great deal but only discussed that after he had died." Austen took "wonderful care" of Vidal, says Vidal's friend Lucy Fisher. "Gore always acted as if he was completely dependent on Howard yet was also a snob. He adored Howard but was not often appreciative. He had a profound gruffness that you could tell was not all of him. He didn't feel it, although he could be gruff too. I think he was embarrassed by the affection he felt for Howard."

The actor Jack Larson, a friend of Vidal's since 1954 and one of America's first television idols, famed for playing Jimmy Olsen in *The Adventures of Superman* in the 1950s, recalls Vidal "as always so offhand about Howard." Larson found this especially odd, as Austen had been so assiduous in helping to raise campaign funds for his 1982 Senate run. "It seemed an equal relationship, Gore always seemed very considerate, and I always took Gore at his word that he it lasted all those years because of no sex." Were they loving? "They were comradely. Obviously Howard was devoted to Gore, and Gore very considerate."

If you take Vidal at his word, that he and Austen were not sexual partners, they certainly had a lot of sex around the relationship, much of it procured by Austen for them both. Over the years Scotty Bowers, Vidal's longtime friend and famous as a pimp for many Hollywood stars of the 1950s and 60s, came to know that Austen would go out cruising, pick up guys and share them with Vidal. "It wasn't just prostitutes but also young men who were available. Howard picked up many men who weren't hustlers and picked up more men in general than Gore. Howard was a nice guy," he says. "They were a great couple and made you feel very welcome. They weren't like two nelly queens. They weren't catty."

Austen told Fred Kaplan, "Who could ask for anything more? I got the company of Gore. Beyond anything I really ever dreamed of...I know people are puzzled by how it works between me and Gore. I've been plagued by that all my life. What do you say, 'Hi, I'm Howard Austen, I'm associated with Gore Vidal, but we don't sleep together?' You assume when two men are living together that [they do]...It was a corner they put me into that I just had to accept. Even today. There's no defense. If it were true, I would not be ashamed of it. People have done a lot worse than Gore Vidal, even though he's fat."

Jason Epstein saw Vidal and Austen's relationship as "a marriage, but it was so peculiar. He set up Howard up so virginally as the man he didn't have sex with while he had sex with so many other people. The outside of that relationship was very cool, but inside it was very heated. Howard took care of everything, Gore would blame him if an airplane was late, but they loved each other. They could quarrel and it wouldn't make a difference." Austen was a wonderful crooner, recalls Epstein, singing old Cole Porter songs. "Gore's arrangement with Howard was very domestic, it was a long-term marriage with a strict division of labor." Epstein, so used to seeing Gore hardened and wry, was surprised in Ravello one evening when, beside his then-dog Rat who had cancer, Vidal said, "Soon Rat's going to die, Howard's going to die, and I'll be all alone.' It was a rare moment of unguarded affection for someone who claimed to be beyond all feeling. I had never heard him speak like that."

They slept separately: in Ravello, as later in his life in Los Angeles too, Vidal would stay up and invite his houseguest that night to stay up with him; a bottle of Scotch would be opened until after four in the morning, the Vidal story machine on full throttle. "The term 'heavy drinker' was no shame to him, quite the opposite," recalls Donald Gislason. "I remember once helping him home drunk from Ravello, getting to the gate and he showed a fence that had been constructed to the side preventing a drop to a vineyard below. 'You know, a person could fall in there,' he said, and I knew by his tone he had."

For Edmund White, "I think it was cruel of Gore to say that he and Howard didn't have sex. That's like denying in any real sense he's your partner and again characteristic of that generation to be evil like that and an awful betrayal of Howard's public role. I remember reading an interview with Marguerite Yourcenar in which she was asked about Miss [Grace] Frick, the person she lived with. 'She's just my secretary,' Yourcenar said, whereas in fact Frick was her partner, supported her, typed her manuscripts, and probably licked her pussy. It probably meant quite a lot to Howard, I would have thought. It's like, if you're the King of Hungary, saying, 'The Queen and I have never consummated our relationship.' How is she expected to reign after that? What position does she have? Why say it? To pack his heart in ice. Men like Gore have companions like Howard who do everything for them: if they can't sleep they stay up all night with them, if they have to have their wisdom tooth pulled they go to the dentist with them."

For White, Vidal had "separated out friendship, companionship and sex, which many people did in the '70s. You would assign those roles to different people—fuck buddies, the lover you lived with, friends, friends with benefits...all before AIDS. There was an eagerness in the gay community to find lots of possibilities, but I'm giving Gore too much credit to say he did that."

Vidal and Austen "had a very civil relationship," recalls a female friend who wishes to remain nameless and who first met Vidal decades ago. Of observing them in Rome in the 1960s, she says: "Although Howard took care of Gore, it wasn't apparent that he was subservient. Howard automatically knew what Gore expected of him. I assumed there was no sexual relationship between them but they were very close, almost a family situation. Gore was a fantastic host. If he liked you, it was a gift, if he didn't, forget it. Luckily I was one of the fortunate ones." Vidal's major domo Norberto Nierras says Barbra Streisand had asked Vidal what the secret was of being together for fifty years. "Mr. Vidal answered her (just as he wrote *ad nauseam*): 'No sex.' I don't know what that was all about. They had their own bedrooms, but they watched TV after dinner in Mr. Austen's room and would call me on the intercom to bring ice and whiskey."

Kaplan tells me that Austen "was a finer human being than Gore, in terms of relationships, honesty and self-awareness. Howard was mostly subordinate to Gore, though took care of all domestic and organizing duties, freeing Gore to pursue his public life. It was a friendship, and as for Gore's statement that they never had sex, well, they were comrades in sex, rather than sexual partners. They had sex with other people, who were bought into the house. I don't know if they had three-ways. They went cruising together. My sense was, when I got involved with Gore in the mid-90s to 2000, was that both Howard and Gore were not engaging in sex in the large way they had in the years before that. Their relationship seemed to be a domestic partnership without sex. It never felt very loving to me, it felt like good friends. It felt as if they depended on one another and were utterly interwoven."

Sean Strub, who saw the couple in Ravello, agrees. "I was struck by how respectful they were to each other. I don't remember the incident, but there was a moment when I saw Gore being very solicitous of Howard that kind of surprised me. I only met Howard twice, in Ravello, but I got the impression that Gore was very protective and appreciative of him. I'm not saying that the reverse isn't true, I'm sure it was, but what I observed was surprising to me because I kind of expected Howard to be more overtly protective of Gore, maybe even in some sort of gatekeeper role. But that wasn't the case. Howard wasn't deferential or secondary, and Gore was very solicitous and caring towards Howard. They were very much equals from what I witnessed."

On one visit to La Rondinaia, accompanied by John Berendt, author of *Midnight in the Garden of Good and Evil*, Strub remembers Vidal telling him not to use the toilet, because the flush would wake Austen. In his forthcoming memoir, *Body Counts: A Memoir of Politics, Sex, AIDS and Survival*, Strub relates that Vidal told him to piss out of the window instead, "gesturing toward the French doors in his library that faced the Gulf of Salerno. As I stood on the small, wrought-iron Juliet balcony outside the window, John joined me and unzipped. Then Gore came over and the three of us stood shoulder-to-shoulder, peeing over the balcony into a dark night sky, our urine splashing on a skylight on the villa's lower level roof." Other of Vidal's friends said he asked the same of guests to do the same on to his patio at Outpost Drive; one wondered if "it was just so he could see your dick."

Austen had relationships independent of Gore, one in

particular with novelist Rona Jaffe, says Kaplan. "Gore told me it was such a special relationship that Howard had contemplated leaving Gore for her. It was certainly romantic, a mutual infatuation. I don't know if they had sex, but it is certainly ironic and amusing that in this gay relationship the possibility of it being broken seems to have come from female 'interests' on either side. But Howard and Gore loved one another very much." Arlyne Reingold recalls two sexual relationships with women in her brother's life. "One was a girl in his teenage years and the other was Rona Jaffe, which lasted a year or two."

Boaty Boatwright, Austen's friend before she became the couple's, said Austen would "never" have left Vidal for Jaffe. "They were together," Boatwright says of Austen and Jaffe, "but he would go home to Gore." Boatwright told Austen she couldn't imagine Jaffe being much fun, Austen replied, "She's good for me." Boatwright thinks "it was a time when everybody liked everybody to think they were in heterosexual relationships, or swung both ways." But Austen and Vidal were "brilliant together," Boatwright adds. "Howard always reminded Gore how brilliant he was. Gore wasn't expressive with anybody. You just sort of accepted they were together."

Jay Parini is adamant that "Gore worshipped Howard and Howard worshipped him. It wasn't true that they didn't have sex, or had it once and never again. They did at the beginning and probably later on as well. When Gore would say 'The secret to a long relationship is no sex' Howard would roll his eyes. Gore did have an intimacy with Howard. Howard humanized Gore. Their social life would have fallen flat without Howard. He was always cheerful and upbeat, which allowed Gore to be grand, remote and acidic. Howard had Gore's number. Without Howard Gore would be miserable." In the late 1960s and onwards, the letters and notes from Austen to Vidal are less passionate *billets-doux* and more chores-focused, centered around financial matters and home improvement, as Austen began to manage his life more and more as Vidal's fame grew. "Do you think we'll ever see each other over a relaxed cup of coffee with a puppy dog or two?" Austen writes.

The playwright Arthur Laurents recalls their upstate New York home, Edgewater, as "a spindly Tara," describing Austen as reddish-haired, freckle-faced," a friendly lad...carried bags, fetched drinks, cooked meals, cleaned rooms, sprayed bugs, and worshipped the master." Austen once jumped into bed with Laurents. "I'm exhausted," Laurents groaned. "Get out and let me sleep!" The next day Vidal informed Laurents, "I'm homoerotic, you're homosexual." Laurents recorded later: "Homosexual being obviously inferior. I was his inferior. The thin semantic line he drew explained his reputation for being a belly rubber." Ironically, for all he himself forswore love or the notion of having a longtime significant partner, Vidal introduced Laurents to his partner, Tom Hatcher.

Austen was a good foil for his partner. When Patty Dryden, who knew Vidal in the last decade of his life, had him and Austen over for supper, she asked Austen how they met. "Gore said, 'Oh, it was probably at the unveiling of another honor for me.' Howard interrupted him: 'We met at the baths.' He just completely cut him off at the ankles. They were well-matched. Howard was very much: 'Come off it, Gore, knock it off, snap out of it' and Gore would. No one else in Gore's life could do that. It was a relationship of love, not physical but very deep. They each had needs and qualities in the other that they didn't have in themselves." Indeed, perhaps they were each other's best foil. In Austen's obituary in the *Los Angeles Times*, the author recalls an incident where Austen swept his hand over La Rondinaia and its surroundings. "You know, Gore, after you're gone all this will be mine." Vidal not missing a beat, replied: "Yes, Howard, that's true, but no one will call." Vidal: eternal king of the zingers.

Austen looked after Vidal very basically too. By 1995, the author was already talking of controllable high blood pressure, a tendency to diabetes, the consumption of a half to two thirds of a bottle of whiskey in the evening, which might give him cirrhosis. But, he writes in *Palimpsest*, "after so many healthy days, why fret over the famous 'one day' that arrives sooner or later—in my case, already later—for everyone?" He swam a couple of laps of the pool and missed his once "vigorous body." Like the Queen, Vidal was too grand to carry money or credit cards. Austen always picked up the tab. Boaty Boatwright once remonstrated with Vidal that he should have a car or a car and driver like "people with serious money" like David Geffen and Barry Diller, although Vidal's "serious money" was never in the same league as Geffen or Diller's. "Gore's money never got over twenty five million dollars."

"They were always the closest of companions," says Jean Stein. "Howard worshipped Gore. He was like his mascot. He would parrot anything Gore said. Howard was Jewish. Yet he even parroted Gore's strong support of the Palestinian cause: it was rather amusing. If Gore had said, 'Hitler was the best person on earth,' Howard would have parroted that too. Howard was dear. He sang in the shower and had a beautiful voice. Howard was so full of life and fun, adorable, loveable, cuddly and warm, but certainly not an intellectual. I don't get their relationship. It seemed so unequal, but it didn't faze Howard in the least that Gore was of a higher order. Yet Gore was a tremendous snob. That he would choose to be with Howard has always been a mystery to me. He might have been turned on by him in the beginning. But all those years? I don't understand it. Perhaps Gore didn't want anybody else to be as original and dominant as he was: he may have just wanted someone who adored him without reservation."

In February 1971, Christopher Isherwood noted that the pair seemed "more than ever a devoted couple, despite Gore's outward coolness." The fact "we [Isherwood and Don Bachardy, Vidal and Austen] are both old couples is the one important thing we have in common." Isherwood felt "embarrassed, because I couldn't ask Howard, 'What are you doing now?' for fear he would have to say, 'Nothing.'"

Matt Tyrnauer notes that Vidal did not like being touched. "You'd never give him a kiss on both cheeks, so commonplace in Italy, or a hug. He'd extend a hand: very papal. I was amused by it. In later years you'd see guys reach down to hug him goodbye in his chair and see his discomfort. He'd allow a grand lady to hug him. But signs of intimacy between him and Howard were nonexistent. However, it was a marriage, they were absolutely connected—and most of *Point to Point Navigation*, published three years after Austen's death, was an apology to Howard. Only Howard, who didn't need constant reassurance and reciprocity, could have survived—someone secure enough and willing to have unreciprocated love or happy to be along for this amazing ride, so grateful that Gore lifted him out of an ordinary life. To keep that up with someone of such formidable narcissism is an amazing feat."

The geography of their house in Ravello was telling. There were at least five levels and terraces; Gore's grand room, in the early years, was at the top and Howard's "below stairs" at the bottom. Later, Gore moved below stairs, one room away from Howard. Vidal even kept his membership card to the Everard Baths hanging, framed, in his Ravello bathroom. Orgies and young men there may have been, but there was a certain formality to how Vidal and Austen presented themselves and liked to be seen publicly in Ravello—and that was certainly not as a gay couple, or as men having sex with the locals. Friends say Austen had "much more" than Vidal. "The villagers knew Howard as '*Il Secretario.*' That's how the locals referred to him," says Donald Gislason. "I thought it was a euphemism because Italians don't talk about gay relationships openly, but it wasn't. That's what they thought he was." Their driver, in thirty years, had never been into the house. Austen told Gislason it was probably best not to make friendships in town "because they led to dinner invitations, which you can't reciprocate because that would mean inviting them here, which is our house and something we wouldn't want." Vidal told Gislason, "I don't have any friends in Italy," which struck Gislason as odd as "they had lived there for thirty years."

Vidal and Austen hated any formality in Ravello and were "unconventional," says Dominique Buonocore-Dauchez, a French teacher who with her husband, Sergio, a communications specialist, was friends of the couple from 1974 to 1984. "They were very modest and Gore always welcomed and accepted them at big dinners with big people. He would walk around the home naked without even batting an eyelid. He was gorgeous and had a gorgeous body. He would read the paper in bed in the morning and throw page upon page on the floor. It was a crucial period for him. He was here to write. He was so modest and anti-conformist, not like any other artist. He was very well-known in the world. I learned a lot from their way of life. Gore was very welcoming with everyone, especially with us."

Steven Abbott saw a different side of the Vidal-Austen relationship when he and his partner stayed in Ravello in 2001: opening their mail one day, Vidal and Austen had been sent a box of chocolates. "Howard said, 'What do you think the motive of sending us these was?' The only power Howard seemed to have in the relationship was in the day-to-day running of the house and the imagined motives of people who they thought had more to gain from Gore than Gore did from them." When Abbott was preparing a book of laudatory quotes for a birthday of Vidal's, Austen said he would help but begged Abbott not to tell Vidal, "because he may not approve." Abbott says, "I remember thinking, 'After all this time, he's scared of Gore.'"

How did Austen put up with the omnipresence of Jimmie Trimble in the relationship? Matt Tyrnauer says, "Howard was willing to put up with it because I think he really loved Gore, and I think he knew Gore loved him and he felt Gore was a great man and there was a price you pay for being around greatness and I think he was willing to pay that price. They were a family." Austen referred to their life together as "family life," says Tyrnauer. "When you were invited to lunch in Ravello and it was a simple meal, pasta and a salad, Austen would say, "We are not eating fancy, because you're family."" Vidal "clearly liked this kind of chatter. If he disapproved, it would have been voiced, with acid."

For Christopher Bram, the mystery wasn't that Vidal "had sex with other people and orgies—who doesn't?—but that he didn't fall in love." Was the tortured memory of Trimble so predominant so as to inoculate against love; had his parents set the ultimate bad example of love and its failure, was Vidal too in love with himself and his work to even conceive of loving someone and all that would entail?

Vidal told another friend, the British novelist and playwright John Bowen, that "The person you live with you should never fuck. You will get tired of them." But he also told Bowen "I should fuck lots of people to have lots of different experiences. For a while I did have sex with lots of people. But David (Cook, the writer) and I have been together for almost fifty years so Gore's influence quickly faded. I never had a sense that there was real equality between Gore and Howard. Howard was very much the junior partner in any decision making."

In 1985, thirty-five years into their relationship, when gay novelist Felice Picano asked Vidal, "Is Howard your lover?" he received the answer, "No, he's my friend and we live together." It was only in *Palimpsest*, forty-five years after they had met, that Vidal first alluded to the depth of their relationship, "because everyone was admitting they were gay and so suddenly Gore realized he had a great love that was Howard and dramatized that for a while" thinks Picano, just as he had done with Jimmie Trimble.

For other friends, the relationship remained a mystery. Richard Harrison "didn't understand, never in a million years" Austen and Vidal's relationship. He didn't think Austen's IQ "much over one hundred...he had a typical whiny New York voice, it drove me nuts and could never understand how Gore could bear to be with him longer than five minutes." Once in Ravello, Harrison recalls Austen telling him Princess Margaret was coming over, but she never arrived: when she heard Vidal wasn't there, and only Austen, she cancelled her plans. Harrison asked Austen how he had met Vidal and said Austen replied, "I was trying to be a singer. I was broke and I met him because he had money." He asked both Austen and Vidal if they'd had sex and received the same answer from both men: "Maybe once." In Ravello once he overheard Vidal on the phone to Austen, "and it was all 'OK, coochy coochy baby baby lovey lovey.' That was very unusual to hear Gore like that. In all the years I knew him I never saw him hug Howard, nothing physical. Gore wasn't a hugger."

Austen threatened to leave Vidal in the late 1970s, "and Gore was beside himself," a friend told me, just as he was when Austen disappeared that night the many years before, and just as he would feel when Austen died. For someone who claimed theirs was only a platonic relationship, Vidal's feelings ran tangibly very deep. In New York, one male friend recalls, Vidal kept certain rituals going. He liked drinks in the Oak Bar at the Plaza. "He never updated. The Oak Bar may have been where the trade was in the past. Now it's a tourist attraction, but the bartenders there were often the same people who had been there for decades."

Once, the friend recalls, Austen was talking about a sex act Gore didn't do—"bottoming," playing the passive partner. "Gore was posturing that he never got fucked. 'Oh, Gore, you're so inhibited,' said Howard, then turned to me and said, 'Are you as inhibited as Gore?' And I said, 'Actually I am.' Howard said, 'Well, I did everything. I had so many venereal diseases I was always getting penicillin shots.' Gore said, 'I have never had one venereal disease.' Another victory over Howard, another way he could be superior to him. But the beautiful thing was Howard's reaction. 'Oh fuck off, Gore, you think you're so superior.' He and Howard tended to take a superior attitude toward 'queens' as they referred to them. He said he the word 'gay' never passed his lips without quotation marks, but he did say it occasionally. If he'd lived another twenty years he may have settled into using 'husband.'"

For Sean Strub, Vidal "seemed very proud of the relationship and the number of years they had together." The true scale of Vidal's feelings for Austen would become apparent when Austen became ill and then after his death, which led Vidal to declare his true feelings for his partner and which also precipitated his own severe decline. Vidal would find coping without Austen, who for those fifty-three years was so much more than a "friend," untenable.

Chapter Five

Rock, Tyrone, Jimmy... Vidal At Play

In December 2011, around seven months before he died, Vidal turned to his good friend Scotty Bowers as the two relaxed in Vidal's Outpost Drive home. "You suppose we could find Bob and bring him over?" the frail, nostalgic Vidal asked. "Bob" was Bob Atkinson, a favorite hustler of Vidal's that Bowers had first set him up with in 1948. They had long lost touch. Vidal's mind was becoming ever more untethered. "Gore liked Bob because he had been in the Navy and he had a cock as big as a baby's arm," says Bowers, who recorded his life as a trick, then pimp, to Hollywood's rich and famous in *Full Service: My Adventures in Hollywood and the Secret Sex Lives of the Stars*. "Scotty was the closest person to Gore in the last four years of his life who wasn't a servant," says Matt Tyrnauer.

Some have questioned the veracity of Bowers' stories. But the biographer William J. Mann, who spoke to Bowers when researching his 2006 book *Kate: The Woman Who Was Hepburn*, said, "I found him forthright and honest and not interested in personal fame or gain," turning down at that stage Mann's offer to write about him or introduce him to a literary agent. "Several people I respect vouched for Scotty's essential truthfulness and reliability as a source," Mann states, including the journalist and author Dominick Dunne and film director John Schlesinger—as well as Vidal. A film about Bowers, directed by Tyrnauer, is in production.

Bowers's book is rich in scandalous gossip, casting a direct and unsparing spotlight on a Hollywood of old, where secrecy was all and the stars protected by a ruthlessly powerful studio system, aided by a media that while frothing in gossip rarely if ever trespassed too far into the sex lives of celebrities. Bowers reveals he had sex with Walter Pidgeon, Cole Porter ("He could easily suck off twenty guys, one after the other. And he always swallowed"), George Cukor (who would "suck dick" with a "quick, cold efficiency") and Cary Grant and his partner Randolph Scott ("The three of us got into a lot of sexual mischief together"). Cecil Beaton would carefully tuck away and de-crease the sheet and blankets of a bed before sex; Bowers had threeways with former English King Edward VIII, the Duke of Windsor ("He sucked me off like a pro") and the woman he abdicated the throne for, Wallis Simpson ("she definitely preferred homosexual sex").

Further, Bowers writes, Spencer Tracy "took hold of my penis and began nibbling on my foreskin," Bowers writes, while Vivien Leigh "had orgasm after orgasm" with him, each one noisier than the last." "Penetrative sex was out" with Noël Coward—"it was strictly oral"—while Bowers made "long slow love" to Edith Piaf "until she dozed off as dawn broke." Charles Laughton liked eating pretty young men's excrement on his sandwiches, while Tyrone Power enjoyed being urinated on; Montgomery Clift was so "fastidious" about the tricks Bowers arranged for him he complained when one trick's penis "was an inch too long."

In this rollercoaster of scandalous revelation there are only four decorous, entirely sex-free sentences about Vidal, praising him as "one of the nicest, brightest men" Bowers has known. Vidal himself supplied a laudatory cover quote for the book, testifying to Bowers's veracity: "I have known Scotty Bowers for the better part of a century. I'm so pleased that he has finally decided to tell his story to the world...Scotty doesn't lie—the stars sometimes do—and he knows everybody." At Bowers's book launch, in what would be his last public appearance, Vidal told guests that he'd never "caught Bowers in a lie" in the many years he had known him in a town "where you can meet a thousand liars every day." Presumably, then, he would sanction as fact Bowers's revelations to me that Vidal not only had sex with him, but also "many" hustlers Bowers arranged for him, as well as Hollywood stars Rock Hudson, Tyrone Power and Charles Laughton.

Vidal's long friendship with Bowers, who was approaching

ninety at the time of this writing, was one of the most consistent of his life: he feuded and broke up with a number of close friends, especially as dementia exerted its grip in the last few years. "There's no one who can say they were friends that long because Gore didn't keep friends that long. I never had a cross word with Gore," says Bowers. "He was very opinionated, I was very easy going."

They met after the end of World War Two. A friend of Vidal's had told him about Bowers's gas station on Hollywood Boulevard, and Bowers had been told Vidal might be coming in. "That's how word got around in those days," says Bowers. "If you had money, you couldn't advertise as well as this. You take a queen, tell him a secret and swear him to secrecy, and you just got the word all over town." The first time he met Vidal, Bowers recalls him driving in one evening just after eight-o'clock at the wheel of a two-tone '47 Chevrolet. He said, "I'm Gore" to Bowers and hung out for around an hour, looking at the trade on display. "Wherever you looked there was someone," says Bowers. Vidal said, "I can see this is going to be a fun place, I'm going to be here often." For twenty dollars Bowers fixed his clients up with hustlers: "If a guy wanted to buy you a car or give you more money, that was his business. I never took a cut."

Bowers and Vidal connected well: Vidal had been in the Army, Bowers in the Marine Corps, which probably made Vidal more open with him than others. Vidal was two years older than Bowers. On that first night Bowers was working till midnight, so sent Vidal "off with someone else he liked, a clean-cut all-American looking guy, his type." A couple of days later he returned and said, "That was great, do you have someone else?" Bowers introduced him to Bob Atkinson, and Vidal saw him "quite often." "Gore had a medium sized cock, seven inches, he looked circumcised but wasn't," Bowers recalls. "He was basically a top [he liked to penetrate, rather than be penetrated], but with Bob he allowed himself to be fucked. With some men I fixed him up with he didn't have sex with them at all. He just talked to them if they were very bright. Gore enjoyed talking to people."

The few times Bowers had sex with Vidal was "pleasant, not mad love." Vidal was always "on the ball, not bashful or shy, rather aggressive and pushy," and was "more or less into a quick trick. He did everything sexually, you sucked his cock, he would suck yours, but he preferred to fuck. Gore and I fucked and rolled around and played with each other's cocks. He'd grab your cock and, boom, he was young and hot and sex was rather quick."

Did Vidal have sex with any of Bowers's other famous friends? "I fixed him up with my friend Tyrone Power, which Gore asked me for as a favor, and he did me a favor and had sex with Charles Laughton," Bowers reveals. "Charles Laughton was not Gore's type, but Gore went with me for kicks." It was a three-way? "Yes, Charles was a dirty old man, but they wanted to meet each other. It was the same with Tyrone Power." Bowers laughs that he "probably introduced Gore to more famous people than he introduced me to." He recalls Jacqueline Kennedy at one party going off to a bedroom with one man: her parting shot to Bowers, "I can't fucking help myself." Bowers says: "They always talk about her husband [JFK] fucking people, but she was a regular little tramp too. She'd fly out here just to see William Holden. So would Grace Kelly. When I fixed up Edward and Wally [the Duke and Duchess of Windsor], I fixed them up with a Beverly Hills hotel bungalow, she was the boss, he was shy and bashful. She told him what to do with guys: 'Suck his cock, do this, do that.'"

When Vidal and Power got together, Bowers recalls, it was a "sucky-fucky thing. Gore put his cock between Tyrone's legs and fucked him between his legs. They sucked each other off and played together." Bowers laughs and adds: "Gore told people I had introduced him to people he wanted to know and that was certainly the case with Tyrone Power. Both Charles and Gore sucked each other off and of course Tyrone liked being pissed on, so we did that. Gore went right along with it."

Bowers introduced Vidal to Rock Hudson; the men "hit it off" and they "buddy-buddied" together as friends too. "We had three-ways just when Rock was getting started as an actor," says Bowers.

"I met him in 1947 when he was living in Hollywood with a little queen who was a car-hop in a drive-in. They had an Irish Setter dog. Gore did a little bit of everything with Rock. He started necking with him and pretty soon he was playing with his cock. Gore was quite into fucking people between their legs. He did that with Rock. Rock had a steam room and that was across the courtyard as you came in. We went into the steam room. Gore was rubbing Rock and sucking his prick. There were hands here and hands there. We were necking, sucking and fucking: whatever position you wanted to be in you got in. We had three-ways a dozen times and I'm sure they did it on their own a few times. When you fix up two people very often they see each other. Separately they both told me how glad they were I introduced them. I know without a doubt they got together other times on their own and I'm sure, when they did, that Gore fucked Rock." Richard Harrison, the former beefcake model and actor who used the same gym as Rock Hudson, recalls: "He would sit in the sauna. His cock was so big it would hang down to the next step. All the old guys would complain about it. But he didn't use it—he was a bottom."

Hudson, Power, Laughton and Fred Astaire weren't the only celebrities Vidal had sex with. The writer John Bowen (a friend of Vidal's since reviewing *The City and the Pillar* for Oxford University's *Isis* magazine under the headline: "Kiss Me, Hotlips, I'm Asbestos") says Vidal described once having sex with Noël Coward. "Coward said to him, 'Let's have a roll in the hay.' And they did. Gore said it was quite enjoyable, but nothing very new." Kenneth Tynan in his diaries wrote that Vidal had told him that Coward asked him to bed in Italy. "When he entered the bedroom Graham Payn (Coward's partner) was already naked between the sheets. Noël bustled in and stripped; Gore buggered Graham, and Noël masturbated with his prick against Gore's bottom. Having rapidly come, he rose and dressed within seconds and went off to work, leaving Gore and Graham to share the post-animal tristesse."

Sean Strub saw Vidal become "very emotional" when talking about the actor Dick York, most famous for playing the first

Darrin Stephens on 1960s comedy *Bewitched*. York had also a part in Vidal's play, *Visit to a Small Planet*, originally written for television in 1955. Vidal rhapsodized about how beautiful York was. When Strub told Vidal York had fallen on tough times later in life, Vidal said, "Don't tell me that," with tears in his eyes.

Vidal wanted Scotty Bowers to introduce him to James Dean, "and I told him Jimmy Dean was a little prick. But I introduced them. Gore thought he wanted to have sex with Jimmy, but after meeting him, he said 'Fuck him. He's into his own thing.'" Bowers fixed Vidal up with "dozens of people," including in Italy men who he knew in Europe: they were, as so many friends recall, "clean-cut, all-American type guys, not rough trade or weird muscleboys, not a bum or someone with long hair." The playwright, director and screenwriter Arthur Laurents recorded that when he first arrived in Los Angeles, Vidal had told him he'd love it there: the hustlers on Santa Monica Boulevard were only $15 before six o'-clock, "and that's when I like to have sex anyway."

Vidal's promiscuous post-war sexual life began at a range of New York venues, including the Everard Baths (nicknamed the Ever Hard, where he met Austen) and the Astor Bar. In *Palimpsest*, Vidal writes of his excitement at finding the Baths, "where military men often spent the night, unable to fund any other cheap place to stay. This was sex at its rawest and most exciting, and a revelation to me." Asked whether he ever worried about his sexuality, Vidal replied to one magazine interviewer: "Never. Absolutely never...I did exactly what I wanted to do all the time."

The Astor was "easily the city's most exciting place for soldiers, sailors and marines on the prowl for one another," Vidal said. In its mezzanine Vidal met Dr. Alfred Kinsey, who was intrigued with Vidal's "lack of sexual guilt." "I told him that it was probably a matter of class. As far as I can tell, none of my family ever suffered from that sort of guilt, a middle-class disorder from which powerful people seem exempt. We did whatever we wanted to do and thought nothing of it." Kinsey himself "had gone through sexual stages with males, females, and groups" while writing his reports into sexual behavior, Vidal said later.

Kinsey told Vidal that Vidal wasn't homosexual, "doubtless because I never sucked cock or got fucked. Even so, I was setting world records for encounters with anonymous youths." He thought Kinsey agreed with him on the issue of unfixed categories, and asked him, had he not known anything about him, how would Kinsey have encapsulated Vidal? Kinsey said as "a lower middle class Jew, with more heterosexual than homosexual interests." Vidal writes, referring to Austen, "Curiously, I have lived most of my life with such a person." Fred Kaplan relates that after *The City and the Pillar* was published, Kinsey gave Vidal a copy of *Sexual Behavior in the Human Male*, complimenting him on his "work in the field."

Vidal told Donald Weise that after Kinsey had found that thirty seven percent of men had had a sexual experience with another male leading to ejaculation, intellectuals "moaned and whined" at the findings. "They asked, 'How do you measure sex by ejaculation?' How *else* do you measure it? There is no way of measuring love, compassion and goodness and all that you value and I value." Vidal cast doubt on another poll that found only one percent of Americans had had gay sex, which was "so palpably a lie. It had middle-class women asking people questions. No one is going to tell these ladies that 'I'm not going to touch you with a ten-foot barge-pole, you are absolutely safe from me and my kind.' It's just an embarrassing situation, and they confessed to having a lot of non-responses."

Most of the youths Vidal had sex with in the 1940s with were his own age and "capable of an odd lovingness, odd considering the fact that I did so little to give any of them physical pleasure. But then, even at twenty, I often paid for sex on the ground that it was only fair. Once Truman [Capote, a lifelong enemy] said to me, 'I hear you're just the lay lousé.' 'At last, Truman, you've got it right.'" Vidal said he never had an affair with anyone. "Sex, yes. Friendships, yes. The two combined? No. Jimmie, of course, was something else—me." For Vidal, Trimble was more than a lost love, but the actual missing half of himself or embodiment of it, an integral part of his soul, rather than soul mate.

Sex and history, the latter his great writing interest, were interwoven, Vidal claimed. "By and large I'm not interested in other people's sex lives, but in history there are times when you think, 'Something's got to explain why someone is doing what he's doing.' What was the relationship between George Washington and Alexander Hamilton? Washington put up with more shit from Hamilton, who as a young aide was rude to him, kept him waiting, treated him abominably. And Washington was a man of enormous dignity and tough as nails. So he'd only do that if he were in love with him in some way."

Hamilton, Vidal said, had a "ferocious sexual energy and was a good-looking boy and obviously he was very flirtatious and very winning. As a boy in the West Indies, fourteen, fifteen, he kept the books for a young bachelor businessman who was twenty-nine. And that guy sent him to New York, to college, got him into the Revolution, got him to the attention of George Washington, who never ceased to be pretty infatuated with him. Whether anything ever happened between them I have no way of knowing and I don't really care. What matters is Washington's passion for him and then the fact that he made him the prime minister of the United States." It was Hamilton, Vidal writes, who created the Republic. "All the hysteria that our poor historians have is because they think that they have to transform all of our great presidents into Ivory Soap monuments. The real subject is sexual energy. Everybody thinks everybody else has about the same degree of sexuality as he himself has. It isn't true."

Vidal certainly relished his own sexual energy. He met Tennessee Williams, who found him sexy (this was not reciprocated), in Rome in 1948, realizing the previous year "he was following me up Fifth Avenue, while I, in turn, was stalking yet another quarry. I recognized him. He wore a blue bow tie with white polka dots. In no mood for literary encounters, I gave him a scowl and he abandoned the chase just north of Rockefeller Center."

Fred Kaplan recounts their wary, funny opening gambits, Williams venturing he liked hot summer nights in New York when the "superfluous people are off the streets." They became friends, Vidal calling Williams "the greatest company on earth"; they shared an acid sense of humor and as a mimic Williams was able to impersonate a dying heroine or "addle-headed piece of trade." The two toured Italy, including going to Ravello where Vidal would later make a home, in a jeep. In Cairo, the men "passed boys back and forth," Vidal recalled later. The plump son of the last sultan of the Ottoman Empire wooed Vidal "sadly and hopelessly...he looked like a sensitive dentist," Vidal writes in *Palimpsest*.

Their sexual whirligig was dizzying. Kaplan quotes a letter from Williams in Rome to a friend, boasting, "I have not been to bed with Michelangelo's *David* but with any number of his more delicate creations, in fact the abundance and accessibility is downright embarrassing. You can't walk a block without being accosted by someone you would spend a whole evening trying vainly to make in the New York bars. Of course it usually costs you a thousand lire but that is only two bucks...and there is never any unpleasantness about it even though one does not know a word they are saying."

In an undated (but likely late 1940s to early 1950s) location-less letter (signed as many of his missives were by his nickname, "The Bird" or "The Notorious Bird") Williams writes in a campy spin: "There has been a terrific influx of dikes...They are a jolly bunch...No word from Fritz and Russell who went off together...Poor La Traube! He has the clap now, the only one of us to be stricken, just when he was getting over the crabs. Afflictions, mortal afflictions! Especially those of love, how troublesome they are. I am glad you did not have carnal associations in Cairo, not only because it would have interfered with the glorious work but because I kept thinking, if Gore is not careful he will catch one of those things from the dirty Egyptians. Franco Brusatti just now climbed in my window but has now climbed back out again, I told him I was working...I close now with an affectionate and mildly libidinous kiss on your soft under lip which I never kissed."

Later, Vidal revealed he had been approached by an academic preparing to write Williams's biography, who "started out briskly, saying, 'Everybody assumed you and Tennessee Williams had an affair.'" Vidal told her they hadn't, adding, "Friends don't by and large, particularly if they are in the same line of business with each other." He then rounded on his questioner: "I do know, all professors of English like yourself are lesbian and do indeed have sex with one another, preferably in the same department." His interviewer didn't answer that, he says; from being offended, a stung Vidal went on the offensive by being as offensive as possible.

In *Palimpsest*, Vidal writes that when Williams had a successful play, "it was like my own. When I wrote a successful play, Tennessee would be distraught. The Glorious Bird...would make hissing sounds through that sharp beak, feathers aflutter, beady eyes wide with alarm, nest invaded." Williams also seems to have been one of the few people, alongside Austen, to call Vidal out on his icy snootiness. Williams once heard that Vidal was upset at Williams's cavalier treatment of some party guests, and thought he could no longer be introduced to party guests. But Williams wrote to Vidal, assuring him of his biding love and loyalty: "Regardless of your crotchety attitude toward me, mine toward you is fixed as a star, not falling. When nervous, you rattle like a window in a bombardment, but that isn't often and most of the time you are one of the smoothest and coolest and effortlessly witty people I've known...and you are steadily more convincing in the part of a grand *seigneur*..."

Once, while cruising with Williams in Paris and both about to go home alone, Williams noted to Vidal, "That leaves only us." "Don't be so macabre," Vidal replied. Williams wrote a friend that "the queens [of Key West] took a dim view of him [Vidal], which doesn't matter...I miss him, for it is comforting to know somebody who gets along worse with people than I do, and I still believe he has a heart of gold." In *Point to Point Navigation*, Vidal writes he is often asked when he and Williams fell out; the real question should be when did they fall in. Despite Williams's paranoia, which Vidal likened to blooming bougainvillea, they got on because they found that the same things and people made them laugh. Williams's "queenly entourage" got on his nerves, but they "defected" and at times Vidal and Williams were inhabiting "the same midsummer night's dream."

Judith Harris recalls Vidal telling her that he had visited Williams's mother in Florida with him. "Well, Tennessee, what did I ever do to you?" Edwina Williams asked her son. "Oh, you only ruined my life," Williams told her. The two men shared complex, painful relationships with their mothers. Vidal "loved Tennessee" says the photographer Michael Childers. "Gore saw him as a literary brother, although at one dinner, Gore said, 'I think Tennessee could have been one of the great writers of the twentieth century if he hadn't become a Hollywood whore." Which was rich coming from another Hollywood whore like Vidal: not only did he write screenplays and TV shows there, he adored celebrity friends. Childers remembers dinners at his home featuring Williams, the agent Sue Mengers (a friend Vidal fell out with), producer Ray Stark, Christopher Isherwood, Angelica Huston, Jack Nicholson, his intimate friends Paul Newman and Joanne Woodward, Diana Vreeland; in Rome where he lived in the 1960s, Vidal entertained Federico Fellini, Marcello Mastroianni, Sophia Loren and Audrey Hepburn.

Vidal parlayed his own fame, and liked to hold court with the famous too. At this Edgewater home in upstate New York were Sunday literary salons with guests like Saul Bellow. The British MP Chips Channon, "who preferred men to women and royalty to either," fell upon him at one London party and once Vidal had defused his ardor, Channon confessed to being in love with playwright Terrence Rattigan. Celebrity made Vidal even more imperious and self-regarding. When a magazine asked Vidal to interview then-British Prime Minister John Major, he huffed that John Major should interview him. At Vidal's fiftieth birthday were guests including Diana Cooper, Jonathan Miller, Clive James, Peter Bogdanovich, Ryan O'Neal, Swifty Lazar and George Segal.

"Gore and Howard had a lifestyle that was the envy of all of us," says Michael Childers. In Ravello, Mick and Bianca Jagger were among the guests. Donald Gislason, his Ravello housesitter, recalls the actor Woody Harrelson as a regular visitor and "Norman Mailer being on the phone. Princess Margaret's room had a bathroom so big you could have a banquet in there." The agent Ken Sherman, at a party at Vidal's Hollywood home, alighted upon an old-fashioned Rolodex. "I scrolled through it to see if I could find Jackie Onassis's number and address and I did. I never used it, of course." Kurt Vonnegut, at one supper, had a more mordant vision of his and Vidal's fame: "Readers know they can always find both of us on the last shelf of the library under 'V.'"

Gislason says Vidal was "very aware of money...He said Woody [Harrelson] made two million dollars a year in royalties from Cheers. Gore would get faxes about his royalties and rights. Along with his intellectual sense came a certain amount of interest in wealth. He was keen to make clear he was part of the ruling class too. 'You know, the family has been owed a president for some time now,' he said. He expected the Gores to be in that league." In Ravello, Steven Abbott recalls the group going to a restaurant and no one paying the bill. He asked Gore if he had an account there: "He said, 'Oh no, these people owe me. I bring enough business here.'" Richard Harrison says: "Gore was cheap, very cheap, he didn't like to spend money and bragged about never having had an expensive car or spending money." Barbara Howar says, "I never saw him pick up a check, he wasn't what you would call extravagant." Harrison notes tartly, "Gore never said 'thank you' for anything. I don't think he knew the words thank you.'"

Having power and being in its orbit remained important to Vidal throughout his life, from his relationship to the Kennedys in the years before and during Camelot, to Hillary Clinton visiting him in Ravello in 1994. Vidal was gleeful afterwards, recalls Dennis Altman. "It showed he still had power and control. He was still a force." Vidal once wrote to a friend of Clinton that "she was braced but edgy. Uncommonly bright with a dry sense of humor that, as a woman and politician, she dares not show the world.

Vidal had particularly close relationships with the men's men John F. Kennedy and Paul Newman. Recalling his carnal affinity with Kennedy, Vidal said in 1993, "There was going to be a different girl every day. And I must say in my youth a different person every day was my ideal, too—we actually had sort of parallel sex lives." Vidal admired Robert Kennedy's political ruthlessness and JFK's sexual ruthlessness, Isherwood said in his diary. "As for himself, he claims that he now feels no sentiment whatever—nothing but lust. He can't imagine kissing anyone. The way he has to have these sex dates set up is certainly compulsive." He and Kennedy were very similar as youths, Vidal said. Neither "was much interested in giving pleasure to his partner. Each wanted nothing more than orgasm with as many attractive partners as possible. I remember that he liked sex in a hot bath, with the woman on top, favoring his bad back."

"Get that ass," Tennessee Williams said to Vidal in 1958, looking at Kennedy's backside when the three were in Miami. His fellow author's leering earned a caution from Vidal: "You can't cruise our next president." Williams said of Kennedy and Jackie: "They'll never elect those two. They're much too attractive for the American people." Kennedy enjoyed Williams's sexual flattery. When Vidal repeated the remark to the future president, he replied: "That's very exciting." Vidal said it was "tragic that both men [Kennedy and Williams] were, essentially, immature sexually...incapable of truly warm *mature* human relations. One could weep for what might have been."

Kennedy, Vidal said later, "was relaxed on the subject of homosexuality, as he was about anything related to sex." In 1999, Vidal said that he was "perfectly sure" that Kennedy and Lem Billings, who met as boys at elite preparatory school Choate and became best friends, had "sex together." The elite are "not like other people, they don't have the same guidelines or horror of adultery," said Vidal. "The rulers of the country are screwing anything and everything they have time or health for...'Anything goes' is their attitude."

Did Vidal desire Paul Newman? "I'm sure he did," says Jay Parini. "Every time Paul walked into a room, Gore's eyes lit up. He said, 'I wish I had him as my husband.' He took a vague sensual delight in Paul and JFK. He liked charismatic and powerful men, I thought it was an attempt to retrieve something of his father." Richard Harrison, Vidal's beefcake model friend, asked Vidal if he desired Newman sexually and Vidal said no, but Harrison and Jay Parini perceived Vidal drawing an equivalence between Newman's looks and charisma and Vidal's father. Joanne Woodward told Kaplan that she wasn't sure if Vidal found Newman "gorgeous." Vidal himself once wrote: "Paul has been a friend for close to half a century, proof, in my psychology, that nothing could ever have happened." A not-exactly emphatic denial.

The actor Anthony Perkins told author Boze Hadleigh that while "bisexual may be the politically correct" way to describe Vidal's behavior, "he has no interest in women. Not that way. And he's not Paul Newman's only friend. We're friends too, and I've heard Joanne [Woodward] saying that Gore's never lusted after her, only Paul." Vidal denied he'd had sex with Newman to Matt Tyrnauer. "Perhaps he desired him like a fantasy object. [The actor] Guy Madison he might have had sex with—if not he certainly wanted to." Judy Balaban in *Vanity Fair* quotes Vidal, saying of Newman, "Men and women all fell in love with Paul for the same reason—he was everyone's idea of what a real guy should be."

The two were close friends: Newman, writing to Vidal in 1965, says, "I am getting sentimental in my dotage and long to crack a bottle with you. It's been a long time since I have seen you face down in the urinal." A later birthday card from Newman to Vidal lists the things advancing age means he cannot do, like "Run the 440 in 3-30 flat; stand in front of the mirror and say 'Hot shit'; match taut buttocks with the corps de ballet; masturbate two-fisted with anyone in their twenties; hang by your toes and learn Russian. Write faster, write better. Smile sweeter."

Christopher Isherwood recorded a "drunken evening" in 1957 at Vidal's rented Malibu house that he shared with Austen, Newman and Woodward, with Claire Bloom who at the time was "madly" in love with Richard Burton. "The Gore-Newman-

Woodward household is curious," Isherwood wrote. "These people who perhaps don't like each other too well but are closely involved. Paul isn't a bad boy, but he's so hard at work every instant proving he is an anti-intellectual nature boy. Joanne has decided, as she puts it, that she is not 'the mother of us all'...Gore is such a resentful unhappy creature. He makes embarrassing references to his books—sort of challenging me to say I don't like them; and keeps bracketing himself with me as a pair of 'literary men.' Howard, I think, is unhappy because he can't have a complete domestic life with Gore, whom he adores." According to Woodward, "Anybody who was anybody" would come to their rollicking Sunday afternoon parties in Malibu.

Richard Harrison calls Vidal "the Paris Hilton of his time. He had a great intellect obviously but told me, 'The most important thing is to be on TV, to get your name out there in public, people have to care for you.' We all know his talent, books, everything. But he was an absolute fame whore, that was everything to him and for that reason I don't think he would have been a good senator. Apart from Italo Calvino, I don't think I ever heard him speak well of another writer. I don't know any president he spoke well of—maybe Lincoln."

The sexual Vidal remained more difficult to decode than the power-player. He ducked so many of Harrison's questions about the sex he liked, Harrison came to think of Vidal as "asexual. I just didn't believe he'd had sex with a thousand men before he was twenty-five. His writing was everything to him. That was his life. Making money was so easy and not important. He told me how hard he had to fight to get his name bigger than the title of his books. That was more important than money or sex to him." That may be true, but the circus of sex around Vidal was fascinating for what it revealed about him.

"Gore was deeply conflicted around sex," Dennis Altman tells me. "He fluctuated between being a gay men and having real hostility to the concept. I never saw any evidence that he was sexually interested in women at all. Very early in his life he separated his emotional and sexual life. Sex was something you paid for." In his book Altman says that approaching Vidal one must recognize that his sexuality and his attitudes towards sexuality are not necessarily the same. "Neither reducing Vidal to his sexuality nor ignoring its significance will suffice."

Vidal "had a healthy sexual appetite, but he had to like the guy too," recalls Scotty Bowers. "He'd come into the gas station and say, 'Scotty, that guy leaning against the car, that's my type.' It wasn't always younger guys. Once in the Beverly Hills Hotel he indicated a handsome guy who wasn't that young. He had good-looking assistants too. I don't know if he had sex with them, but Gore was the kind of 'put your hand down there and grab the cock' type. Anybody around Gore knew that score. I don't know if he had sex with Paul Newman, but that's not impossible. He always said Paul had done it with guys." At other times Vidal would claim differently or dismiss such gossip as rumors. He was both a writer and his own author: with words he could stoke controversy, ferment gossip and mischief, and also bring the shutters down. For Vidal, sex and storytelling were intimately linked.

Chapter Six

The Label Game

If Vidal wasn't gay, but mostly, if not exclusively, had gay sex, why did he believe in the model of sexuality he constructed? How did he see himself and the world around him? The novelist Edmund White believes that Vidal's "no such thing as being gay, only gay sexual acts" dictum matched the theories of Michel Foucault, a friend of White's. "He was against the same thing. I think Gore was deeply grounded by research in the classical period: in classical Greece the men really were bisexual and weren't definitely one way or another. But in his case it was muddled. He wanted to run for office, he was from very political family. Perhaps his rejection of labels also came from how bitter he felt about *The City and the Pillar*, which was crucified by many critics. He felt the *New York Times* wouldn't review him for years after that. I think that affected how he saw homosexuality generally."

The author Adam Mars-Jones wrote after Vidal's death that Vidal's position was different from Foucault's—"more libertarian than radical. It could come to seem positively conservative," noting that, post-Stonewall, Vidal "would have made a superb figurehead for the gay movement as it emerged a couple of decades later, with his fearlessness, his media skills and his sense of entitlement, but he distanced himself sharply from any such role." As Vidal once said, "I think when it comes to writing about subjects like sex, people want reassurance. I'm not terribly reassuring."

This lack of "reassurance," his innate desire not to fit into any category, dovetailed neatly with Vidal's general radicalism. In 1950, two years after the publication of *The City and the Pillar* and two years before the publication of another gay-themed novel, *The Judgment of Paris*, Vidal sketched in an unpublished essay his views around sexual identity for the first time, reported

Fred Kaplan: in the essay, Vidal said gay sex was as normal as straight and that men who had sex with men did not need to be cured. However, "the queen world frightens and depresses me, and in its hysteria I see all the horror of the world brought into focus." Vidal was impatient when asked why he wouldn't define himself or anything else as "gay." To Donald Weise, Vidal laid out his view of labels bluntly. "I too got to second base or third base with a girl or boy. And what mattered was penetration." If this was with a girl it could lead to "baby-making."

"Homoerotic" to Vidal "means lust for one's own sex, which I certainly did a lot of in my youth. 'Homosexual' implies really an organization of one's life around it and I never did that and always kept my options open. Needless to say I was immediately categorized with *The City and the Pillar* when I need not have been and never regretted it for one minute. I always thought it was my opinion of others which mattered, not their opinion of me. I was less distressed than you might think for being so categorized but always hesitated to categorize anyone else unless they insisted on it."

Vidal's "quarrel" really began with "the people who ran *The Advocate* in the '60s, '70s and '80s" when "they started in on 'gay sensibility'...If there's a 'gay sensibility' there has to be 'heterosexual sensibility' and I've never come across it..." Vidal doesn't explain why one would necessitate the existence of the other; arguably some kind of gay sensibility or sensibilities flourished because gay sex and sexual expression was once so proscribed. "Trying to make categories is very American, very stupid and very dangerous," Vidal said that categories led ultimately to the Nazi doctrine of "We don't like your category." At one extreme maybe, but not all categorization leads to mass slaughter. But for Vidal, "To make a category means a hierarchy of categories, at the top of which is breeders, at the bottom is same-sexualists." The "generalist, humanist point of view is that you start out with everyone is a human being capable of good and bad. Larry Kramer wants me to be a spokesman for the cause. I couldn't be a worse spokesperson."

Noting that Kramer chided him "for not being a role model to today's gay movement. Well, you know everybody's so bored with my line, but I don't really feel that this thing exists...There's nothing binding...It's oppression that's binding. And to lose a career or lose a job or not be able to go in the Army or teach school or whatever, yes that's oppression and that should be fought. I have actually on several occasions come close to suggesting violence. I was a large boy, and while I'm an old man I still think like a large boy. And I'm something of a bully, as well. It's not my most pleasant trait. I'm for taking no shit, I'm not for putting up with shit. To say that there's gay sensibility and something that holds these wonderful, wonderful people together, I mean, here we go, black is beautiful, woman is naturally nurturing."

He may have been right, but he was speaking to a society and legal system which hadn't yet adapted to his sagacity. Vidal was a powerful spokesman and many gay men and women might agree with his views, if only society was as evolved around sexuality as Vidal wished; the truth is that much of society and the law discriminates against gay people, so some kind of campaigning and political organizing under the heading of 'gay' was, is, vital to bring about legal equality. Vidal didn't agree, though at the same time he campaigned for sexual equality according to his own intellectual constructs and beliefs.

He was, he told Donald Weise, "perfectly happy to be active politically to get laws changed," though harked back to the ancient Greeks for his favored model of sexuality. The Greeks "never had a word for 'faggot' or 'dyke' the concepts didn't exist," Vidal said. "They knew about feminine men and sometimes thought they were funny—more 'ha-ha' than peculiar. They certainly knew about lust, they didn't make a fuss about it. This was a world I understood and was bought up in: it was, sexually, extremely free. Homosexuality was institutionalized, because it was useful for training soldiers—the thieves in Sparta specifically. You also got married to have children so there would be more babies. It never occurred to people you would be one thing or the other."

The word "homosexual," said Vidal, was invented in the 1890s, while "heterosexual" was made up in the 1930s. "To create categories is the enslavement of the categorized because the aim of every state is total control over the people who live in it. What better way is there than to categorize according to sex, about which people have so many hang-ups?"

Weise asked whether Vidal could understand the use of categories like "gay" as an organizational, political tactic. That would mean "acting as if indeed the non-existent exists because your enemies do," said Vidal. "It's as clear as clear can be, particularly in a country like the United States which is very savage in all its relations."

"He didn't want to be seen or identified as what he called a 'queer,'" says Judith Harris. "He wanted to be seen as what he thought of as a 'normal' man. Being 'queer' meant dressing or behaving in a way that he wasn't. He considered being 'queer' a weakness. He said that a number of times in my presence. He didn't approve of anything or anyone overtly 'queer.'" For Harris, this was sourced in Vidal's upbringing, the heritage and stature represented by his beloved grandfather, running through to his connection to the Kennedys. "Gore did not want to be shunned by that Establishment. He didn't want to be seen as odd or separate." Vidal was not going to be screwed in bed, or in public.

"The whole pattern of his life seemed to be gay," Fred Kaplan tells me. "He came out of a world in which the image of gay people was not only negative but unmasculine. That's what he couldn't stand. He couldn't stand the idea of people not considering him masculine. He wanted to be a powerful force in the political world when the notion of 'gay' was limp-wristed. He was all about being masculine, dominant."

For Vidal's bibliographer Steven Abbott, Vidal "only identified with the most intellectually powerful people. During most of his life gay people were considered neither intellectual nor powerful, they were a group under the radar. For him to proclaim to be part of such a group, when the essence of his personality was that he existed only among the powerful, would have been utterly contrary to his self-image." Abbott, like others, also saw Vidal's attitude to his homosexuality as being "a product of his generation." Discreet as he was, he could also be brilliantly smutty. Nina Straight remembers, "He once said Doris Lessing had told him when she was writing *The Golden Notebook* that she had masturbated twelve times a day. He told her, 'Oh, for the thirteenth time.'"

For Sean Strub, Vidal was "totally a gay man, but I understand, and to some extent agree, with his rejection of the 'gay' label. I like 'homophile' myself, although I don't have the conviction and perseverance to campaign for it. I think if Gore understood 'gender queer' as it is used today, he would approve, as that is more consistent with my understanding of his preference for 'homophile' over 'gay' or 'homosexual.' I think he rejected any label that would pigeonhole or limit him or potentially deflect from being defined by his intellect."

His friends and peers wonder what underpinned his desire to remain undefined. John Rechy, most famous for his 1963 hustler novel *City of Night*, shared a "significant long-distance [platonic] relationship" with Vidal, who he found "fascinating. For all his bravery and courage, which he had in spades, he never came out. He did not want to be identified as a homosexual. In an incredible way he was trying to define homosexuality in a way to fit him perfectly: a mode of never really coming out or this empty bisexuality, which people doubted. He was discomfited with overt homosexuality."

Alongside his crusading for sexual equality, there were elements of the scared closet-case about Vidal, not wanting to reveal himself publicly. The actor Anthony Perkins said of Vidal, "To me, he's a climber. He cares desperately what other people think, but always pretends he's insensitive to it. He's so above it all. At least Capote wasn't as pompous or paranoid. You could count on Truman for his ratty, little genuine opinion. With Vidal, it's all so *calculated*...He won't even say he's allegedly, supposedly bisexual. He only says that acts are this or they're that, but he's...*above* it all. He won't commit. So he's not that brave." Dennis Altman questions why Vidal called himself bisexual while "most of his sexual interests were homoerotic." His clumsy terminology—"homosexualist," "same-sexer"—and his insistence that categories of sexual preference are misleading, "make sense given his history and age." He wanted to both "stand above homosexuality" and flaunt it, says Altman.

Vidal stayed true to never saying he was gay and believing in a lack of labeling, all through his life, disputing in one essay how one word—gay/homosexual—can characterize "people as different as Frederick the Great and Eleanor Roosevelt." People who prefer homosexual sex, he writes, "range from the transvestite who believes himself to be Bette Davis [funny, as Vidal himself reportedly did a great Bette Davis impression] to the ordinary citizen who regards boys with the same uncomplicated lust" as straight men desire girls. In a 1993 interview Vidal said he "hated using words like "homosexual" and "homoerotic." He added, "The American passion for categorizing has now managed to create two non-existent categories, gay and straight. Either you are one or the other. But since everyone is a mixture of inclinations, the categories keep breaking down; and when they break down, the irrational takes over. You have to be one or the other...Many human beings enjoy sexual relations with their one sex; many don't; many respond to both. This plurality is...not worth fretting about."

Vidal told the author Patrick Higgins that "If there is such a thing as a homosexual identity you must then admit that there is such a thing as a heterosexual identity...Since I don't recognize such a thing as a heterosexual personality, how can I define or detect a homosexual personality?" In an illuminating interview in *The Nation* in 1993, Vidal references *The City and the Pillar* as emblematic of this wider thinking. "I think it was the first book...that made the point that perfectly normal boys fall in love and have sex with each other—a subject on which I was expert, having spent three years in the Army, in the Pacific and aboard a ship. This was the great secret of the male lodge. Despite all this nonsense today about gays in the military—I just wish the word had never been invented. It's men in the military—[who]

have always had homoerotic feelings. They have to have homo-erotic feelings or they can't stand each other. This can edge over into homosexual—I'm using words I hate, you know—relations, and it's no big deal. Now, mind you, the age of psychiatry had just got America by the throat in the forties, so it went from being a hideous crime of nature like witchcraft to being a mental illness. So the atmosphere was pretty lousy, but the practice and the ease of it all, particularly overseas...The Pacific was a great sexual riot of same-sexuality."

Asked by Donald Weise why gay people in power like Roy Cohn [Senator Joseph McCarthy's aide, who died of AIDS in 1986] could be so vicious towards gay people, Vidal first dismissed the language of the question. "By using the dead adjective [gay] again, a screen goes down in my head. I don't know what a gay person is. There are quite a few psychopathic characters drawn to politics and extreme danger, and I have known quite a few of them. They go to the john, commit an act against nature, then go on to the floor of the House and denounce perverts. It's very exciting for a certain kind of psychopath. I prefer words like that to 'gay.'"

Vidal was emphatic on the need for as few labels as possible. He told the producers of *The Celluloid Closet*, "Well, there is no such thing as a homosexual person or a heterosexual person. I am the last person to ask about this, as I don't believe in these cate-gories. Only a country as crazed as the United States would invent categories. Other countries call it sex...We have to have a good team and a bad team and so we have a good team called 'straight' and a bad team called 'gay,' but they don't really exist.... And we can go into the roots of this, religion and so forth and so on but it's part of the sectarian nature of the Americans because we are slightly slower than most First World people, more primitive, certainly more deeply bigoted religiously and racially than let us say our European equivalents." Vidal said that Christianity was "a permanent enemy; the sooner we get rid of it, and Judaism and Islam, the better off human race will be."

Vidal believed that in the "faggot world" there were similar-ities of style, "but it's really in communities. The Castro [the

well-known gay area of San Francisco] will set a tone; fag New
York back in the forties and fifties was very chi-chi, and Truman
Capote was the sort of icon of that world—with which I had absolutely no connection at all and rather disliked." On why the
word "gay" irritated him, he added, "You can change attitudes if
you change words. Well, you have to change the attitude. Then
the word changes, or it is dropped or it is no longer loaded with
false resonances. All my life there was a category to which I had
been assigned. Well, I don't feel like I belong in any category.
And, yes, it's like a labor union. I will go to war if it is necessary
for people to get their rights, but that's it. There is no fellow
feeling particularly."

Vidal was also, more simply and understandably, a product of
his generation: an era when "gay" meant effeminate or camp,
someone outside society, a freak—not things the patrician,
Establishment-inhabiting Vidal saw himself as. "Gore was not a
gay person, not a queen," says Bowers. "He would say, 'I have gay
sex but I'm not gay.' I heard him say that numerous times. He
meant he wasn't what he thought was a queen, the kind of guys
where it's like 'How much was the operation to have all those
bones removed from your wrist?' You can spot a queen. Gore was
not gay at all in appearance."

But that's a narrow definition: you can be gay without looking or behaving in a stereotypically gay way, I say to Bowers.
"Gore was gay but didn't look gay, act gay, but he had gay sex,"
says Bowers. But he was also a gay person, even if he didn't say
it? "Yes." And in that knot lies Vidal's sexuality. Richard Harrison says he found Vidal's "'I'm not gay but have gay sex' so much
double talk. He didn't have sex with women as far as I could tell.
Anyway, when you're fucking someone in the ass it has to mean
something."

However, Vidal did not subscribe in any way to clearly defined
views of sexuality, personally and intellectually. In the afterword to
a later edition of *The City and the Pillar,* he wrote: "All human
beings are bisexual. There is no such thing as normality." Vidal's
half-sister, Nina Straight, says, "Gore fancied what he wasn't. Sex

for him was perpetration—being able to do something he wanted to do when he wanted to do it—not penetration. I think he thought, 'I have sex. None of the issues about my sexuality are resolved so instead of masturbation I'll do something equally contained and the other person won't get anything from it. This sex is just for me, my own fulfillment.' Think of ideas of domination and class superiority and slaves in chains. People like that are totally out of control."

There were "a lot of contradictions" with Vidal, says his nephew Burr Steers, "but ultimately he believed everybody should do what they wanted to do and not have prudish hang-ups about sex. But, of course, he seemed to. He resented being tossed into the same group as some 'stupid faggots,' as he'd call them. Elizabeth Taylor had a clique and he hated that she assumed he would fall into that group. He detested Truman Capote and didn't want to be lumped in with homosexual authors. He used words like 'fag,' 'queen' and 'sissies' and had a line about his mother: 'For her affections many men tried and all succeeded.' Her sexuality was not an exclusive club, she had a very strong sex drive, and so did he, right up until the last couple of years of his life."

Vidal may have been ensconced in a gay literary milieu, but "I loathe the word 'gay.' I'm sick of gay," Vidal once said to Michael Childers, who told me that Vidal "wanted to go back to a simple, pre-liberation age when queens just had 'trade,'" i.e. straight-acting men who had sex for money. "He didn't like complicated sex. They were different times, he hated labeling. In the '50s and '60s one could have a few drinks with straight men and sleep with them. After gay liberation, they were labeled 'cock-suckers.' It all became so institutionalized."

Vidal's world was "pre-labeling," says Matt Tyrnauer. "His big problem was with the post-'gay lib,' as he would have said, world. He and Howard always said, 'We never knew any queens.' There was a queen world so pervasive, even in the closeted world before gay liberation. The most famous was Truman Capote. Gore and Howard wanted to draw a very firm line between them and those people. It was a very feminizing world he didn't want to be part of, although he knew of those worlds—in *Myra Breckinridge* he nailed it. He is entitled to his thesis of no labels, even if it's out of fashion at present."

For Dennis Altman, Vidal's claim of bisexuality "perhaps showed him to be a product of his age, generation and class and particularly the kind of Southern family he came from, where homosexuality would have been unacceptable." What stopped Vidal from defining himself as gay wasn't just intellectual and genuinely based on a belief that such strict labeling was bogus; he was also, like many, a product of his times.

Occasionally emotion broke through the brusque Vidal facade. Emphasizing that labels around sex and sexual identity were redundant, Vidal told the makers of *The Celluloid Closet*, "We're all everything, and considering under the great heterosexual dictatorship that we live in this country the vast amount of propaganda, schools, television, everywhere you look, this taboo is even more as the religious right rises, is more and more great...Despite this great taboo, this great Satan that has been built up, that same-sexuality, even in the age of AIDS, is so powerful and so enduring that somebody might someday figure out that this is our normal condition just as much heterosexuality is a normal condition. These are manifestations not only of sexual outlets, quote the physiologists, but also of something larger, which is human affection." What a piercing conclusion and all the more so, and ironic, as Vidal rarely openly expressed affection himself.

Chapter Seven

Vidal's *Dolce Vita*

Vidal's sexual adventuring reached an impressive zenith when he and Austen settled in Rome in the early 1960s so that they could have access to the library at the American Academy, where Vidal researched his bestselling novel *Julian* (1964). In that period, mid-"*Dolce Vita*," Rome was embracing the glamorous, bustling café society popularized by Federico Fellini's classic 1960 film of the same name; Vidal later appeared in Fellini's 1972 film, *Roma*. The city "was a very good place to meet really attractive young guys willing to do anything. That was another big point of the Rome move," says Matt Tyrnauer. "The other city contender had been Athens, which they decided was too ugly. Gore had been humiliated by Bobby Kennedy at the White House, and things were deteriorating in his relationship with Jackie Kennedy. He'd lost his race for Congress in 1960. Capote was literary king of New York and Gore could not abide that."

Cruising for sex in Rome was "the best it could have been for them," a longtime friend told me. "It was exactly their speed: up, down and everything." Vidal and Austen would go to the Pincio [a hill near the center of Rome] where the hustlers gathered back then. They had a Jaguar convertible, which was immediately surrounded by young men, the longtime friend of the couple told me. "Italians are very innocent and sincere to this day and obviously, besides seeing these rich guys, they'd want to talk about the car. Then Gore and Howard would pick which boys they liked. I asked Gore what his line was and he said, 'I'd try, "You're the most beautiful boy I've ever seen" and see how that works.'"

Vidal once asked Sean Strub, "Do you know what the difference is between American boys and Italian boys? Italian boys have dirty feet but clean assholes, while American boys have clean feet but dirty assholes." He also repeated to Strub his contention that "he had sex with hustlers in the afternoon, so in the evening he could focus on conversation rather than cruising."

The couple would take one or two young men to the penthouse at the Via de Torre, 21 Argentina where they lived. The sex, the friend says, was conducted separately. Vidal's type was "basically a straight masculine guy." In *Palimpsest*, Vidal says he was only sexually active, that he was never passive. That was certainly the impression he wanted you to have. Although he says he never performed oral sex, he once told a friend of the long-time friend quoted here that he had done it once and "it didn't work out" and he never did it again. Austen was known to take Polaroids of some of the young men they met in Rome.

In 1961, Vidal said Rome was "a sexual paradise...every evening hundreds of boys converged on the Pincio in order to make arrangements with interested parties." The literary critic Richard Poirier, a friend of Vidal's, told Fred Kaplan that Italian gay life was "very seductive. It was sort of older to younger brother, and in the sixties it still wasn't that easy for a young Italian guy to sleep with a young woman, a young girl. He may have wanted to get married but didn't have much money. This sex for money and favors was sort of a common thing to do...And you'd meet very, very sweet boys. The other advantage of it was that you didn't need to cruise, that is, you knew where these guys were and you got to know them and they'd introduce you to others, so you'd have a whole social life. That was perfect for Gore, and he liked the types, the Italian boys who were available, as I did. In a sense, whenever we went out, we'd be looking at good-looking people...In Rome it was the practice to take the boys back to the apartment. He'd pay them and give them clothes. They were very sweet. A few times I'd be sitting out in the front room with Howard. Gore would come in with someone and introduce him. One time he was passing through with someone I had met before and said to me, 'Say goodbye to Antonio.'"

In 1999, Vidal told Donald Weise that "these things—men with boys—has been going on throughout recorded history." Ninety percent of men go on to get married and have children,

Vidal estimated, though that was "stopping now" with birth control, over-population and a fear of AIDS. "There's a good deal less heterosexuality, less sex going on. People are scared. Every last one of the boys we knew in Rome are fathers and grandfathers now. But they weren't just lying there. They were eager participants in a normal activity." Both Vidal in *The City and the Pillar* and Kinsey were saying "same-sexuality" was normal, Vidal added, then qualified himself. "'Normal' is the incorrect word. 'Normal sex' is that which is most done which means masturbation, 'normality' is masturbation, so we must use another word which is 'natural.' Same-sexuality is as natural as other-sexuality, neither to be preferred to the other unless you want to make a baby in which case do not try it with another boy. It just won't work for some obscure reason."

At night in Rome, Vidal and his friends would go to nightclubs like 84 and the Pipistrello, recalls Bernie Woolf who met him in Rome in 1960. "They were laughingly called nightclubs, not gay, but popular with glamorous rich gay people," says Woolf. Vidal would eat and drink at Harry's Bar, Tullio's, Campo dé Fiore, Nino's ("the best food I've ever had in my entire life," Vidal once said; the T-bone steaks a particular favorite), and the downstairs bar at what was the Flora Hotel. Female prostitutes, and the "fancier" male prostitutes, would parade down the Veneto. The trade Vidal liked was ostensibly straight; his friend George Armstrong would send his sexual partners to Vidal, says Bernie Woolf. "There was definitely traffic there."

Austen would go to the beach at Ostia and pick people up, adds Woolf. "Gore was an embroiderer of stories: he could sit at a dinner table and make himself the center of the story. He was an entertaining son of a bitch, though. I sat down at many dinner parties to hear him tell a story of something that had happened which I knew hadn't happened as he described it: he didn't lie, he just made stories more interesting than they were. You couldn't believe half of what Gore said. It would change day to day, like the weather. One to one he was absolutely charming, without guile because he knew you knew him. But in a group of people he was 'on.'"

The writer Judith Harris began a lifelong friendship with Vidal in Rome in 1962. "I was unthreatening to him," she says. She spoke better Italian than he did and her first husband, Aldo Ajello, a senator, gave Vidal a connection to political power. She recalls the plaque on Vidal's apartment block, reading "*Volere è potere*"—"To want is power"—which made Harris smile: it wasn't Vidal's, but it encapsulated him. One night she went for supper with Armstrong, her best friend, Vidal and some friends. The men wanted to put on a porn film, but wouldn't until Harris left, instructing her to take Vidal home and not to stop at a bar as he was already drunk. But Vidal insisted they did, and then shouted, "I could have any boy in here for thirty thousand lire [about twenty dollars]." She told him he wasn't allowed one that night. Harris remembers Vidal shouting he would never allow himself to be fucked: "He had to be 'the guy.'"

The author Tom Powers, who first met Vidal in Rome in 1965, recalls that Armstrong had a portrait of Vidal, signed by Vidal, "with something intense and intimate, like 'Lest we forget.' Gore and George were really close. Gore was obviously sentimental about certain people." At a supper of mostly gay men, which Powers attended with his wife Candace, "there was this unbelievable sexual electricity. Gore, who was very handsome then, had a way of focusing on a person with such intensity it made them giddy."

Powers recalls another supper at Armstrong's where Vidal "ate all the *hors d'oeuvres*, all the bread at dinner, finished his drinks at machine gun rate, poured himself wine faster than his carafe could be filled. I asked him if he felt much different now. 'Closer to the end,' he said. 'I'm dragging my own corpse around'—pointing to his swelling belly and adding that he had been a good deal fatter yet. He said he still went off the booze three or four weeks—or was it months?—a year, occasionally fasted to get his weight under control. He lost thirty pounds last year, he said patting his belly, but had half of it back. He has a way of breathing in deeply through his nose, straightening his back, smiling absently into the middle distance as if expecting someone to take his picture. He does it when he's said something clever and is pleased with himself, not overweening or arrogant but just happy, proud, at peace."

Italy was "great for Gore," says Harris. "Rome was very much a gay capital and Naples had a tradition of gay aristocrats settling there. Gore felt accepted there." He would spend six months there—any longer and he'd have had to have paid full Italian taxes—then the next six months in the US.

The theater director David Schweizer visited Vidal and Austen in Rome in 1971, three years after Vidal had published his scandalous bestseller *Myra Breckinridge* and the year after his autobiographical novel, *Two Sisters*, came out. Schweizer was a twenty-year-old Yale student and the lover of Tennessee Williams, who he had met on spring break in Key West. "He became infatuated with me, I was perfectly happy to let the relationship happen," Schweizer tells me. "I thought he was fascinating." At the party they met at, Schweizer recalls Williams's mother sitting "wrapped up by some queen in a feather boa and looking like a snowbird." Williams's chat-up line to Schweizer was, "Have you been here all evening? I don't know how I could have missed you, I won't the next time." Thinking that being "eyeballed by Tennessee Williams" would be a story to take back to Yale, Schweizer slipped a poem under his door about what it was like to be in his home, and when Williams saw him at an outdoor party later he invited Schweizer to join his party for supper.

"I stayed with him for about a week until I went back to school," Schweizer recalls. "He was kind of a romantic, he wasn't real evolved (sexually). I was a lot more evolved at twenty than he was at sixty after his lifetime of having sex." But Williams swam every day and was "no physical wreck." He invited Schweizer on a European trip, taking in readings at poetry festivals; Schweizer found people surprised he "had a brain" and wasn't just some pretty boy-toy. In Rome, Schweizer "could tell the stakes were getting higher" when Williams "pimped me out" to Rudolph Nureyev. "Tennessee retired from the ring briefly and wanted to hear all about it. Nureyev and I had sex: there was a tragic neediness and loneliness about him."

Williams said they were to "spend a certain amount of time with Gore and that awful Howard." Austen had a "dry, undercutting humor" that Schweizer didn't find charming. Schweizer recalls the taxi bumping along the teeming streets to Vidal's house. Vidal had recently written the film adaptation of Williams's "horrible" play *Last of the Mobile Hot Shots.* In the taxi, Schweizer recalls, Williams "was babbling, 'I don't know if I have the strength for Gore. You know he's so full of himself. Baby, you know he can't write—he could never write.'"

Williams's jittery mood, says Schweizer, was partly down to the intense memories Rome evoked for him of spending time there with his great love, Frank Merlo, who died of lung cancer in 1963. Williams's relationship with Vidal was rooted in deep affection, despite occasional squalls and rivalries. *Palimpsest* features some delicious scenes, such as Vidal turning up alone in Cambridge to visit a gloomy E.M. Forster, without Williams ("I do not choose to lunch with old gentlemen with urine-stained flies"), much to Forster's disappointment.

In the introduction to *The Mutilated*, a one-act play that premiered in 1966 about a bar and its queer (in every sense) denizens, Williams writes: "Gore and I have been friends since the winter of 1948 in Rome" when Vidal had already published the bestselling *The City and the Pillar* and Williams's *A Streetcar Named Desire* was playing on Broadway. "When we first encountered each other...I thought it was illegitimate for a writer to be that young and good-looking and a witty talker as well. These attributes made me suspicious of his capacities as a writer until I read some of it and discovered that it was authentic and serious work...To my face, Gore calls me 'Glorious Bird,' with a friendly kind of mockery, but I have heard from other sources that he describes me as 'a sad little door-mouse.' He is not one to pull his punches with friend or foe, but he never fails to be...good-looking and witty. It no longer irritates me; in fact it gives me a reassuring sense of an element of permanence in the world, despite the assaults of time."

When Schweizer met Vidal for the first time at his home,

"My first impression of Gore was standing at the top of his stairs, peering down. I'm a small, compact man and my impression of him was of a giant. He seemed so tall: big chest, long legs, so handsome and so deft. Dazzling." Schweizer first properly spoke to Vidal at a supper at an outdoor restaurant, where the sex chatter was "who was a top or bottom, a little cock or big cock. Gore took a liking to me, it wasn't sexual. I was so used to everyone coming on to me sexually and he did not. He was intrigued why someone as smart as me would drag around Europe with Tennessee. 'How are you faring with the Bird?' 'How's it going with the Bird?' 'Watch your step.'" Schweizer asked why. "Just...he can turn," said Vidal. "I don't think you're protected. Protect yourself."

In *Palimpsest*, Vidal remembers why he called Williams the Bird or Glorious Bird: "The image of the bird is everywhere in his work. The bird is flight, poetry, life. The bird is time, death..." His last story, "The Negative," featuring a poet no longer able to write, poses the question: "Am I a wingless bird?" Schweizer thought Vidal was just "being bitchy but I found him incredibly compelling and so handsome. He was manly and had a deep voice and kept himself very well. I would have snuck out in the afternoon and thrown myself on him in a second." His attitude towards sex fascinated Schweizer who, even coming out at a "wildly promiscuous" time, still believed in a "romantic taint" to homosexuality. Vidal was far more "clinical, he lined people up and had sex with them every day."

Vidal invited Schewizer to have tea in the afternoons, where his tone was "brusque, tough love." "We would talk politics and suddenly Gore would say, 'Now it's time for my afternoon...' and some gorgeous young man would walk in. 'David, this is Gabriel', he would introduce us, then say I could stay and talk to Howard or see them later for supper. It was almost like clockwork. They were very high quality trade, extra presentable, their beauty was aristocratic and some were American. Gore insisted it was paid-for sex." Schweizer asked him why. "That's the way I want it." But why, Schweizer persisted. "It becomes only itself. It is what it is,"

Vidal replied, meaning, says Schweizer, "'It's a service, it's an activity, I am pleasured and someone is rewarded.' It was very important for him to keep it at that level." Vidal introduced many of his friends to the young men. In a letter to Vidal in 1973, Ned Rorem says he's planning on publishing a diary from 1970, including a trip to Rome: "It's all very favorable, but some of it could be construed as compromising (i.e., our young friend Leonardo…)."

So intriguing were Vidal's contradictions and persona around sex, Schweizer one day asked him to explain his private life and desires. The young men he hired seemed very handsome, Schweizer said to Vidal. "Yes, of course, they have to be," said Vidal. In *Palimpsest*, Vidal writes that Italian "trade has never had much interest in the character, aspirations, or desires of those to whom they rent their ass." "Do you ever get involved with any of them?" Schweizer asked him. "No, why would I?" Vidal replied, aghast. "It would be hard for me not to," said Schweizer. "Oh, you'd better get over that: it doesn't make any sense," said Vidal. "Well, it makes sense to me," said Schweizer. "Well, my way is my way," said Vidal. "It suits my life and will never be any other way."

Schweizer asked him what Austen meant to him. "He's my companion, we've never had sex," said Vidal. "Even when you were both young and cute?" asked Schweizer. "I needed someone I could trust," Vidal replied simply. Schweizer today admits he found Vidal's attitude "so perplexing but I liked he was so candid. There was something so vehement and legitimate about him, I accepted what he said. My radar was always up for a slip, a contradiction, a chance to say, 'You say that, but you just did this…' but it never happened. I trusted him."

Vidal's warning to Schweizer over Tennessee Williams's behavior certainly proved prescient. Schweizer went back to his and Williams's lodgings and found a letter on a typewriter written to Williams's agent about Schweizer, calling him a "viper companion" who was driving Williams crazy and "stifling him." Schewizer thought Williams meant for him to read it, so Schweizer left a note saying they needed some time apart.

Vidal admired that he had left Williams. "There's nothing else to do," he told Schweizer. "It might have been a kindness, because he might just have to think about it. It's very hard to get the Bird to think about anything." A week and a half later Williams called Schweizer to say "all was forgiven," though Schweizer wondered what he had to be forgiven for. They flew back to the US and became friends.

Vidal was less sexually inclined than Austen, says Bernie Woolf. "Howard was very promiscuous. He picked up sailors, he worked the streets and picked up trade. George [Armstrong] was a procurer of sorts and very friendly with Gore. He had a million tricks. Rome was a very advantageous place to live: if you were a homosexual of a certain age at that time you could have almost anybody. I don't mean all the young men were gay, but for a certain amount of lire they were yours. If that was your proclivity and that's what you wanted to do you were home free. It was just part of growing up for these kids: they felt no compunction about hiring their bodies out."

George Armstrong would boast that he had never had a lover in his life, "and I've never wanted one, I paid for sex every time and I'm the happiest person who ever lived." Armstrong was "extraordinarily promiscuous," like Vidal, "literally a revolving door," says Woolf—yet unlike Vidal he was more at ease about being gay. "But then Gore was a celebrity and consider that time when nobody was out," says Woolf.

"I think Gore and Howard had a shared sex life, but as in all things Gore was boss and Howard the facilitator," says Matt Tyrnauer. "It was an open relationship in which they relied upon what they referred to as 'trade.' I heard the word from Howard mostly: in Ravello he would point to some of the locals and say, 'He's trade, he's not trade.'" Fred Kaplan tells me, "Gore's sex drive was tremendous up to fifty five to sixty. He was extraordinarily good looking, and he was very aware of it and into his fifties kept very fit. He was a gym-goer and liked to have a good torso and nice musculature. He used his good looks." Later, Vidal had "work" done on his eyes, he told Richard Harrison. Vidal was aware of his good looks and what time had done to them.

Edmund White remembers meeting Vidal for the first time at a cocktail party at Peggy Guggenheim's Venetian palace in 1974. "She was very cheap, you know," says White. "She never served *hors d'oeuvres*, but might have some Prosecco. She was the kind who would count the apples in the fridge to see what the servants had eaten." Vidal was "handsome, frosty and nice. He was definitely cute, but I was sort of an ageist. I was thirty-four years old and he was almost fifty, just enough older not to make me interested. There was no spark there. I was sure he didn't know who I was, I'd only published one novel, *Forgetting Elena*, by then."

White had heard stories about Vidal as they lived a few blocks away from each other in Rome. "The main story I would hear is that he was irritated by his friends cruising for guys, he would hire hustlers in the afternoon. In Rome in those days you would eat outside on the Piazza Navona on a big table with ten to twelve friends. It was very cheap and you'd look at all the trade going by and there were these really cute but preposterous-looking boys who would be swinging Maserati keys, but they didn't have a Maserati. Everybody could be had for money."

"Gore's homosexuality came out most easily when he was drunk," says a female friend of many years standing who wished to remain anonymous. "If he was drunk and there was a man in the car he might try and make pass at him, put a hand on their leg. He liked young men. One night I was over there [at his Californian home] for dinner. I'd had a haircut and he put his hands on my shoulder and said, 'You'd make a beautiful Italian boy.' He liked his sex down and dirty, he liked beautiful boys but not his equal in education. That's not unusual. He wanted to keep those parts of his life separate."

On one occasion, an American friend of White's, indicating a cute guy on a Rome street, asked how he could "get" him. White said it was very easy: find two blonde women, go over and say how lonely-looking the guy is, why doesn't he join you. Go from club to club, get drunker and drunker. At the end of the night, say, 'Why don't you stay at my house tonight?'" White smiles: "Then you get to suck him." People of Vidal's era, and even "somewhat" his own, says White, "weren't interested in sleeping with gay people, but just into sleeping with straight trade. You might say, 'Why don't you go out with my good-looking gay friend Bob?' to someone like Gore, and he'd say, 'And do what—bump pussies?'"

White sighs. "I have never met so many weirdos as the gay men in Italy. They lived with their mothers, they had to be home by dawn, they never had affairs, just one-offs. When I lived in Rome in 1970 people went to the movie theater, sitting with their raincoats on their laps, jerking each other off, or they went to the Coliseum late at night, when you could still get into it, and have sex. Nobody was 'out.'"

Italy's sexual attractions continued to be enjoyed by Vidal when the couple moved to Ravello in 1972. In his book *Defying Gravity*, Dennis Altman describes how Vidal advised him how to procure Italian men in Rome and the Amalfi Coast and reward them appropriately. "I first learned the rules of commercial sex from Gore Vidal in Italy," Altman writes. On the beach near La Rondinaia, Altman "had met two young men who seemed interested, as most Southern boys are, in a little adventure. Through Gore's assistance, appropriate arrangements were made and the men and I went off to their rooms in town for the evening. On Gore's advice a small financial incentive was offered, more it seemed to reassure them that they were really not faggots than for any other reason. At the time it seemed to me that one of the men was clearly interested in doing it for more than just the money."

In Ravello the locals knew Vidal as *Il Maestro* or *Il Scrittore*. According to Altman, there was an unspoken rule that Vidal and Austen wouldn't bring men back to La Rondinaia: one day, Vidal pronounced "apropos of nothing" to Matt Tyrnauer, "I've never had sex in Ravello." Austen said, "I have." Tyrnauer asked Vidal why. "Well, when I moved here I didn't want to be viewed as the pederast who lived at the end of the road, so I made it my business to never have sex with anyone who lived in this village." Tyrnauer asked, "What did you do?" and Vidal replied, "Well, I would go to Minori, which is right down the hill."

Some locals dispute this. Piero Cantarella, a friend of Vidal's, said, "This is a village of 1,500 people. Everyone knows everything and we love secrets and to gossip." A few people think he created a sexual hideout in Minori as a myth, just as some people believe he did with Jimmie Trimble. Some locals say letters arrived for a period from a woman reputed to be his daughter, others say that he had affairs with men who worked in the villa, now dead. Vidal was reserved and private; as Vincenzo Palumbo, now one of the current owners of La Rondinaia recalls, "A strange person. Not easy. Very intelligent but he was a friend just for 'good morning,' 'how is the weather,' but you cannot speak of important things with him if you didn't understand politics." Austen was seen as friendlier.

Before he built a swimming pool at La Rondinaia, Vidal swam at the Lido delle Sirene in Amalfi. The man who would rent him the boats (and maybe drive them) said he was very reserved and he did not pick men up there. He always rented a boat and went with his guests, often hunky American men, local say. In 1983 Judith Harris recalls Vidal being awarded honorary citizenship of Ravello.

La Rondinaia, perched in the cliffs, is nicknamed "the birds' nest." Jason Epstein recalls you would sit and have your breakfast on the terrace and watch planes going between Naples and Salerno fly beneath you. The men would dine in local restaurants such as Da Salvatore, one of Vidal's favorites, with its spectacular views of the Mediterranean, or Villa Maria, a hotel and restaurant owned by Vincenzo Palumbo. Vidal would sometimes frequent the San Domingo bar at night and café by day or the Luna Hotel's nightclub down below on the coast, the beach clubs in Amalfi and restaurants such as Da Zaccharia along the coast. Vidal's love of cats, a constant, was evident on one occasion at Da Salvatore. One time, he was there eating a meal on its terrace and a cat kept wandering in. Another guest, a woman, kept saying, "Waiter, can you throw the cat out?" Cesare Calce, the owner, threw out the cat and it kept coming back in. Finally, Vidal called the proprietor over and he said, "Cesare, can you throw the lady out?"

Vidal was seen as a difficult man, private and reserved, say many locals; a "hermit" who came there to work. One reason Vidal and Austen moved to Ravello was because the cruising in Rome had gotten too dangerous. "We thought we might be exposed to HIV or be murdered by a bad trick," Austen told Tyrnauer, who says: "When they had first moved there all the boys were Italian, but by the eighties there were more immigrants and they said Albanian prostitutes, for example, tended to be rather violent."

Tyrnauer recalls, "Gore and Howard talked about sex a lot: it was pretty much all they wanted to talk about. If you were in Ravello with them you would sit at a cafe and survey the piazza, assessing and commenting on who was passing by. Howard was not shy about saying that he had sexual encounters with multiple generations of the Ravellaise. However, Gore maintained he never had sex in Ravello. It was all put on Howard. I was sitting with them in the piazza and they would say, 'See that boy over there? His grandfather was the most beautiful man when we first came here.' Then they would go through three generations of that family: the implication was these guys had been trade for Howard over the decades. There was a long tradition of fluid sexuality among young and older men, they said. Young men in Italy seemed very sexually available: even if they didn't identify as gay they would have sex with men for fun or money. Howard used to say that all Italian men were bisexual. And the Italian approach fit very well with Gore's thinking on sexual acts and sexual identity." A priest in Minori once told Vidal and Austen's housesitter Donald Gislason how hypocritical the Italians were. "All women cheat on their husbands," the priest said. How did he know? asked Gislason. "I hear confession."

According to local lore and those that knew the couple, there were regular parties, often wild get-togethers, hosted by Austen who would come regularly to the main square in Ravello and announce that a party would take place on a particular evening. Sex with straight men and drinking were all part of La Rondinaia's pool-side activities, although most people agree that Vidal was rarely present, instead staying in his room working while the parties went on. Residents say Austen had a lot of sex with the locals and the parties were wild. "It was Howard who was the whore," said one shop owner who often talked with Vidal. "Gore. Never."

Lucy Fisher, a film producer who knew Vidal for thirty-five years, says that in Ravello Vidal would dress in mismatched clothes, and often in shorts "like a ragamuffin, quite the opposite to the elegant Gore. Every morning he would read the International Herald Tribune on the piazza in Ravello and "make fun of or flirt with the boys. To him they were all gay, and he would joke about them being cute, hot or stupid or say, 'This one Howard's gonna fuck.' He would brag about Howard's sexual exploits and was proud that he'd have studly guys around."

Dennis Altman visited Vidal and Austen at their Rome apartment in the mid to late 1970s. "I was going out for dinner with them. Gore opened the door and with a big wink said, 'Would you like a pre-dinner appetizer?' He took me to a bedroom in the apartment where there was a rather attractive Sardinian boy laid out on the bed. It was clear the boy was available. Gore would provide and you would pay. The assumptions were quite extraordinary: I don't know how he would have reacted if I had said, 'I don't want to have sex with this guy.' I suspect he would be displeased, he was obviously very pleased with himself for setting things up." In Ravello, down on the beach, there were guys hanging around who were "obviously" available to richer men, recalls Altman. "Gore would say, 'Are you interested in any of these boys?' He would pick up the ones who were available."

Like Vidal's sister, Altman thinks Vidal used prostitutes "as a way of maintaining total control and also a way of dealing with his own rather confused attitudes towards his own sexuality. He kept on saying he was bisexual, but he clearly wasn't in any real sense. There is no question his sexual interests were not with women, but men and specifically in 'trade' or 'rent.' He liked young, good-looking working class men, an old English tradition Gore seemed keen to take over. Cruising for him meant cruising for young men."

Rome, and the liberating sexual circus it embodied, would always be special to Vidal. In a 1992 letter to his friend Judy Halfpenny, he said, "I was never lovelier, as Marlene used to say with absolute seriousness glaring at old stills, than when I was in Rome." Vidal wrote that he was forty-seven, still worked out in a gym, "and there was sex and motive. At sixty I said to hell with it and now people make most unkind references to my lack of beauty. I find myself peculiarly unbothered," Vidal said. "So much for vanity, which is only useful, necessary if you're after something. No pursuit, no beauty. I'm a utilitarian finally."

Chapter Eight

The Rules of Attraction

A certain kind of sex lasting a certain amount of time at a certain time of day with a certain kind of intimacy and a certain kind of man: Vidal was very controlled in how he sought and approached sex. For Matt Tyrnauer "the core of his psychosexuality" was that Vidal saw sex "as a temporal thing. After a certain point in his life he compartmentalized sex and it was a transactional thing that was meant to be temporary, not relationship-based. He used to mock the overuse of the word 'relationship.' If sex was repeated, as it was on occasion for him, it would have to be something good enough to go back to or for convenience sake. But the idea of having a romantic love affair attached to an ongoing sexual relationship was something he was not open to. It would not have worked for him intellectually or psychosexually to have sex with someone he viewed as an intellectual peer or near peer."

He parried the question, in a magazine interview, over whether his first sexual experience was with a man or woman by replying, "I was much too polite to ask...A gentleman never asks the sex of the person he is going to bed with." In 1977, a *New York Times* reviewer of a book of his essays talks of "unresolved hostility toward his father, further evidence of which, some would argue, is Mr. Vidal's cheerfully admitted homosexuality." Vidal replied stingingly that not only is "unresolved hostility" towards his father non-evident any of his work, but also, "Nowhere in my writing have I 'admitted' ('cheerfully' or dolefully) to homosexuality, or heterosexuality. Even the dullest of mental therapists no longer accepts the proposition that cold-father-plus-clinging-mother-equals-fag-offspring." He and Austen had been together twenty seven years at this point, not to mention the many men he had slept with. Life, he once said, was "as promiscuous as I can make it."

Did Vidal love, or believe in love? "He believed in it but he thought he was above it all," Ned Rorem tells me. "He wouldn't allow himself to fall into certain traps. I was very different, very romantic. I was 'married' nine times." In his biography, Fred Kaplan observes "the romantic Rorem and anti-romantic Vidal enjoyed one another's conversation." Rorem writes in his diary that he is sympathetic to Vidal, "except the cynical stance. Those steely epigrams summing up all subjects resemble the bars of a cage through which he peers defensively. 'It's not that love's a farce, it doesn't exist.' Defensible. Yet it's just one definition of something without definition. Rather than be accused of being called a softie he affects a pose of weariness," that Rorem thought Vidal had learned from Paul Bowles. Vidal told Rorem, "It's too bad I can't love anymore." Rorem observes, "But of course he doesn't mean it."

In *Palimpsest*, Vidal wrote that he didn't know what other people meant by the word "love" and so avoided it as a word, although he had been in love with Jimmie Trimble, he says. Vidal told Mike Wallace in a CBS *60 Minutes* interview in 1975, "I don't like the word 'love.' It's like patriotism. It's like the flag. It's the last refuge of scoundrels. When people start talking about what wonderful, warm, deep emotions they have and how they love people, I watch out. Somebody is going to steal something. Romantic love as Americans conceive it does not exist. Hence, the enormous divorce rate. When sexual desire cools there's often not much left." Vidal followed this with something that must have been lovely for Austen to hear. "Haven't I proved my point by living with somebody for twenty four years? That's obviously not being in love. You don't live with the person you love. At least I've known very few cases of it. You live with a friend, which is something quite different from having a grand occasion or a love affair."

So, Vidal rejected the notion of love, lived with his "friend," and paid for sex with hustlers. Diana Phipps Sternberg reveals a darker element of control Vidal enjoyed in the transaction. "I remember Gore saying to me, 'There is nothing more pleasurable than if a partner doesn't like it.' He meant going to bed with someone you didn't know, and paying for it, and knowing what you wanted them to do paying for it, knowing they wouldn't be doing it for pleasure."

In 1957 Vidal's desire for control led to a particularly nasty incident, according to Vidal's sister, Nina Straight. Newton Steers, her then-husband, told her Vidal had been one of a gang, including the English poet and novelist Stephen Spender, who had all fucked a hustler under a bridge. The story was well-known within the family, says Burr Steers. "I guess these guys had a kind of contempt for him bending over and picking up the sap. It was brutal sex and then they beat him up," says Straight. It's one thing to be in complex retreat from your sexuality, and quite another to beat up a hustler you've just had sex with, I say. "I guess it was the attitude, 'If we beat him up, it's like we haven't just done what we know we've done sexually. This is what I want, how dare you make me want it.' You know, it happens to women also," says Straight. When I later ask Straight for clarification on the incident—when and where exactly it had taken place, whether Vidal had been arrested or charged with committing an office—she declines to comment fruther; Burr Steers thinks it had been in England.

Her half-brother's use of hustlers was rooted in his desire for control "and an attitude of contempt," Straight believes. "He just paid for it and didn't have to do anything. They would do whatever had to be done for him and that would be that. It allowed him to feel superior: 'I'm paying for you. You do whatever I say, you piece of you-know-what.' I'm sure the contempt that Gore had for the people involved was huge because he had contempt for himself and his own homosexuality, which is there in the fact he was saying he was bisexual, which was total rubbish. You had the money and you said, 'Well, you contemptible person, you're coming in here for me to do something to you. And you're letting me pay you for me to do what I want to do.'"

Vidal's formality with hustlers was observed by many. In New Orleans, Vidal's friend J. Winter Thorington recalled Vidal paying for sex. "He said he liked it that way because then nobody owed anything to anybody." After one encounter with a hustler, Vidal was "a bit cool toward the guy…He didn't seem interested in carrying on a conversation…he probably figured that everything was even-Steven at that stage of the game and he didn't owe him any conversation or any money or anything else." Geoffrey and Penelope Moore, who visited New Orleans with Vidal, told Fred Kaplan that Vidal would boast about "getting certain guys when out on the town." Vidal said he was into belly-rubbing, not fucking. Another friend recalled Vidal making remarks about young men being just for sex, no love involved, and being in Paris with a "disreputable-looking" very young man. Vidal told Jack Larson that the actor Doug McClure "was the quintessential hustler type."

An actual quintessential hustler, Denham Fouts, was recalled in by Vidal as an *homme fatal*, kept by multi-millionaire Peter Watson, who had established Fouts in his own Parisian apartment, where the handsome young man "spent his days in a great bed beneath a Tchelitchew painting, the paraphernalia for his opium pipe close by." Vidal didn't think Fouts as stunning as his many admirers. "He looked like the ghost he would soon be, dead of a malformed heart."

Jack Larson once said to Paul Bowles that he was "mystified" about Vidal's sexual activity, and, Larson tells me, Bowles, who was one of Vidal's longest-standing friends, "said Gore had only ever been interested in 'prep school sex'—mutual masturbation." In late-night conversations in Rome and Ravello Vidal would tell Richard Harrison "the boys in Rome were easy to get undressed: you just tell them 'You're good-looking.' He thought it was because Italian mothers treated their sons as babies." Harrison asked Vidal what he liked to do in bed: blow jobs? anal sex? "He knew all the words, but he'd go 'Ugh, agh.' Everything was disgusting. I thought, 'What the hell does he like?'"

Vidal never "sucked cock or got fucked": this "deprivation is presumably what made him homoerotic rather than homosexual," noted Arthur Laurents in a memoir. "Gore thinks role-playing is all important, i.e., it's the position in the sexual act, what the male does and does not do, that makes him more masculine and less queer. Not generational, this struggle with it until some, at least, grow up and realize it isn't the act that determines whether a male is homosexual, it's the sex of the person he consistently chooses to do it with. Over a thousand young men before the age of twenty-five seems a fairly consistent indication of homosexuality."

Gay men aren't alone in confusing role playing with masculinity and masculinity with sexual behavior, writes Laurents, noting that Vidal has written he wanted nothing more than orgasm with as many attractive partners as possible and he wasn't interested in giving pleasure to any of them. "He adds his friend Jack Kennedy's endorsement of that view presumably because a presidential endorsement endows glamour. It does, but doesn't make it special. Scores of American males behave that way, that's why they remain boys all the way to the end. Boys don't realize they have cheated themselves as well as their partners. Making sure to pleasure a partner is making sure to increase your own pleasure. Gore's partners, of course, were anonymous quickies; he didn't care about them or believe he should or could, for that matter: he was homoerotic." In his diaries, Christopher Isherwood writes of having lunch with Vidal in 1955, with Vidal depressed "because he finds himself unable to care for anyone seriously."

Patty Dryden, a friend later in Vidal's life, says Vidal talked about sex "in the abstract: he would talk about men's wee-wees [penises]." Yet on the square in Ravello, in the San Domingo bar, one of his favorite hangouts, Vidal would turn to Richard Harrison and drunkenly shout, 'Well, that fellow over there looks like he's got a big cock. All around tourists were whispering, 'That's Gore Vidal.' Nobody recognizes writers, but Gore was a writer who was on TV."

John Mitzel, who interviewed Vidal for *Fag Rag* magazine in 1974, recalls Vidal coming into Boston's Glad Day Bookshop that he owned at the time—since superseded by Calamus Bookstore—in 1990, asking for Madonna's book, *Sex*. "I didn't know you were a fan of Madonna," Mitzel said. "I'm not," Vidal said. "It's for Howard." "I didn't know Howard was a fan of Madonna," Mitzel answered. Vidal "looked at me like the dullest piece of lint you ever picked out of your belly button and said, 'Howard's not a fan of Madonna.' 'I hate to ask you the question, but why are you buying it then?'" "It's so Howard can show it to the boys when they come to up to the palazzo," Vidal replied. Staying overnight in a Boston hotel, Vidal also rented a gay bondage porn video from Mitzel's store, *Tie Me Up*, by Tom "Ropes" McGurk. After Vidal's death, Burr Steers found "a lot of gay pornography, tapes and things" at Outpost Drive.

Vidal was a keen observer, intellectually as well as across Italian piazzas, of gay male aesthetics. In 1974 he told *Gay Sunshine* magazine that he had noted a changing ideal of male physical and sexual beauty. "I have noticed a very interesting change in my own lifetime. And that has been the quality of the trade has fallen off. When I was young there was a floating population of hetero males who wanted money or kicks or what have you and would sell their ass for a period of their lives. Later they would marry and end up as construction workers or firemen or in the police department. And that was that. Their phase was over. But these were really all-American types, masculine in the old sense. There has emerged a new physical type who seem feminine to me, and I use the term in its old sexist sense. Very schmoo, soft shoulders, flat muscles, broad hips, high voices...I wonder if the body is changing physically, whether there might be some kind of mutancy taking place, and that nature is instinctively saying that we don't need any more babies. And the men are becoming a bit less masculine and the women a bit less feminine."

Dennis Altman says, "He struggled to understand why people appropriated a gay 'identity' in the 1970s. He was uncomfortable around theoretical discussions around sex and sexuality. I once asked him why there was racism in his novels. He said, 'Well, what do you expect given my background?' That also applied to his homosexuality. It was easy for him to find men to have sex with, but in no way was that a basis for an identity. That was an irony for Gore: he was open about his relationship with Howard, they lived together for fifty years and at one level he was comfortable with it and had a wonderful life. Later on he was active at certain gay events. Then he'd still maintain there was no such thing as a homosexual. You'd need a psychoanalyst to filter an explanation of that; he was both denying and asserting his homosexuality at the same time."

Christopher Murray, a therapist with many gay clients in New York's Chelsea neighborhood and well-versed in Vidal's work, life and beliefs, observes that there was little healthy—for Vidal—in his rejection of all labels. I assumed Murray would have found Vidal's "no such thing as gay, no labels" attitude liberating and radical. Vidal, he thought, had "terrible self-esteem," sourced in his difficult childhood, from which he had developed a personality disorder. Like many gay men he was traumatized by the early experience of "performing your gender wrong."

His mother, having expressed her concern that he would be gay and behaved in the destructive way she did, left him with shame, humiliation and guilt. As he grew up, thinks Murray, he developed an "armor." He became macho, a swaggering peacock, "he had to be top dog as a rejection of the message that he was a sissy boy. Everything he did, and how he behaved, his public image, was compensatory. He had a mask constructed of superlatives, he had to be the haughtiest, smartest guy in the room." But "he was clearly miserable" and, far from rejecting labels, "he was about labels for everything," says Murray. "He just didn't find a way to embrace his own identity: it was a rejection, containment, denial of who he was. 'I'm not gay because that's being a sissy, and I'm not that. I'm *sui generis*,' and he was. Gore wasn't part of anyone's community. I think he probably occupied a very lonely place, and it's to his credit he was a very smart guy, creative and able to have a long-term relationship."

It's wrong to say "there's no such thing as 'being gay,'" adds Murray, because like race or gender identity, it "transparently just is, we say they 'are' and so they 'are.' Vidal wasn't fooling anyone, everybody knew he was gay. He had low self-esteem after being humiliated and shamed as a little boy and didn't have a truly intimate relationship because he was scared of being rejected and humiliated." In his relationship with Austen "he was not secure enough to be vulnerable, he could only operate 'Battleship Vidal' and that's sad. He was able to marshal an intellectual defense but it came with a price tag: authentic relationships with intimates. He created a prickly protective shell because his identity was under attack." But he did a lot for gay people in his writing, he was an eloquent advocate however he defined himself, I say. "Yes, but it came at the price of a shutdown. He was a miserable man. You marveled at him on TV, but you were scared of him. You didn't want him to turn that rage on to you. He wrote books, ran for office: all admirable, but not healing."

Jimmie Trimble, for Murray, is a frozen, persistent early experience of romantic obsession, "an adolescent fantasy of the love object, older brother, the captain of the baseball team." Murray is a Vidal fan: sad he didn't form the kind of "safe circle" around him for a warm and nourishing private life. "But he wasn't an axe murderer, he didn't commit suicide. He was vigorous in his public and private lives. He was intellectually engaged and had a long-term relationship. He was absolutely a gay radical, a transitional figure from the century that defined modern homosexuality—and he sort of bore the brunt of that for the rest of us and paid a high price for that. I like him for that and for being out there in the world, swinging."

Vidal once wrote to a friend that Freud was "god for far too many Americans. I fear he thinks exclusive heterosexuality is normal." Ruminating to Judy Halfpenny on the possibility of a gay gene, he writes, "Where then is the straight gene? Confusion begins with the boy in the army who has a dozen and perhaps emotionally fulfilling affairs and then leaves the army and goes back to girls. His poor genes must be twirling like dervishes while his hippocampus or whatever it is in his brain keeps expanding or shrinking in order to accommodate what is now known as situational sex (like a homosexual prison term), ignoring the fact that all sex is situational." It was "interesting that bisexuality is now in the news, if not fashion," he writes. "Of course even Freud realized that everyone was bisexual but who practices what is—well, situational." In a "cul-de-sac" lay, for Vidal, "our barbarous religions and ongoing peasant superstitions."

David Schweizer thinks Vidal was "pre-, during- and post-gay. He was old enough to remember sneaking around, that illicit thing was a little bit of a key to him: he wasn't so interested in permissiveness. He had these people in, paid them…on some silly level that was what was hot, what turned him on. What he wanted as a companion was Howard." Marriage is the "glummest situation of all," Vidal once wrote to a friend.

Vidal's view was that sex and intimacy were open fields, says Dennis Altman. "He had a Kinsey view of sex: that there was a continuum of sexual identities, and he was very proud of the fact he was able to fuck ostensibly straight men for money. He was also deeply discomfited by the idea his sexuality defined him publicly. Yet he made dramatic interventions for the gay community. There was a deep ambivalence."

Sometimes this ambivalence erupted at home. When Steven Abbott stayed at La Rondinaia, Abbott and Jim Stephens, his partner, moved the two beds in their room together. After they left they received a furious letter from Vidal criticizing them for doing so: the maid, he said, had been horrified and he and Austen had had to "explain things." It seems astonishing that this was an issue for Vidal: the maid was working for a gay couple, albeit one with two men who slept separately. Abbott was extremely upset by the letter and author and bibliographer were estranged for a year.

Visiting England, the sexually voracious Vidal hired prostitutes "occasionally" says Vidal's friend John Bowen. "He would pick them up at the 'Meat Rack' [where the hustlers hung around at Piccadilly Circus] and take them back to the Connaught Hotel. The only time he spoke about it with me he intimated the guy had behaved rather badly, demanding more money than they had agreed. Sex was important to Gore. It was one of the pleasures of life. What was important was that he stayed in control."

Another story related by a friend of Vidal's features the writer staying at the Savoy Hotel, a hustler in his room, the two unable to agree on a price. Vidal called the butler, had the young man removed and then when he checked out, the bill has a listing for one hundred pounds for sundries. The first time Vidal heard a hustler in the US charge one hundred dollars he wanted "to leave the country," he said to a friend; Scotty Bowers had charged twenty dollars.

Vidal and Austen also went to Numbers, the L.A. gay restaurant of the 1980s and '90s, where "trade" stood at the bar, waiting to be bought by horny customers; Numbers itself was a slang word for "trick." "It was fabulous, a fantasy," recalls the photographer Michael Childers. "You came in via a descending staircase with mirrors behind, so you could be seen from all sides. Everyone could see the legs, then the basket, then the face—and if all that was disappointing they would turn back to their food." The Numbers telephone number was written, in Austen's handwriting, in the couple's Rolodex. Childers recalls, "You'd send the young guy a drink, for example. He'd come over say, 'Thank you, Mr. Vidal, that's so nice,' and so the introduction would take place." The *maitre d'*, remembered as "Ernest" by regulars, would advise Vidal, says Childers, "Gore, that one's trouble, stay away from him."

When I mention Numbers to Burr Steers, Vidal's nephew, he laughs. "You couldn't parody it. The whole thrust was that the hustlers were these hot guys from Oklahoma, while the customers were these old Hollywood queens with blue hair. It was the last vestige of that world. I went there with my wife and two guys and a guy came over and, looking at all of us, said, 'I'm really into scenes of five people.'"

Altman's fondest memories of Vidal are of the author his late forties and early fifties. "He was still very good looking: ironically if he had gone into a gay bar he could have picked someone up very easily. I once took him to a Sydney gay bar in the early 1970s. He looked around and said, 'This is like New York in the 1940s.'" Maybe therein lay another basis of

Vidal's need for hustlers, thinks Altman: they afforded him privacy. "My impression with sex partners was that he was the dominant partner. I'm not saying he was a top—we never discussed the anatomy of it—but part of buying the hustlers was being in control. Gore needed to be in control of every social situation. His egotism was overwhelming."

Vidal's many sexually-themed stories "never seemed lecherous or unseemly," notes Matt Tyrnauer. "This, after all, was one of the great storytellers. Even in private, he seemed to be playing it for the history books. Gore knew how to present. This was not someone who wanted to come off as a gossipy queen or seem prurient or disgusting. He played it very straight in both meanings of that term and was more like an old schoolboy. He was very circumspect and discreet. However, he was not above dishing the dirt. Sex was an extremely important topic for him. It's underneath the surface in all his books and very above the surface in *Myra Breckinridge*, *Myron* and *Duluth*. Sex was politics. But considering how much sex he claimed to have had he didn't talk about it much. He was more likely to talk about what Howard did."

In his later life, Jay Parini saw Vidal's sexual energy decline. "Howard would find trade, he would get Gore dates. Gore didn't want intimacy, he wanted sex without intimacy. Gore liked non-intellectual men who looked like rugby players. But he wasn't into sex: I always felt he would be happier not to think about it." Parini believes the couple "had really stopped having sex with that much trade in Ravello. Howard liked to hang out with twenty-year-olds. They would invite these young men to parties at their pool and just hang out. Gore wildly exaggerated his sex life: in the last twenty to thirty years it had reduced to the bare minimum. I saw very little sex in Gore, it exposed too much to the possibility of intimacy. He liked the cozy, comfortable, asexual. Howard would constantly say, if we were having lunch in the square in Ravello, 'Look at that ass, Gore, holy mackerel mamma.' Gore would roll his eyes."

Vidal had "a very particular patrician masculinity," says David

Schweizer. "He was an American aristocrat, all his training to be a political figure, all pushed towards this masculinity. He had every qualification, he had the brains and background but he knew deep inside himself it wasn't going to happen. He ran for office twice, half-heartedly. But he knew his political destiny would be betrayed by his gay sexuality—this taint. So he boxed it up. He's like the Roy Cohn figure in *Angels in America* who says, 'I'm not gay. I fuck men.' That gets a big laugh, but is it that funny? Gore Vidal provided us with decade after decade of color and intellectual challenge to savor. There's no need to belittle or despise him, but he had not a dissimilar male schism to Cohn's—a very, very classic example of gay self-hatred, a highly functional version of it."

While having so much gay sex in private, Vidal made no public speeches or stands in favor of gay equality (though did write about it), and arguably the most pronounced omission of public speaking on an issue where he could have made an impact was around HIV and AIDS. In private Vidal talked about HIV and AIDS intermittently, says Scotty Bowers. "When AIDS first started Gore said to me: 'I can see your point in not fixing people up anymore and I'm very concerned about meeting people.' He said, 'You never know,' but Gore said if a guy looked healthy and clean-cut it's possible he doesn't have it, but he wouldn't fuck anyone looking drawn." What poor, ill-informed judgment, I say. "That's what people thought at the beginning," says Bowers. Did it change his sexual behavior? "He met some guy: he just wanted to jack off and watch the other guy jack off, not touching. I never saw him use a condom but he might have. Possibly." Did he ever bottom? "Not really. I knew him as a top, so he worried less about contracting HIV."

Michael Childers agrees. Vidal wasn't concerned about AIDS "as a top, active sexual partner." He was never passive? "No, no, no." Vidal was "very moved by the AIDS struggle. He lost good friends. But ACT UP and all that he called 'the Kramer Hysteria.' He didn't like [Larry] Kramer much. But he was very touched by HIV and AIDS and felt a sense of loss."

In 1986, David Schweizer recalls Vidal coming to a theatrical piece derived from Plato's *Symposium* in Los Angeles that Schweizer directed to benefit the American Foundation for AIDS Research. "I'd never seen him entirely enthuse about anything, but he was deeply moved by it and said it was one of the seminal theatrical productions he had seen. Maybe he was so moved because the word 'gay' is never uttered. It's just a stage full of brilliant men making competitive speeches about the love that dare not speak its name, an army of lovers, and he was just blown away by it."

Schweizer and Vidal "talked a little bit about AIDS. He told me he hated the politics of AIDS, the way it was being parsed as punishment for homosexuals." Yet in *Point to Point Navigation*, Vidal explains his silence with the shockingly blithe, "I am also chided for not doing enough about AIDS; but my virological skills are few." In an interview with *Playboy* conducted early in the pandemic, quoted by Christopher Bram in his book *Eminent Outlaws*, Vidal said people were over-reacting about AIDS: he had grown up with syphilis in the years before penicillin, he was used to sexual diseases. While his arrogance could be impressive, it could also be witless.

Behind his silence, and like many gay men of that era, Vidal lost friends to the disease, such as Rudolph Nureyev. In *Palimpsest*, Vidal recalls getting to know Nureyev when he moved to an island off the coast around Positano, near Ravello, and would visit Vidal at La Rondinaia to "let his AIDS-wasted body collapse beside the pool." On his last visit, the August before he died, Nureyev ruminated on the big cock of a fellow dancer, Vidal noting "the upper body has begun to waste away, but the lower is still unaffected, legs powerful, and the feet—for a dancer—not too misshapen, no hammertoes." In *Point to Point Navigation*, Vidal writes of a doctor coming regularly to "change" Nureyev's blood. "When this happened, he would be full of energy for a few weeks." He would dance and "sweated like a horse." He'd strip off and swim in Vidal and Austen's pool, then drink wine and watch TV. At La Rondinaia, Vidal showed Sean Strub the telescope he had trained on the chaise longue next to Nureyev's swimming pool at Gallo

Lungo, an island once owned by the ballet dancer off the Amalfi coast, where he liked to sunbathe nude. "He referred to how large Nureyev's penis was," recalls Strub.

Nureyev hated being seen as a Russian defector, he told Vidal. "I get out only to dance more. Is frozen there, the great dance companies. So I left." He also rejected criticism of not being open about having AIDS. "If I do, I cannot reenter US. Law says no one with such a disease can be allowed in. So I must be silent." Bidding farewell at the gate of La Rondinaia, Vidal made a sign of the cross over Nureyev's chest. Nureyev bowed gravely and died soon after.

Vidal had become friends with Strub in 1995. Strub had just married Doris O'Donnell, twenty-five years older than Strub, and a longstanding childhood friend of Vidal's. "It wasn't a romantic relationship," says Strub, who is gay, of his marriage. "Doris was a very close friend and we married so she could qualify for Social Security and Medicare." When Strub met Vidal for the first time he was critically ill with AIDS. Strub had KS (Kaposi's sarcoma) lesions on his neck "and I could tell he was disturbed by them. I was working on a column for *Poz* that raised the prospect of reparations for people with HIV. He read it and marked it up, making all my gentle, tentative sentences much more declarative. 'If you're going to say it, don't pussyfoot around and just say it!' he said."

Strub "had an instinctive sense" that Vidal "hadn't spent much time around anyone with AIDS," he writes in his memoir, *Body Counts*. "I understood. People were inherently curious about such things. Later, he admitted that mine were the first Kaposi's sarcoma lesions he had seen up close."

I ask Strub why he thinks Vidal was silent about HIV and AIDS. "In the earliest days, the only people saying anything about AIDS were gay, and some lesbian, community leaders, particularly the political activists, all part of a milieu Gore had already rejected. The association with identity politics I suspect made it something initially of less interest. Then, of course, he began to lose his own friends and I think a combination of his geographic distance (living in Italy) from the visible epidemic in the United States and his age were both factors. He famously denied having anal sex and I'm guessing he early on figured out he personally wasn't at much risk. He asked me questions about the risk of transmission via oral sex, but generally didn't have much to say himself about the epidemic."

But, in person, Vidal seemed open-hearted and open-minded. "When we met for the first time in person, I still had lesions on my face and I think that was somewhat of a shock to him," Strub tells me. "He asked if they were painful and was clearly compassionate in his response towards me. The KS lesions were the mark of death and the marriage only happened because it was expected that I would die soon. So that kind of frankness about my impending demise sort of put everything on the table, most importantly the status of my health. So it was talked about, including the most visible manifestation of the disease, the lesions on my face."

When Strub visited Vidal a couple of years later, again in Ravello, Vidal "was astonished that the lesions were gone." In Strub's memoir, he recalls Vidal and him discussing how the epidemic had changed since the introduction of combination therapy. Vidal told him that when he had seen the lesions "he didn't expect me to survive much longer." "*Front nulla fides*," Vidal said to Strub, testing his Latin: "Appearances can't be trusted."

Strub recalls a supper with Vidal at a restaurant in New York with a mutual acquaintance, George Armstrong. "I was railing about something concerning epidemic politics. I realized George was uncomfortable with the subject and conscious of who in the restaurant might overhear us. George was totally out as a gay man, but AIDS stigma adhered even to engaging in a conversation about it in public. I can't say that would be the same for Gore, as he could talk in intellectual terms about anything in any context, but I think there was something distasteful about the topic for George and I suspect the same might be said for Gore. That didn't get in the way of their compassion or concern, it just was an uncomfortable topic because it necessarily brought up subjects they weren't comfortable discussing."

More personally, the disease struck at the heart of Vidal's family. Hugh Steers, a painter and brother to Burr, died of AIDS in 1995. He was gay and had beseeched Vidal to take a public, campaigning stand. "He very much fought the fight politically and was very outspoken," Burr says. "He and Gore had been very close, but Gore didn't do a lot during the AIDS crisis and Hugh called him on it. Like Gore he was gay, they resembled each other and had similar personalities. Gore had a lot of things he was not totally good on when it came to the gay community, including the 'no such thing as gay, only gay sexual acts' thing. Maybe it was generational. Maybe identifying as 'a top' for him meant in his eyes he was the man, masculine not feminine. Hugh was effete and androgynous and Gore was odd with him about it"—Steers pauses—"actually 'homophobic' is the word." Nina Straight, Hugh's mother, says, "I don't know what it was that Gore didn't want to deal with. He loved, cared and was scared like the rest of the world. That's big human emotion, that you're vulnerable that you're open to the shot."

Letters and cards Hugh sent Vidal sketch both the intimacy and frustration he felt towards his uncle's inaction; he confided in Vidal and also asked him for money, which Vidal gave to him. In one note from Paris, dated 1984, Hugh writes: "My libido has been unbounded of late... I seem to spend all my weekend fucking—but the fucking is very good." On August 9, 1989, Hugh sent his uncle literature on the direct action group ACT UP: "Though the development of a gay community in the US has created a certain ghettoization and made homosexuals an obvious target, it has also provided us with an efficient, ready network to deal with this crisis."

In 1990, Hugh tells Vidal, "I'm doing well enough. No major health problems aside from a few viral infections which are normal and not that wreak danger—that being bacterial infections...My real problem is depression. I think it's chronic and clinical and I might go and see someone finally..." A year later, on the back of a newspaper clipping about a contemporary art show in Denver featuring his work, Hugh says: "Well, I'm famous in Denver, whatever that means. Obscurity seems to dog me still in New York. It's impossible to get critics in just to give the work a look, let alone review it...The two consolations are that things can't get worse and those who do see the work are very moved and impressed."

The last notes are from 1992. On June 24, Hugh tells Vidal, "My physical health is good; my mental health, which may be connected to a physical problem, is not so great—stressful times." He asks for money. "I'm sorry to burden you with this problem. I feel pretty messy." Then in the final note Hugh writes the most personal of political pleas Vidal did not heed: "We, I don't mean just gays and PWAs [people with AIDS], need someone of your intellect and articulateness to seize the field. The times are such that I think you could have quite an impact raising some hell."

"Gore forked over a substantial sum to support Hugh," says Nina Straight. "He was great in that and did say how awful it was Hugh had died so young, that he had a full life." How did she cope with her son's illness and death? "The fact is I needed Hugh. He was such an influence, such a sound thinker. He didn't have to come out to me," she says with a laugh, "do you think I'm deaf, dumb and blind?" She's proud of her son's AIDS activism: "You should have seen those guys, what they were doing changed the face of medicine." She shivers recalling the wards of AIDS patients in the New York hospitals of the day. "My god, the halls were lined with guys, the next day they were dead. Our lives were so shattered, but Hugh was so frank about it. He was suffering a long time before he was diagnosed. But you go out fighting, he was so busy fighting. He just went out swinging, painting, eating, exercising." In *Palimpsest*, Vidal refers to Hugh only to condemn Jacqueline Kennedy for ignoring the nephews they had in common, including Hugh ("the brilliant painter with AIDS"). To Strub, Vidal conveyed a fondness for Hugh, but also a sense that he hadn't done enough or wasn't in touch or supportive enough. "He was very interested when I told him about Hugh appearing in a public service campaign, I think for the Community Research Initiative on AIDS," says Strub.

Rather as he would do after Austen died, following Hugh's death at thirty-two in 1995, Vidal finally expressed what he thought about his loved one. He composed a moving testimonial to his nephew, and not only that, finally said something about AIDS. It was delivered not by Vidal who did not attend the funeral but by Burr, Hugh's brother, and Vidal later printed it, alongside some of Steer's work in *Poz* magazine, in April 1997. Vidal "read and admired" the magazine, says Strub. "When I first asked him to write something, he said he didn't know what he would have to say and then started talking about Hugh. I asked if he would like to write something about Hugh for *Poz*. He paused for a moment and then said he would like to do that."

In the testimonial and piece, Vidal wrote, "I'm not an art critic and can pass no judgment on Hugh Steers's other than to say that it very much moved me thematically," wrote Vidal. "But I am a professional judge of character and I think that my admiration for the way he conducted his life and death is well-grounded. Now that he is done with both, we should try and recall that the victims of this plague have often had splendid lives and, certainly, they did a lot else other than die. This should never be forgotten in Hugh's case, or that of anyone else.

"Nearly ten years ago, when he learned that he was on the downward slope, he contemplated suicide, fearful that he would not have the time to make his work other than mediocre, incomplete. Happily, he remained alive and in the most heroic fashion worked until the end, completing, as it were a charismatic talent; then, that done, he went, knowing that he had pulled it off. There is a real triumph here. He liked George Eliot so I shall quote her in this regard, from *Adam Bede*: 'Our deeds determine us, as much as we determine our deeds.' So he has left himself, as good artists do, to us in his work. His deeds are all down now. Occasionally in a family as supremely incoherent as ours someone does manage against the odds to complete him or herself, and so I am most honored to have been his half-uncle."

Burr Steers says another George Eliot quote, this time from *Middlemarch*, was inscribed on his brother's headstone: "If we had a keen vision and feeling of all ordinary human life, it would be like hearing the grass grow and the squirrel's heart beat, and we should die of that roar which lies on the other side of silence." Strub interpreted from Vidal that he felt what he had written "could enhance Hugh's legacy, or he hoped that it would." Strub thinks he might have felt "guilt" over Hugh's death, of not being there for him "emotionally and practically. The magazine article meant he had been able to burnish Hugh's legacy."

In later notes to Strub, Vidal said it was "a pity [Hugh] lived in such a fifth-rate era for the arts, particularly cabinet painting, which must either be soothingly abstract, like tasteful linoleum or just carefully tricky. He was a latter-day Goya with an even harsher subject." He also wrote to Strub, "I hope Hugh's posterity goes better than his 'terity. He was luckless on a grand scale. But this is progress, I suppose."

This return to habitual balefulness notwithstanding, Vidal's more moving testimony, at the funeral and in *Poz*, don't simply speak to his love and respect of Hugh, but also to a hitherto unknown wider understanding of AIDS. It echoes what would flow from him—feeling, love, raw emotion—after Austen's death; both reminders that behind the haughty Vidal mask was a gentler, more empathetic writer and man.

Chapter Nine

Lovers or Just Good Friends? Vidal's Women

Was Vidal truly bisexual and, if so, how actively bisexual was he? In *Palimpsest*, Vidal said he told a "riveted" Jimmie Trimble about the first sex he had had with a girl at twelve or thirteen. "They fumbled about" at Merrywood, he more interested "in what I was going to tell Jimmie about the great mystery that I had at last barely penetrated." Note that Trimble is the focus of this first sexual experience with a girl, not the girl: Vidal simply wants bragging rights. It also doesn't sound too thrusting, an appropriately inconclusive, barely convincing attempt at heterosexuality that Vidal would repeat throughout his life. Women were "sometimes tempting," but the examples set by his family "proved to be a reliable, unbreakable prophylactic." To Donald Weise, Vidal said he felt "close to women," who were "more likely to pick up on body language and unspoken statements. They interest me more, I suppose."

"It suited Gore to put out these rumors he was having affairs with women," says Matt Tyrnauer. "A lot of Gore's statements about heterosexual sex really have to be taken with a grain of salt," Fred Kaplan tells me. "I found no hard evidence he and [the English actress] Claire Bloom had sex; or that he and Rosalind Rust had sex." Rust was Vidal's first long-term girlfriend in 1940. Vidal "is so divine-looking," she wrote in her diary, detailing his handsomeness, including "an aristocratic nose and a nice rather mocking mouth." In his biography, Kaplan quotes Rust telling a friend that Vidal was "my first beau and the best man I ever had. The best man I ever had in bed." He double-dated a few girls; his Exeter years were without "romantic longing or sexual angst," writes Kaplan. "We were used to each other in a low-key, comfortable way," Vidal says of Rust.

In 1942 he and Rust, both seventeen, decided to get married;

his grandfather advised him, "Be *not* fruitful, do *not* multiply."
He told his father that he'd need about a hundred dollars a month
to live on. Jimmie Trimble, at the dance at the Sulgrave Club
where both men orgasmed over each other while talking about
girls, told him he was "crazy" to consider marrying Rust. In 1943
Vidal broke off his engagement with Rust, according to Kaplan's
biography, apparently greatly affected by a novel called *Fling
Out the Banner*, whose male character Paul, breaking up with
his girlfriend and affected by the suicide of a friend who has sex
with men, seems to have conflicting sexual feelings. Rust went
on to become a successful commercial artist.

As a young man in New York, while having sex with men at
the Everard Baths, Vidal was also stepping out with socialite
Cordelia Phelps Claiborne. Vidal also had an intense relationship
with Alice Astor, who had a home in Rhinecliff, upstate New York
(he would buy his own home there, Edgewater, in 1950). Astor
had already been married to a gay man and her daughter Romana
recalled to Fred Kaplan, she was "sort of aware of Gore's homosexuality." She added, "I was also aware of my mother's penchant
for having love affairs with homosexuals. She was the sort of
woman that if Gore was going to have an affair, she would have
one with him."

Vidal, writing in 1974, equated the sexuality of heterosexual
women with that of gay men, both paling unfavorably compared
to straight men. "Women are actually much more interesting,
because you're getting exactly the same psychic charge from a
faggot, and it isn't as comfortable. The hetero in the old days was
always more fun to go to bed with...There was a kind of kinetic
energy about it, it really could get wild. An enormous kinetic intensity, like a lightning storm, is exciting for its own sake, or, to
use that word Norman Mailer always misuses, 'existential.'"

The photographer Michael Childers says Vidal told him he
had had sex with a "couple of beautiful women" when he was
young. He also had close adult relationships with women, especially Claire Bloom, Joanne Woodward, Barbara Epstein, a
founder and co-editor of *The New York Review of Books*, and

Susan Sarandon, who all stayed with him at La Rondinaia and in years of conversation and letters shared their innermost thoughts with him. Claire Bloom recalls meeting Vidal on New Year's Eve, 1956 at New York's Plaza Hotel: "We got on very well and afterwards went to El Morocco where we talked till about five in the morning," she tells me.

Bloom was twenty-five, Vidal thirty. She later recorded in a notebook, held in her archive at Boston University, "Handsome, charming and, needless to say extremely witty, he was already an established and highly regarded writer. According to his own testimony bisexual, he was as attractive to women as to men." Their friendship "has been one of the most sustaining and precious of my life, and the love we have always felt for each other will continue for the rest of our lives. Through all my marriages he has remained a constant, the person I could always telephone, visit, call on for help and advice. Above all, who could make every kind of trauma I was agonizing about seem ridiculous and laughable."

At the time they met, Vidal was living with Austen in Edgewater on the banks of the Hudson River. Bloom was renting an apartment on East 51st Street belonging to Joanne Woodward. Bloom was seeing if she could "make a life" in New York and was "needless to say, very lonely indeed. Gore invited me to Edgewater and our friendship began." She lived in Rome with her first husband, Rod Steiger—"who belonged in a deli," Vidal told his friend Elinor Pruder—at the same time as Vidal lived there. "I was very attracted to Gore, but, mistakenly I now see, thought he was purely interested in young men and had no romantic interest in me whatsoever," says Bloom. "He later told me that I was quite wrong and that he made many attempts to seduce me that I completely ignored. None of this has ever stopped our loving each other. Horrified as he may have been by my choice in men, he accepted them as part of my mental aberrations. To my daughter Anna, he has always been an honorary godfather."

Their letters have the easy intimacy of friendship. "Skin cancers fall away; but hypochondria mounts: why so many extra white cells, doctor?" Vidal writes to her in 1975. "What—you always use cobalt for a minor sinusitis? Nothing serious of course. What an anti-climax death will be!" Vidal loathed Bloom's third husband, Philip Roth, and it was rumored Vidal had asked Bloom to marry him. "Not seriously, maybe jokingly," Bloom says. "It was a slightly romantic joke. We were romantic friends," Bloom tells me. "I think we said we planned to adopt Howard." She laughs. Did she and Vidal have sex? "No, he was homosexual," says Bloom. "Gore liked beautiful young men, not women. It was romantic in a lovely sense. It was absolutely not sexual: he adored Howard. Howard was his life." Austen seemed to think the rumored wedding proposal was serious, I say to Bloom. He joked about Bloom joining "the family." "Howard would not have liked it," Bloom tells me emphatically. So what exactly was her and Vidal's relationship? "I think it was more than friendship on both sides. We loved each other. He was a fantastic friend. But he was drawn to beautiful young men." So, why did he say he was bisexual? "There may have been relationships with women when he was young, he implied to me," Bloom says. How would she describe their relationship? "It was love between a man and a woman. But who cares what sex we were? And that was that. There was no more to it—yet that was still a great deal."

In Ravello, the former model and actor Richard Harrison recalls Bloom "really coming on to me strong and she made it very obvious that she wanted me to come to her bedroom. Gore grabbed me and said, 'I want you to know that she's the only woman I've ever been interested in.' I could certainly tell she wasn't interested in him, and I certainly didn't do anything with Claire Bloom. I don't believe Gore screwed any woman."

"I didn't ask any question of how Gore saw himself," says Bloom. How did she see his sexuality? "Who cares? It was obvious he lived with a man for over fifty years. That has to mean something. You couldn't put labels on Gore. There was nobody like him. There was no person in the world as witty and funny and clever and serious. He was a great man, quite honestly. He gave great advice, very good and very funny. I had many problems in my life and he was very kind and constructive. When my ghastly second marriage fell apart [to producer Hillard Elkins] we went to Greece together; to go with a writer and historian of that stature was simply wonderful. I know he could be tremendously acerbic, to me he was kindness itself. My happiest times with him were in Rome, with my first husband, Anna's father [Rod Steiger]. We went on wonderful trips, to Etruscan sites and temples—you couldn't have wished for a greater guide. There were fun, wonderful lunches. Gore was very strong: we climbed unclimbable hills."

"Claire Bloom was another fantasy, his ideal woman," says Jean Stein. "He'd always rhapsodize about her. I think Gore loved women. He loved Joanne Woodward too, but I suspect he loved Paul Newman as much as Joanne, if not more."

Bloom's affection and love is clear in our conversation and in her and Vidal's correspondence. After the death of Vidal's father, Bloom wrote to him, "You have many friends who love you, know how you must feel, and give you their strength and warmth. Perhaps that is all any of us can do for each other. It is a poor comfort but, I hope, a true one." In another letter, after he has stopped working mid-book to be with her, she writes, "I think you know how much our friendship means to me, and that I do love you. I mean that completely, and see no reason ever to change. We are very lucky, few people have as much between them as we do."

Though Vidal "definitely preferred" men, he talked about Woodward and Bloom a lot, says Fabian Bouthillette, his caregiver from 2008 to 2010. "He loved them as great friends. 'Claire was very bad in her selection of husbands,'" Vidal told Bouthillette. "I think Gore had a bit of the romantic hero complex," Bouthillette says, "swooping in and saving her from the heterosexual riff-raff and taking care of her. He did not want to see her abused by other men. Joanne told the story of Gore's marriage proposal to her as a way of getting Paul Newman to propose to her. It's a cute story, but it says a lot about Gore's concept of love: it was very intellectual and based on respect for people's characters." The agent Boaty Boatwright, a longtime friend of Vidal's, said he could be "unbelievably kind out of the blue, most women will tell you about that much softer side to him." After the breakdown of her marriage, he called her up to invite her to be his guest at a function. "Except in writing and interviews, I don't think he thought of himself as particularly unkind. That got worse when he drank too much, coupled with age and dementia."

Bouthillette said Vidal was attracted to women, "but he was a boy at heart and liked hanging out with the boys, so women bored him. There was a female bartender at the Beverly Hills Hotel he liked because she had a tight body and small breasts. He found her attractive and thought I should ask her out on a date. I did and it didn't work out." "Why do you like breasts?" Vidal would ask Bouthillette. "I don't know Gore," the younger man would reply, "but when I'm fucking a woman I like something to hold on to. Vidal didn't understand that: he didn't like big breasts. Bouthillette would shrug to his baffled questioner, "It's an A-type macho guy thing to like big breasts." When they went to Rome, Vidal would point to big-breasted women and say "You like that?" "Yes, I'm attracted to that, Gore," Bouthillette told me he would reply, wearily.

Vidal may have had close friendships with women, but those closest to him doubt many, if any, became sexual. "I never really bought that package," says Bernie Woolf. "Maybe he was just protecting his ass because of the times he was in." "He had sex with two or three women," claims Jay Parini, most notably Anaïs Nin, who wrote in her diary when they first met that he was "not nebulous, but clear and bright." Jay Parini recalls, "I asked Gore if he had slept with Anaïs Nin. He said, 'I did but I didn't like it, so I didn't count it among my conquests. You have to enjoy it for it to be real,' he told me. He was bisexual in name only."

Vidal told Patty Dryden that he had had sex with Nin. "He was young and she was in her forties." The author John Rechy says, "There was probably something there but no big thing. There was such a lot of venom between him and Anaïs Nin. He was forever doing parodies of her in his books in nasty, nasty ways." The only romance with a woman Vidal told Diana Phipps

Sternberg about was with Nin. "He said that she was a disaster in the end." In her diaries, Nin quotes Vidal in an early letter telling her, "You see, if I could have loved a woman, it would be you. Now I know my homosexuality is incurable." Vidal paid for an abortion for her. Later, she visited him in Guatemala and seemed to be in love with Vidal, thought one visitor.

Nin, wrote Fred Kaplan, found Vidal's sexual evasiveness baffling. She quotes Vidal telling her that he lived "detached from my present life...I like casual relationships. When you are involved, you get hurt." In *Palimpsest*, Vidal dissents from this "tune she has written for me in the opera of herself." Nin wasn't shocked when he told her about his sexual feelings for men—she had had relationships with women—but she strongly believed Vidal's homosexuality was partly a response against women, rooted in his dysfunctional relationship with his mother.

Their passionate then vituperative relationship can be charted in Nin's letters to Vidal. In 1947 she writes, "*Je t'embrace cheri, de tout mon tendresse. I love you deeply cheri, my mystical self follows you in your long voyage.*" But she is aware of his gay sexual leanings: "I see you still...always with some boy or other...no matter how real your love for me is, you are motivated by compulsions deeper than any love for me, compulsions which have nothing to do with me, of which I am merely a symbolical victim." "The flowing megalomania" of Nin's diaries, says Vidal in *Palimpsest*, contains the voice of the character who became *Myra Breckinridge*.

Vidal, Nin writes, had "a deep lying desire to escape and to frustrate women, fear and revenge for the initial destroyer"—his mother. His homosexuality, she says, was down to his desire for twinship, "doubles," narcissism. In 1946 she asked him not to "out of your deep gentleness and tenderness, sustain this illusion that I have no competition." She was offended by a female character in *The City and the Pillar* who is aging and vain. "No woman wants to read that about herself," she hissed at him, Vidal writes in *Palimpsest*, also denouncing the "promiscuity of same-sexualists." Vidal was polite about her own "powerful and eclectic appetites, but I did suggest that there was both a beauty and fulfillment in sex with strangers that one seldom enjoys with people one knows."

Judith Harris says Vidal told her that Nin had warned him not to publish *The City and the Pillar,* because it would cause trouble for him. By 1952 their relationship was in freefall. "I am afraid that when it comes to destruction your talents are greater than mine," writes Nin to Vidal. "Let us acknowledge defeat and abandon this false relationship altogether...I have one more favor to ask of you. Please do not talk about my writing. It represents everything you have denied and do not believe in. It would be another act of insincerity. It takes great hatred to produce caricature and that is what you are engaged in writing and living out." Vidal went on to write poisonous portraits of her in his books, particularly *Two Sisters.* Then, in 1971, Vidal reviewed volume four of Nin's diaries in the *Los Angeles Times:* "Not only does she write an inflated, oracular prose, but she is never able to get outside her characters...Anaïs is dealing with actual people. Yet I do not recognize any of them (including myself) had she not carefully labeled each specimen." After that, Vidal and Nin didn't speak to each other, or see each other, again.

In 1974, in a note to journalist Ann Morrisett Davidson, Nin wrote, "Gore Vidal is a hypocrite...he did all in his yellow journalism power to harm the diary [the publication of her expurgated diaries, the first volume of which was published in 1966], told lies...you only have to read the monstrous *Two Sisters* to measure the extent of his distortions. He is the only person in all my life I am ashamed to have befriended...there is no interrelationship between us, he is homosexual, hates woman, and my romanticism of him at an early age proved completely lacking in insight into his real venomous character."

Vidal once wrote to Judy Halfpenny of the idea that he was set to marry Nin, "I can't believe this whopper appears anywhere in Anaïs's diary, though God knows the stories she invented over the years...As a rule twenty-year-olds of my class do not want to marry raddled 'old ladies' of the same age as their mother, particularly bizarre old ladies." Vidal recalled Nin pursuing him to East Hampton, Vidal insisting "we go to the public beach by the back lane so that I not be seen with her." It was wrong, he says, for Nin's biographer Deirdre Bair to imagine Nin "as a *femme fatale* and I so smitten or carried away I would want her as a front! She also ignores the fact that I was the famous one even at twenty, and she a fringe."

In Nin's papers at the University of California, Los Angeles, the author and screenwriter Kim Krizan uncovered a letter from Vidal from 1947, saying he would "never have a satisfying homosexual relationship," and that while he was "attracted to youth, to beauty," he was, separately, attracted "unphysically" to Nin and enjoyed the "spiritual emotional rapport" they had. "I need that more than the other." Krizan quotes Vidal as suggesting to Nin, "We can get a small place near Antibes or wherever there are interesting people and cheap living." He envisions a "tranquil if not complete" life with Nin, one in which she would be "free of America, Hugo [Hugh Guiler, her husband from 1923 to 1977], all the mess." Again, as with Austen, Vidal's feelings for Nin appear more profound than he was prepared to admit. The unknowable truth about their relationship and connection survives both of them and the many words they wrote to and about each other.

Vidal had other very close relationships with women. He and Joanne Woodward, before she married Paul Newman, were "certainly engaged," says Jay Parini. Vidal's friend Lucy Fisher thinks he was "genuinely in love with Claire [Bloom] and Joanne." In a 1956 letter to Vidal, Austen wrote, "From what I gather, Joanne has cooled down considerably in the idea of getting married. She admits that she still loves Paul (they had sex) but that she can do without him."

"There was a time when Joanne thought Paul was never going to get a divorce [from Jackie Witte, his first wife with whom he had three children] and marry her," says Boaty Boatwright, Woodward's agent and friend. "She was madly in love with Paul and she, Howard, Paul and Gore were practically living together"— indeed they did in Malibu later. But Joanne and Gore did not have a physical relationship. He embellished the story. He might have said, 'Let's find a way of getting Paul to ask you to marry him by pretending we're engaged.'"

Woodward told Fred Kaplan that she and Vidal thought they could never go to bed together because they would laugh. She thought that if she was never going to marry Newman she may as well marry Vidal. Then she thought, "What about Howard?" They decided Vidal should run for president, win the election, over-run the government, and create a constitutional monarchy. But again, Woodward said, the question was: "What about Howard?" If Vidal had asked her to marry him, she says she would have accepted "because I was very fond of him. Many people have had those sorts of marriages. I can't imagine how long it would have lasted. I would have driven Gore crazy, or he would have driven me crazy."

In an article about Vidal and his friendships with women published in *Vanity Fair*, Woodward said her relationship with Vidal was "a long and complex one." Vidal confirmed that the marriage idea cooked up between him and Woodward "was at her insistence and based entirely upon her passion not for me but Paul."

Woodward hoped it would provide the impetus to give Newman the "push" needed to commit to her. Woodward said that Vidal's mother or grandmother wanted him to get married (this despite him already being with Austen for a few years by this point). "We pretended that we were having an affair or something. We got a kick out of it, because it was in the newspaper. I couldn't see Gore and me getting married—oh heavens—but we did have a great time together. Gore, Howard, Paul and I had one of those rare life experiences where we shared special, special times. I certainly miss those times." In *Palimpsest*, Vidal writes that in 1958 Joanne and Paul "were married at last and we all lived happily ever after." They honeymooned in London with Vidal and Austen, "where, in great secrecy, she promptly miscarried."

Edmund White believes Vidal was "genuinely bisexual," pointing to Vidal's friend of the late 1950s and early 1960s, the author Elaine Dundy, who wrote in her memoir that "once, and once only, Gore and I went to bed together. Next day everything was back to normal. Let us say we chose to bathe in the pure, refreshing streams of friendship rather than shoot the perilous rapids of physical love. Which is not to say I wasn't in love with Gore because I was. I saw nothing odd about this. If platonic love is not based on passionate feelings, how can it sublimate itself and ascend the heights?" Vidal quotes this in *Palimpsest* without confirming if it is true or what his thoughts were about it. Dundy told Vidal's friend, the actor Jack Larson, that she and Vidal had a "major affair." Dundy was married to Kenneth Tynan, "so she liked sardonic men," says Larson. In 1955, Vidal told Tennessee Williams that he was thinking of getting married, but to whom it is unknown.

Nina Straight says she has "talked to the ladies" Vidal was supposed to have had sex with and they all denied it; she thinks actresses sometimes said it to boast—in the sense of "I converted Gore Vidal." Why did Vidal maintain the mystique then? Did Straight ever ask why he said he was bisexual when he was gay? "He would bash you shitless, excuse my language," she says. "He would tell you 'What do you know? You nothing, you housewife. What have you ever done?' He wanted to let himself off the hook, he couldn't face the fact he was homosexual."

Vidal said a woman once told him he made love like Picasso: "Just in and out and back to work." There were rumors, never substantiated, that he had fathered a child with a Key West waitress in 1953 or 1954 and that the doctor paid to perform the abortion had placed the dead fetus on his Christmas tree. On whether Vidal was the father of the child, Vidal said in an interview in 2008: "Possibly. I don't believe so. The father was either me or a German photographer. I believe the mother is dead. The child was a girl. Every Christmas, I would receive a picture of them all around the tree, and there's the little girl, looking like me. I could have a daughter, yes." Have you tried to contact her, the journalist asked Vidal. "No. Why would I?...I sent her mother money for an abortion, which she used to go to Detroit, where she found a rich man." Researching this book, I heard rumors of another child, uncovered since Vidal's death, although his nephew Burr Steers denies this is true. "It suited him to keep all these rumors alive," says Steers. "I always thought he was gay."

Another friend was Eleanor Roosevelt, who Vidal became

close to while living in Edgewater, upstate New York, once interrupting her arranging a dozen gladioli in her toilet bowl at her home, Hyde Park. "It does keep them fresh," she said. It was "perfectly clear," Vidal said, reading the private correspondence between Mrs. Roosevelt and her long-rumored lover Lorena Hickok, "that they were having sex. The writing is full of tactile images which are erotic." Later Vidal said that Roosevelt "had these funny veins in her temple which would pop out when the subject of sex came up. She was very non-judgmental about others: 'People are what they are, there's nothing you can do.'"

Vidal told Judy Balaban that "Eleanor was in love with Amelia [Earhart], and Amelia was in love with my father." Vidal hoped they would marry, so she would become his stepmother, but when he asked his father why they didn't marry, his father told him, "She was like a boy. I never wanted to marry another boy." Vidal cried, his friend Boaty Boatwright remembers, when he heard in New York restaurant P.J. Clarke's that Mrs. Roosevelt had died. "It was one of the only times I saw him cry," she says.

Vidal "never made any bones about his proclivities," says his friend Barbara Howar. "I once kidded with him, 'I'm going to turn you' and he said to me, 'If Joanne Woodward couldn't do it, no one could.'" Boaty Boatwright is sure Vidal had relationships with women, "because women adored him," like the actress Diana Lynn. Austen once reported seeing them writhing on the floor of her Hollywood apartment in 1955. "It was important for him to maintain he had affairs with women," says Matt Tyrnauer. "He frequently alluded to an affair with Diana Lynn, who was said to have been a lesbian, but it always rang false. 'Whenever Diana and I went to a party we were the golden couple,' he'd say. 'Oh, why this fluffing?' you wanted to say to him."

Vidal could also be very open with his female acquaintances about being attracted to men. Alice Denham, the beautiful cousin of Denham Fouts, related in her book Sleeping with Bad Boys having lunch with Vidal and Leo Kelmenson, an ad agency colleague, in the King Cole Room of the St. Regis Hotel in spring 1956. She tells Vidal she read The City and the Pillar: a lie. She's disappointed that he isn't as handsome as his jacket photo but does find him seductive and sensual. They talk about Eugene O'Neill's play *Long Day's Journey into Night*, which they both admire. Then they compare notes about the dancer, Jacques D'Amboise. "Not only is he nimble and emotional," Denham sighs. "But his delicate turns with those long sexy muscular legs. Drives me wild." She laughs. "I'm in love with Jacques D'Amboise." "Oh, so am I, darling," Vidal replies, "leaning forward, not quite flapping his wrist," Denham recalls. "I'm mad about the boy," Vidal tells her. Denham writes: "Then I knew. My face didn't fall, but I plunged inside. It had never occurred to me that suave Gore was gay. He didn't hide it. He simply didn't broadcast it. Finally Gore declared himself bisexual, which everybody felt was code for gay, back when homosexuality was barely tolerated and mostly denied...If I had actually peered into *The City and the Pillar*, I would've known it." That summer Denham appeared in *Playboy* as both a centerfold and author of a short story. She later published two novels.

Whether Vidal had sex with some women, his relationships with a small group of women, like Bloom, Sarandon and Woodward, were close and clearly important to him. Diana Phipps Sternberg, who had first met him as a seventeen-year-old society beauty, said, "He was one of the most interesting people I've ever met in my life. He was a fantastically good friend. He was terribly kind, which doesn't come across in his public image. Gore took me under his wing." Was there romance? "Absolutely not. He was like a brother. He gave me advice about a lot of people who might have been on the cards for me. It was always sensible, if a little extreme and hard. 'This person is perfectly dreadful, under no circumstances go out with him.' He liked women more than men, but not sexually. He liked the company, the gossip, it was easy. He didn't want involvement and possibly that's easier with men than women: women are more demanding of affection than men. When we took houses together he'd disappear during the day. I didn't ask where he went."

Boatwright says Vidal "loved the fact these women adored him and I think he would have loved to have been straight. I don't think he wanted to have babies. He didn't like children unless they were smart enough to listen. I always thought he would have loved to have had a relationship with a woman like so many homosexual men, especially back then, who got married and had beautiful wives and children. He was like a lot of men who don't like to think of themselves as gay. Has there been any woman that's ever come forward and said, 'I had a mad passionate relationship with Gore Vidal'? No." For Boatwright, Vidal's claim to be bisexual was "fantasy. He wanted to be straight *and* gay. He liked the idea of being with women, the idea of being able to control both situations perhaps."

Scotty Bowers recalls Vidal once wanting to watch Bowers have sex with a woman: "There was something about her he liked, so he sat and watched us fucking and jacked off. He liked her because her personality was like his. I had a good-looking guy who was gay. Gore liked him, and used to fuck him too. I would stop fucking this guy and Gore would plunge his prick in, and boom, blow his nuts." Matt Tyrnauer thinks "voyeurism was a huge part of his sexuality" linked to Vidal-the-writer, "in control, the fantasist and observer."

When Vidal and his good friend Susan Sarandon were watching a film with Debbie Reynolds, "he said she was adorable," then added, "Oh yes, we had a little dalliance." Margie Duncan, Reynolds's spokeswoman and longtime friend, denies this. "I know all the fellas she dated and I'd have to say a 'no' to this," she told me. "In over sixty years of friendship, Gore Vidal's name never came up between us." In 1960 Vidal told Christopher Isherwood, "in deadly confidence," that he was "planning a marriage of convenience" with the actress Phyllis Kirk.

Walking beside a river arm in arm one day in the late 1950s, Vidal turned to his friend Elinor Pruder and said, "If I marry, you'll be the one." Pruder had met Vidal through Austen in 1956; she had become the Baroness de la Bouillerie by marrying a French count in 1950, though they had separated. "I was a stylist and very involved in the theater world where I met Howard. All the theater people would come up to my apartment: Rex Harrison, Kay Kendall, it was better than a bordello. Howard was a stage manager and he, Gore, and I soon became like three sisters. We'd met late at night and became a clique. We had the same rotten, terrible sense of humor, we'd be saying, 'Oh, look at whoever it was, and she thinks she's an actress.' Pruder's father, who was president of Bendix Aviation, knew Vidal's.

"We did have a deep relationship but, no, we didn't have sex," says Pruder. "Not at all, although he tried to kiss me once. If he'd had a heterosexual man's instincts he would have grabbed me. I wasn't sexually attracted to him but loved his intelligence and sense of humor. I think he was afraid of women. There was a lot of inner turmoil left over from his mother. He had grown up hating her. He was attracted to me and Claire Bloom." Pruder had introduced Vidal and Bloom the New Year's Eve they met in New York's Plaza Hotel, with Joanne Woodward and Paul Newman. "If she gets fat, she's had it," Vidal joked about Bloom. "He adored her, especially her Englishness and her daughter Anna," says Pruder. At the end of that "wonderful" New Year's Eve, Vidal said, "We'll meet every New Year's Eve from now on." "Of course we went our separate ways," says Pruder.

Vidal would depend on Elinor Pruder when Howard wasn't around for weekends at his country home in Rhinebeck, "where I became a permanent fixture, an elegant housekeeper. I would say, 'You only keep me around because I'm a half-assed baroness.'"

Pruder was also a "beard" for social occasions. "I would stand in for Howard. Whenever Gore needed to go to a gala, dinner or drinks party, he would take me. He didn't want to be seen with Howard at those events. 'You're using me,' I would say. 'That's right,' he would reply. Gore was attracted to me on a certain level. He loved to use my baroness title. It helped his image. Once, at a dinner for Princess Margaret at Annabel's in London, he put her on one side of him and me on the other: 'You're using me again,' I said. I don't think he minded if people thought I was his girlfriend. I didn't. I thought it was funny. Howard didn't mind either. Before an event he'd say 'Wear this.' What I was doing shielded Howard too: neither of them wanted their relationship in public. My presence kept that away."

Pruder isn't "sure" if being gay disturbed Vidal: it seemed to occupy dual, conflicting positions for him. "He felt it made him unique. But he also hid it, using me as a shield. He hid his gayness, but then he took Howard wherever he went and said he was his secretary. He didn't want to be thought of as gay, or have the image of himself as 'gay.' Yet he was arrogant about his sexuality in some way, he didn't care what people thought. But he said to me that he thought Bobby Kennedy had had him banned him from the White House when JFK was president because he was homosexual. 'That sonofabitch bastard,' he'd say. After that he used me more and more as his companion at events. He never got over that. It hurt him so much. 'I'm related to Jackie, for Chrissakes,' he'd say. The columnists at the time made it pretty darn clear, without actually saying it, that Gore was gay, and although Jackie liked Gore, Bobby thought it would present the wrong image of the First Family if Gore was around. I'd never seen him so hurt and angry, and it destroyed his relationship with Jackie." In *Palimpsest*, Vidal writes of Bobby's own "homosexual impulses," alluded to by Rudolph Nureyev. "Nothing happen," Nureyev said. "But we did share young soldier once. American soldier."

Jacqueline Kennedy's "boyish beauty and life-enhancing malice were a great joy to me," writes Vidal in *Palimpsest*. He recalls the "erotic shock" of her skin against his when water-skiing in the late 1950s ("No, nothing happened"). Selfish and self-aggrandizing "beyond the usual," Jackie was a slyly humorous presence in Vidal's life, he writes. They lunched together in New York, Vidal introduced her to actors and his television and theater worlds. Richard Harrison remembers Vidal telling him of staying in the White House one night "next door to John and Jackie fucking. 'My god, they made a lot of noise. Believe me, they really fucked hard.'"

Vidal talked "about 'the new Athens' which will arise when Kennedy is in power," Isherwood writes in his diary in 1960, and that Kennedy wanted Vidal to be his minister of culture in a future administration, although Auden told Isherwood someone else had been approached for the position and turned it down. After Kennedy was elected, he joked with Vidal that the ambassadorship of Mali was open for him.

Vidal told Fred Kaplan about a November 1961 party where he had his hand on the back of her chair, his arm brushing her back. Robert Kennedy removed his arm from its position. Vidal followed him and told him, "Don't ever do that again." "Fuck off, buddy boy," Kennedy replied. Vidal said: "You fuck off too." His friendship with Jackie continued, then dwindled; the White House invitations dried up. In later interviews, he said while he had been seduced by the Kennedy charisma and power, he would never again be taken in by a charming politician.

After Kennedy's assassination in 1963, Vidal told Christopher Isherwood that once at a horse show with Kennedy Vidal had said how easy it would be to take a shot at Kennedy, but the bullet would most likely hit him (Vidal). Kennedy replied: "That'd be a big loss." Vidal thought Kennedy, at the time of his assassination, was "losing his grip," having crying jags over the death of his son (Patrick, on August 9, 1963), and losing confidence he could get people to see things his way. He believed Kennedy had been assassinated by the Mob.

Barbara Howar remembers the powerful Hollywood agent Sue Mengers bringing Vidal to her Georgetown home for a party to celebrate the Washington opening of his play, *The Best Man*, in the 1960s. Howar lived opposite Janet Lee Bouvier, Jackie Kennedy's mother and third wife of Hugh D. Auchincloss, Vidal's stepfather (Hugh had been married to Nina Gore from 1935 to 1941). Austen asked Howar, "Would you mind if I used the powder room?" Vidal cut in, "Just go across the street and pee on Janet's lawn."

In *Palimpsest*, Vidal ruminated after Jackie's death of "the cancer" going to her brain. "She loved money even more than publicity," Vidal wrote, "and her life was dedicated to acquiring it through marriage, just as her mother had done before her and my mother before her mother, to the same rich man." She had the "good sense" to ally herself to Kennedy patriarch Joe Kennedy and accepted her husband's promiscuity. Kennedy had the income from a $10 million trust fund—adequate at the time, says Vidal, but not nearly enough if she was to live like her role model, Bunny Mellon. Contrary to popular belief, Aristotle Onassis was "more charming and witty" than she, writes Vidal. He recalled seeing her in 1975 in the Ritz Hotel's elevator in London. Their friendship was all but over; they did not speak, she "sighed in her best Marilyn Monroe voice, 'Bye-bye' and vanished into Piccadilly."

One of Vidal's most glamorous female friends was Princess Margaret: they spent a lot of time together, exchanged letters and—according to one guest of Vidal's in Ravello who requested anonymity—"he sent her out on a boat with a young Italian guy with a big cock and she came back very satisfied. For Gore, being a host meant providing young men if necessary."

The two were close confidantes. After she divorced Tony Armstrong-Jones in 1976, Princess Margaret wrote to Vidal: "Yes, it's all over, isn't that a relief? Having asked T for a separation for three years which he'd refused consistently he suddenly agreed (with a bit of pushing form both families). But he managed one last blow to the midriff" as Armstrong-Jones chose the time when Margaret had had some "unwanted publicity about a...young man I had staying with me in Mustique who'd come to do the garden."

Armstrong-Jones had put her through "years of torture...not to mention his drunkenness, which was the last straw." She had to pay him a "thwacking great amount" in the divorce settlement. "Isn't it ignominious on his part to accept it after all this—I'm livid. Anyway, he can't come back to the house, so we are at peace." In *Palimpsest*, Vidal recalls swimming with her in the pool at the Royal Lodge in Windsor and them both rescuing a number of bees from drowning, "she exhorting them in a powerful Hanoverian voice to 'go forth and make honey!'"

"PM," as Vidal calls her in *Point to Point Navigation*, told Vidal that the Queen is "uncommonly talented in ways that you might not expect." Vidal asks in what way. "Well, she can put on a very heavy tiara while hurrying down a flight of stairs *with no mirror.*" Princess Margaret wrote in another note that she is going to Los

Angeles, "to collect some money for the Royal Opera House, Covent Garden. We only need £30,000,000. You don't happen to know thirty millionaires do you? It would be neat." "She was too bright for her role," Vidal told Judy Balaban. "It was a tough role—thankless! When she got bad press and deserved to be smacked down, I think she could take it. But when it wasn't deserved, she'd tell me, 'Look, you're the youngest sister of the Queen, who is the source of honor, grace, righteousness, and all that is good. You're not going to be understood, so you just have to take it and accept that there's nobody who understands a word you're saying.'"

The actress Susan Sarandon recalls first meeting Vidal forty years ago when she made her Broadway debut as Tricia Nixon in his play *An Evening With Richard Nixon*. His birthday, October 3, was the day before hers. "He was involved in a lot of debates around Cambodia around that time," she tells me. "I really got to know him when I stayed at La Rondinaia. He loved people showing up to have a good time. I was never supposed to get pregnant by Eva's father [Franco Amurri, the Italian film director, producer and writer]. It was a miracle. I did my pregnancy test at La Rondinaia. Gore was the first one to find out. He said, 'Well, of course you'll give your baby neuroses. The only important thing is that they're productive.' Later he told people I had conceived Eva by the pool."

At two months old, Eva had a series of allergies and never slept. "It was very stressful and Gore let us stay with him, which probably saved my life," says Sarandon. "Gore recalled that when he was a baby, when she was nursing him, his mother would put a napkin on him so the ash wouldn't fall on him from the cigarette she was smoking." The two shared witty correspondence for years. Before she filmed Thelma and Louise, Sarandon wrote to Vidal, "I start a film with Ridley Scott and Geena Davis late May. It's an existential female road movie. I get to drive off the Grand Canyon—I'm not sure I get it to be honest, but it's the most interesting though possibly full of shit screenplay I've read in a long time—and Geena is taller than most leading men I've worked with lately."

Certainly Vidal lavished attention on the offspring of friends like Bloom, Sarandon and Tim Robbins, all of whom would take their children to La Rondinaia. "I had great times with him, great meals, great class," says Hubert de la Bouillerie, son of Elinor Pruder. "He paid for our summer camps. He was a father figure to me and my sister Annie." "Gore was very tolerant of children," says Sarandon. "He was the godfather of our youngest, Miles, who he felt a special connection to. He said he saw him as the reincarnation of Jimmie Trimble, his first love." Was that a little spooky, I ask. "I thought it was great he felt that way," Sarandon says. "It was a real kinship: I would send Gore things Miles had written or music he had made."

Vidal "really loved women, certain women," claims Sarandon. "He was flirtatious, fun and witty to be with. He was really fascinated with Claire Bloom. You got the feeling that there were women he just adored. He liked stylish women who were funny. He implied he was romantically attracted to them in his younger days and had had relationships with them; he presented them as love stories. I had a sexual relationship with a gay man: I was the only woman he had ever slept with. So it can happen." Sarandon, like Vidal, hopes "that kind of sexual fluidity is still around, although today certain categories seem to be so fixed."

Vidal would have agreed heartily. He felt close to women, for sure. Like many gay men, some of his closest friendships were with women. In his early adult years, he had had sexual experiences with women. But his life partner was a man and his sexual partners in later adulthood were men. His "bisexuality" seems to have been a construct, rooted partly in the generation he grew up in where open homosexuality was *verboten*. It was also partly intellectual, rooted in Vidal's mistrust of categories, and partly down to his innate contrarianism. But he believed it and believed he was living it. Vidal had created and crafted his own sexual history. However much sex he had with women or men, he did not want it to define him, or he define it: his definition of his bisexuality remained as uniquely singular as its owner.

Chapter Ten

A Literary Sex Life

In 1994, Allen Ginsberg told Vidal that the Beat writers had read *The City and the Pillar* "because of the sex. Nobody had gone that far then." When Vidal told Ginsberg he was preparing a new edition of it, Ginsberg said, "Put more sex in." "But everybody does that now," Vidal replied, contrarian torch on full beam, "Maybe I'll take it all out." In 2000, Vidal said the Beat writers had been "scared of the subject" of homosexuality. "They didn't want to be labeled quite rightly. They had watched it done to me."

Away from what he did in bed and with who, Vidal's sexuality also occupied an intriguing, contradictory place in relation to his career and ambition as a novelist and public figure. As one of his friends, who wished to remain anonymous, told me, "Gore was homosexual and struggled under the burden of the public life he wanted and the kind of man he should be." In 1993, Vidal said his sexual identity "certainly gave direction to my fury. And out of that I took quite a strong, plain style that was absolutely...if not on target, it was unmistakable in its energy and anger. I had been very much in danger, as my whole generation was, of being School of Henry James, and the beauty of higher sensibility. And suddenly something like James M. Cain [hardboiled crime novelist, most famously of *The Postman Always Rings Twice*, *Mildred Pierce* and *Double Indemnity*] took over the controls."

The City and the Pillar, Vidal's third book and the first postwar American novel to feature explicit gay sex and gay characters, made Vidal, then twenty-three, famous when it was published in 1948. It still stands out as a coming out story—the protagonist Jim contemplates if he is gay and meets many different kinds of gay man—but also as an evocative portrayal of a number of gay worlds, from glossy Hollywood homes to dive-y hustler bars. It is also an intense love story. Bob is Jim's true love;

the ending of *The City and the Pillar* featured in its first incarnation a murder, which Vidal changed to rape (Jim's rape of Bob). It ends with, if not hope, then a sense of Jim's life, wrecked, going forward: "Soon he would move on."

Vidal thought the original murder ending was ambiguous, as if Jim was "killing off the obsession…for my character who had forfeited an emotional life for love of a boy, now a man, who had forgotten him." To placate those "who felt I was making a case that same-sexualists were homicidal psychopaths, I made it clear that Jim does not literally kill Bob, only the idea of him."

However he came to see homosexuality and gay rights later, writing *The City and the Pillar* was a singularly radical act. There was so much nonsense written about homosexuality at the time, Vidal said in 2010 of the political impulse behind writing it. Christopher Bram tells me that *The City and the Pillar* "certainly sent the message to other gay writers that if this gay man can have this success with a wider population of readers, so can we." There were other novels that included gay elements around at the time: John Horne Burns's *The Gallery*, Calder Willingham's *End as a Man* and Willard Motley's *Knock on Any Door*. "Vidal may have originally published it as a tactical move for fame and to be noticed, but he stayed true to it," says Bram. "He wanted to own homosexuality as a subject. He wanted it to be his. And then he didn't want it to be his anymore. He had a weird love-hate relationship with the notoriety of it. He didn't want to be a 'gay writer,' but he wanted the book to be a classic."

Vidal recalled to Donald Weise that he and Burns were put on a "hot-writers-to-watch" list, adding caustically that "within ten years Burns had been driven out of America and died of drink, and I'm off every single list and no longer mentioned as a major American novelist." In the same interview, Vidal claimed *The City and the Pillar* was "not autobiographical," although the sex scenes were based on Vidal's life. "I had to make a decision whether to go into politics or become a writer. I couldn't stop being a writer. If I could have stopped it I would have. But it's something you're born with, there's nothing you can do about it." Whatever he felt about being labeled, Vidal said the book was born out of a sense of injustice around homophobia. "I was born with an aggravated sense of justice. Very few Americans know this trauma. I suppose it goes back to my grandfather [who] represented the Indian tribes against the government." Vidal liked to invoke a wry quote of Elaine May's as a touchstone of his own: "I like a moral problem so much better than a real problem."

Vidal said he was "institutionalized by the Army. Everyone had such good time, particularly overseas. The bases at home were like Auschwitz, very controlled, a lot of faggots locked up and tortured. I came out with such a rage about what had been done to a minority by a majority whose opinion wasn't worth anything on any subject. So what would fuel my energies as a writer was this total hypocrisy about same-sexuality." In *The City and the Pillar,* in the messy, deeply felt story of Jim and Bob, Vidal "got into the dark side of it, sexual obsession, which is what Romanticism is...slightly demented."

The City and the Pillar had advance orders of 5,000 copies. Vidal told me in 2009 that "it's still going strong." Thomas Mann praised the novel, Anaïs Nin—then at her most devoted to Vidal—hailed his success and said Vidal's only enemy was doubt and lack of confidence. The at-the-time scandalous content generated publicity: the first print run ran to 10,000 copies, and became a bestseller. Vidal said the only good review had been in *The Atlantic Monthly*, although there were others. What hurt the most was to be ignored by the daily *New York Times*, while the Sunday Book Review section said: "Presented as the case history of a standard homosexual, his novel adds little that is new to a groaning shelf. Mr. Vidal's approach is coldly clinical...this time he has produced a novel as sterile as its protagonists." For much of his life Vidal nursed a grievance against the paper, claiming for the next ten years they didn't review seven works by him. "One of his 'best' subjects was the *New York Times*," recalls Bernie Woolf, Vidal's friend from his Rome days. "If I had to hear that one more time...'They're out to get me,' he'd say, he was convinced there was a cabal there."

His British publisher John Lehmann, telling him to not dwell on bad reviews, wrote to Vidal in 1950: "You always count your losses, not your gains; foolish honey child." Over three years the book sold 30,000 copies. In *Palimpsest*, Vidal after years of victimized grizzling, said he had just made a "tentative peace" with the *Times*—this in the mid-1990s. In 2010, he claimed not to care about "losing" its support, it was such a "dreary paper" anyway, he told the Canadian interviewer Allan Gregg.

For Vidal's close friend Nancy Olson Livingston, in *The City and the Pillar* Vidal "told the truth in the most touching, revealing way possible. And like the rest of us, he was vain and had an ego, he wanted to be loved for himself." Vidal had no idea of the kind of repercussions that *The City and the Pillar* would have, says Steven Abbott. "He said he was blacklisted by the *New York Times* and never forgot that for decades afterwards. Right up to his death he said the blacklisting had forced him into screenplays, plays and detective mysteries." If the experience with the *New York Times* remained a bugbear, he knew that the book had also bought him what he also craved: fame and notoriety.

One of the first letters Christopher Isherwood sent to Vidal was a detailed critique of *The City and the Pillar*, dated December 19, 1948. In its profoundly moving and sensitive way everything it says holds true and fresh today. It also embodies the differences between Isherwood and Vidal, and how Isherwood represented, openly and proudly, a belief in sexual equality and liberation and a belief that novelists like him and Vidal had, at that moment, a wider responsibility than simply to themselves as artists. "I think *The City and the Pillar* is certainly one of the best novels of its kind...It isn't sentimental, and it is extremely frank without trying to be sensational and shocking. These are enormous virtues. I believe it will be widely discussed and have a big success, well-deserved."

But Isherwood writes that he has "reservations." There are certain subjects, "including the Jewish, Negro and homosexual questions" that are social and political, alongside discriminatory laws that could be repealed and prejudices eradicated. An author writing around these subjects inevitably has a "propaganda value,"

Isherwood writes. "I am sure that you, personally, would wish to see the homosexuality laws repealed or at any rate revised?" he says to Vidal. How could *The City and the Pillar* affect public opinion, Isherwood wonders, particularly its ending, Jim's murder of Bob. Isherwood says he finds it "dramatically and psychologically" plausible, though wonders what "moral" the reader will take from it—that "this is what homosexuality brings you to...tragedy, defeat and death," and homosexuals themselves—well maybe we shouldn't send them to prison, but rather be "put away" in clinics...Such misery is a menace to society."

Isherwood writes that, yes, "many homosexuals are unhappy; and not merely because of the social pressures under which they live. It is quite true that they are often unfaithful, unstable, unreliable. They are vain and predatory, and they chatter. But there is another side to the picture, which you (and Proust) don't show. Homosexual relationships can be, and frequently are, happy. Men live together for years and make homes and share their lives and their work, just as heterosexuals do." This, he says, undermines the "romantic, tragic notion of the homosexual's fate." If, under the social conditions of the time, gay relationships were tougher to sustain than straight, says Isherwood, "doesn't that merely make it more of a challenge and therefore, in a sense, more humanly worthwhile?" The success of gay relationships "is revolutionary in the best sense of the word," demonstrating "the power of human affection over fear and prejudice and taboo," and as such, gay relationships are "beneficial to society."

Isherwood says he is "really lecturing myself" because he too has "subscribed to the Tragic Homosexual myth in the past and I am ashamed of it." Isherwood emphasizes that he doesn't think *The City and the Pillar* will have a negative effect on "public attitudes to homosexuality," but instead create discussion; "it's absolutely unpornographic nature will force readers to view the whole subject without disgust," Isherwood says, which is all "to the good. In fact, it is excellent."

The original "murder" ending led novelist James Baldwin, later famous for *Giovanni's Room* and *Another Country*, to accuse Vidal of "homosexual panic," Vidal said later, adding indignantly, "If ever was a book of homosexual panic it was *Giovanni's Room*. What is this homosexual panic? Bob Ford (in *The City and the Pillar*) suffers from it, and rejects the other one because of it, and gets himself beaten up because of it. But there was no 'panic' on the part of the writer, which should have been perfectly clear to Jimmy [Baldwin] although he wasn't clear headed." Vidal noted that Baldwin "had more to carry than any writer I know" as a "black writer who then turns out to be a queen and also a preacher of the Lord: it was one of the reasons he was so often hysterical and very often made no sense at all, because he was living too many contradictions." Being black on its own, said Vidal, was "enough to blackball him in the literary world. Blacks were generally not accepted out there."

Vidal said that *The City and the Pillar* meant Vidal "became a figure of great interest to the fag world, about which I knew rather less than the book suggests." "Grand queens" disliked the book "not only for its lack of chic," but also because the "hetero" boy gets fucked by the protagonist, "an act very much against his nature," Vidal wrote. Even though he'd written a radical gay-themed novel, Vidal saw himself as far removed from those "fags" and "grand queens," both things he was not.

In the afterword to the 1965 edition of *The City and the Pillar*, Vidal made an odd declaration: "I decided to examine the homosexual underworld (which I knew rather less well than I pretended), and in the process show the 'naturalness' of homosexual relations, as well as making the point that there was no such thing as a homosexual. Despite the current usage, the word is an adjective describing a sexual action, not a noun describing a recognizable type. All human beings are bisexual." In fact, he knew a lot about "the homosexual underworld" evoked in the book, as he'd been occupying it, with sluttish élan, for a few years. But there is his thesis, bold as ever: "gay" doesn't exist, bisexuality is the only meaningful sexual label, even though he was far from the active bisexual he marketed himself as.

The novel, if he came to feel had harmed him, also fit with his self-honed image of the renegade. "Nothing I say charms corporate America, which owns the place and owns the media. It gradually dawned on them I was extremely articulate of the country they had created." Vidal was proud of identifying in the late 1960s that "the United States has one party, the property party, which has two right wings, the Republican and Democrat." From the Kennedys to the neo-cons, Vidal said, "I have been so demonized." He was against any prevailing current or orthodoxy, stubborn and singular.

The City and the Pillar is impressive in many ways, not least how it evokes so many kinds of gay worlds and voices, and Bram's history of gay fiction rightly places Vidal as one of the key creators of contemporary gay literature, although Vidal would have objected to that term. In his colorful and illuminating book, Bram writes that "Vidal was a godfather of gay literature, in spite of himself—a fairy godfather. He would cringe at this description. He would have said, 'You've made me into a vulgar fag writer,'" Bram says with a smile. But The City and the Pillar, whether Vidal liked it or not, was trailblazing and much cherished by an older, more isolated generation of gay readers.

The journalist Doug Ireland, a friend of Vidal's, calls the novel "an extraordinarily courageous thing, especially at the young age at which he did it. He took a ton of shit and really suffered for it. By writing it, he did a great deal for gay people. For many of us, it was the first time encountering being queer presented as part of nature. It was very liberating and helped a lot of gay people. He was a pioneer in that sense." Ireland affectionately calls Vidal "Uncle Gore," as did Ireland's good friend Christopher Hitchens, when Hitchens and Vidal were close.

The City and the Pillar transformed Vidal's public life in many ways. He became a famous figure whose sexuality if not stated was implicitly obvious given the material of the novel, though in more decorous times, his sexuality was not open to question, until his explosive television confrontation with William F. Buckley in 1968. But neither did Vidal publicly parade relationships with women, like many closeted Hollywood celebrities. If Vidal occupied a closet, it wasn't founded on a publicly voiced declaration of heterosexuality; and on TV and in print he held true to fighting for the tenets of gay liberation, if on his own terms, never defining himself.

Clearly Vidal felt aggrieved at being marginalized because of *The City and the Pillar*; he exerted much effort in the subsequent years to be as widely known in the mainstream as possible. But he knew his sexuality set him apart. In 1959, he opined that "each year there is a short list of OK writers. Today's list consists of two Jews, two Negroes, and a safe, floating goy of the old American establishment just to show there is no prejudice in our loving land; only the poor old homosexualists are out." Vidal said the comment was sardonic and focused on how marginalization operated in the literary establishment in favor of the WASP.

"It was a combination of bravado and naivety that led Gore to publish *The City and the Pillar,*" says Dennis Altman. "That effectively ended his political career." In 1960 Vidal ran, unsuccessfully, for a seat in the House of Representatives in the heavily Republican Dutchess County in upstate New York. In 1982 he ran, again unsuccessfully, for the Democratic nomination for the US Senate in California. Armistead Maupin, author of Tales of the City series of novels, interviewed him that year for *California* magazine, before the Democrat senatorial race: his sexuality was a private matter, Vidal told Maupin; he and Austen, whom he had been with for thirty-two years, were "old friends...he's lived various places, I've lived various places. We travel together, we travel separately." Rock Hudson offered to work on Vidal's campaign, but Vidal was advised not to allow him to as he and his friends were well-known gay men. (Hudson's homosexuality became known in 1985, when he died of AIDS.)

The first time he ran it was for greed and vanity, Vidal once said, the second because of "terror" at the Reagan-era America unfolding. "I almost won the most difficult seat in the country," Vidal told *The Independent* in 2008 of the 1960 campaign. Robert Chalmers, the interviewer, says, "And yet even today, any admission of a sexual inclination that doesn't involve two children and a well-manicured back yard is likely to be used against you in politics." "The book was fiction. That it could be exploited by political enemies is—yes—kind of proof of something," Vidal replies. Chalmers reminds Vidal he had said, "I might have had a life in politics if it wasn't for the faggot thing." "You're right, I did say that," says Vidal. "And it is true. But now I am old, I realize that I probably didn't want that [political career]." If he hadn't published *The City and the Pillar* he would have been president, "like George W. Bush," Vidal tells Chalmers, "with just the slightest hint of sarcasm." Chalmers says "we" would be a lot better off if Vidal was president. "We'd be safer," Vidal replies.

While talking about their respective losing campaigns in the Hudson River Valley (Vidal's in 1960, Strub's in 1990), Sean Strub asked Vidal, "How much of an effect do you think your homosexuality has had on your career?" Vidal replied, "Well, it kept me from getting elected President." After a quiet pause, Strub recalls in his forthcoming memoir, Vidal added, "If not for that, it would have all been so different." Strub asked, "You mean your career would have been different?" Vidal said, "No, I've had a wonderful *career*," exaggerating the word, "making it sound like a pathetically inappropriate word, his monumental body of work," notes Strub. "I mean the *country!*" continued Vidal. "The *world!* If I had been elected President, it all would have been so different."

His opponents in the 1960 Congressional election used broad references to Vidal's sexuality, but nothing overtly hateful. But Vidal considered the shadow cast by *The City and the Pillar* long and profound. Journalists were "amazed" Vidal ran for office, he wrote in *Palimpsest*. "They did not realize that their sort of inside gossip was almost impossible to transmit to the public in those days. If one had not been in a courtroom, there was nothing to talk about. More to the point, I had been visible to the public for years on national television and the people were comfortable with me, if not with my politics." Austen told Fred Kaplan he had had nothing to do with the campaign: "I was running away from that kind of world, and Gore was running to get into it after he had left his aristocratic world. I couldn't understand it."

"What one feels and rather loves in Gore is his courage,"

Christopher Isherwood writes in 1960 in his diary. "He's most definitely not a crybaby. He has a great good-humored brazen air of playing the game." The night previously he had almost gotten into a fight with a car driver; no young delinquent would dare challenge him, he boasted, because they sensed he would fight back. Isherwood noted Vidal was "rather playing the role of the reckless young political gambler, rushing to fame or disaster. He enjoys playing with the idea that the Republicans will launch some terrific smear campaign against his private life—but I don't seriously think this will happen."

Later, Vidal conceded he had "a truculent nature. I had to make a great choice between publishing *The City and the Pillar* and having a conventional literary career. I mean, the very whisper that Thornton Wilder was a fag had cost him for decades, and he was the most popular good writer in America. He was a very repressed man living with his sister in New Haven, and he was appalled by it. Read the...reviews of Tennessee; they're maniacal...I knew I was doing something. What I really admired was the *Satyricon*. That was my idea of the way the world runs. That was the world I'd observed. And *The Golden Ass* [the well-known Latin novel otherwise known as *The Metamorphoses of Apuleius*] was a great turn-on. But I didn't have any ancestors for that book [i.e., *The City and the Pillar*]."

The experience with *The City and the Pillar* "intimidated" Vidal, says Steven Abbott. "The McCarthy hearings began soon after." "Vidal always said *The City and the Pillar* had messed up his literary career," says Dennis Altman, "but he seems more unaware of its consequences for his political life. He took the 1982 race seriously, though very few people thought he had a chance. I thought he was desperate to rescue some of what was lost when he was expelled from the Kennedy camp years before. He never got over that."

For Altman "it seems inconceivable" that Vidal could publish *The City and the Pillar* when he did "and think you could have a political career. Gore was angry and said the literary establishment ignored him afterward, but the real cost was to his political career.

Maybe that explains some of his conflicted feelings around his sexuality: though ahead of its time, it altered the course of Vidal's public life. *The City and the Pillar* was written in that small window, pre-McCarthy, where things seemed they could be getting better, the problem for Gore was that he wanted to be US President and Poet Laureate and you couldn't do that in the America of the 1960s." Bram doesn't believe that Vidal wasn't at least a little affected by the attacks on the novel: "I think it did really traumatize him." Vidal had at least one fan. Ethel Merman told him: "Don't read much but love books about homos."

Whatever the impact of his novel, after losing the 1960 race Vidal called his agent. "I've lost the election. Get me a job." Vidal told me in 2009, "I would have liked to have been president, but I never had the money. I was a friend of the throne. The only time I envied Jack was when Joe [JFK's father] was buying him his Senate seat, then the presidency. He didn't know how lucky he was. Here's a story I've never told. In 1960, after he had spent so much on the presidential campaign, Joe took all nine children to Palm Beach to lecture them. He was really angry. He said, 'All you read about the Kennedy fortune is untrue. It's non-existent. We've spent so much getting Jack elected, and not one of you is living within your income.' They all sat there, shame-faced. Jack was whistling. He used to tap his teeth: they were big teeth, like a xylophone. Joe turned to Jack and he said, 'Mr. President, what's the solution?' Jack said, 'The solution is simple. You all gotta work harder.'" Vidal guffawed heartily at the memory.

By the time of the 1982 campaign another famous "Vidal" was causing confusion while Vidal was running for office. The famous hairdresser Vidal Sassoon had his own TV show and became used to being confused with Gore Vidal. Once, at a health farm, Sassoon was given the writer and essayist's enema by mistake, while Vidal, perhaps even more hilariously, was told to stop sexually harassing the female guests. When Vidal ran for the Democratic nomination for the Californian Senate seat against Jerry Brown in 1982, Sassoon was mistakenly sent checks by his donors. "Send them over, dear boy," Vidal asked him, "I need every penny."

On April 1, 1982, Sassoon wrote to him: "Dear Gore, One of us has to drop out of public life...Over the many years now, I have been flattered, and sometimes concerned, by the people who think I am you. Your problems obviously have been even greater: an international figurehead of great intellect, from a noble family yet, stooping to sit in the Senate, being mistaken for a lowly barber!" If Vidal beat Brown in the primaries, Sassoon promised to combine all the energy of both their names and to "go into bat for you." On April 12, Sassoon sent Vidal a newspaper cartoon of "Vidal" saying, "I have thirty-eight percent name recognition." A reporter then asks: "And how will that translate into votes, Mr. Sassoon?" On May 7, Sassoon sent Vidal a check himself—"not an endorsement, it is a gesture of appreciation for all the initiative and novel things you talk about inside and out offside of politics." Vidal and Brown have "two such abnormal minds" making it difficult for "us, mere mortals" to choose who to vote for.

Vidal linked the failure with of his 1982 candidacy with his sexuality. Randy Shilts, then a reporter with the *San Francisco Chronicle* and the first openly gay mainstream newspaper reporter, asked Vidal about his sexual orientation; Vidal doesn't address this directly; instead he quotes another journalist, Richard Rapaport, in *Point to Point Navigation*. Shilts, who went on to write *And the Band Played On*, the definitive early history of the AIDS pandemic, was taken aside by Vidal who on several occasions "patiently explained to him that although it was no secret, his sexuality was his own damn business and not a thing gentlemen of his generation comfortably advertised."

Here then, two gay generations came face to face. Vidal, still quoting Rapaport, says Shilts "took it upon himself to punish Gore with some unnecessarily, pointedly nasty reportage...His *Chronicle* stories continued to damage Gore's campaign and helped, I felt, secure the nomination for Jerry Brown." If Rapaport's interpretation is true, then Vidal felt a gay man had derailed his second attempt at a political job with Vidal's semi-closeted life the aggravating factor. Even in his memoirs, Vidal couldn't, wouldn't address the knotty, very personal politics of his sexuality and its impact on his life. Vidal, who didn't come close to beating Jerry Brown in the primary, doesn't acknowledge Shilts's right to question him and uses someone else to criticize Shilts rather than say anything in his own words. But there was Shilts's *The Mayor of Castro Street*, a biography of Harvey Milk, a true gay hero who advocated the power personally and politically of coming out, lying on Vidal's study desk the day, many years later, I visited Vidal's Los Angeles home after his death.

If Vidal really did feel his political career had been compromised by being so open in *The City and the Pillar*, why did he continue to write sexually radical novels? Vidal's desire to blur sexual boundaries was fully realized in the transsexual central figure in Vidal's *Myra Breckinridge* (1967), the inspiration for which came from being asked to write an erotic sketch for what became *Oh! Calcutta!* Immediately the phrase, "I am Myra Breckinridge, whom no man will ever possess" occurred to Vidal, the character an amalgam of memorable, against-the-grain literary heroines like Becky Sharp, Isabel Archer and Moll Flanders. Some readers now may see it as less radical and queer and more transphobic and misogynistic, but the central character's sex change operation "embodied" her capability for bisexuality, says Kaplan.

Vidal dedicated the 1967 novel to Isherwood, whose criticism of *The City and the Pillar* had proven so pointed nearly twenty years before. In a note to Vidal, Tennessee Williams related, "Overheard a faggot say to another in Bloomingdale's: 'That's Tennessee Williams! Why, he sounds like Mae West in *Myra Breckinridge*!' You are becoming a household word!" Vidal intended *Myra*, and its sequel *Myron*, in which the male and female parts of Myra/Myron battle for supremacy over his/her body, to convey his own beliefs in a more just, equal society, where the state could not hold sway over personal freedoms. The movie version of *Myra Breckinridge*, with Raquel Welch in the title role, was a critically derided flop.

It is Vidal's lesser-known 1970 book *Two Sisters*, part-autobiography, part fiction—and Vidal obscured which was which—that most fascinates those disentangling Vidal's own story.

Jimmie Trimble is referenced right at the outset: "Death, summer, youth—this triad contrives to haunt me every day of my life for it was in summer that my generation left school for war, and several dozen that one knew (but strictly speaking did not love, except perhaps for one) were killed, and so never lived to know what I have known—the Beatles, black power, the Administration of Richard Nixon—all this has taken place in a trivial after-time and has nothing to do with anything that really mattered, with summer and someone hardly remembered, a youth...so abruptly translated from vivid, well-loved (if briefly) flesh to a few scraps of bone and cartilage scattered among the volcanic rocks of Iwo Jima. So much was cruelly lost and one still mourns the past, particularly in darkened movie houses, weeping at bad films, or getting drunk alone while watching the Late Show on television." "Is it Jimmy?" V, the narrator, wonders of one "familiar face" in battle scenes.

"I chose not to be young," says V. "I began with the autobiographical intensity of the young person I was. The young search not for love but for someone they can talk to about themselves or, best of all, to find that most marvelous of creatures who will, without fatigue or apparent boredom, analyze them by the hour...Of all the disappointments of my own youth, I recall not so much love affairs gone wrong as those moments of intimacy when at last the dominant theme of the duet was clearly myself."

The narrator sleeps with women, making love with one until dawn leaving them "pleasantly exhausted." At another moment a girl is in his bed and he records: Her clothes are on the floor, mixed with mine...I can smell her on me, in fact the mingling of her smell with mine, bottled, would put Chanel out of business." A tender moment with an actress, thought to be inspired by Claire Bloom, unfolds: "Recently I spent an afternoon full of silences...with someone [an actress] I did not have an affair with a dozen years ago—too much silence at a crucial moment on a midnight beach, and a sense she was distracted by someone else—yet we continue to see each other year after year and affection grows, unstated and undefined and all the deeper perhaps for that." Bloom herself was between marriages, and V notes, "I think how remarkably beautiful she is, as one marriage ends and another begins, and how we are once again together, in transit, emotionally. I prepare myself for the new husband, hopefully an improvement on the old, an emotional cripple who used her—much to her initial delight, it should be noted—as crutch, wheelchair, iron lung. But the masochism of women tends to be limited, and usually stops altogether when they give birth. Hers stopped, and so did the marriage."

Heterosexuality, or the ability of men and women to truly connect, is questioned by the narrator. "Why is it that whenever women speak of love, I reach not for a gun but my cock? As an offensive weapon, that is, and not as an instrument of fulfillment. I suppose it is the dislike of being just a thing and despite women's constant talk of their need for a truly meaningful relationship, as opposed to the male desire to tear off a quick piece, it is the men who are usually more sentimental or at least more responsive to the whole experience (no matter how brief) than the woman who is thinking not of the man who makes love to her but of the end product of that act, the egg she means to lay. We are at hopeless odds, the two sexes, and ought not to live with each other except for what pleasure can be obtained on those occasions when egg-layer meets cock robin in some neutral nesting place."

V lauds the fluid sexual connectivity of the Bloomsbury Group as a model to emulate; given Vidal's own beliefs in fluid sexual identities, it seems reasonable to assume he would echo V's praise of "that bright short-lived world I have always found attractive...Of course my view of Bloomsbury is deliberately romantic, echoing Voltaire's similar dream: 'What a delicious life it would be to share a home with three or four men of letters with talent and no jealousy, who would love one another, live agreeably, cultivate their art, talk about it, enlighten each other! I dream one day to live in such a little Paradise.' So do we all, and never will."

V mulls the memory of an "Eric" who he thought one summer so much about sleeping with "that my memory of him...is entirely sensual. I didn't know him, only the dream I had of him, an erotic fantasy never translated into actual life because of shyness—no, not shyness, pride. Neither of us would make the first move and so I took another turning; abandoned Eric as unfinished business, now quite finished."

While V enjoys sentimentalizing "what might have been." "The cult of love" is not for him. "Invariably my interest wanes as my partner's increases and, alas, the other way around." He ponders his and Eric's possible "game...a fierce duel if prolonged for there is nothing so brutal as a contest of similar masculine wills. Yet what, paradoxically, makes impossible a long knowledge of each other adds extraordinarily to the excitement of the brief coupling." Nothing compares, he says, to "those moments when two bodies separate themselves entirely from personality in that kind of beautiful war" D.H. Lawrence captures in *Women in Love*, where he confesses to wanting both man and woman "and fails to possess either in a way he would like."

The narrator responds to a journalist querying why V talks about "having sex" as opposed to "making love." Having sex "is a fact and describable, while making love is an illusion and indescribable. I have always thought it wiser and more honest to deal with facts than evoke illusions, no matter how self-flattering."

Vidal re-emerges as himself talking about walking into the Astor Bar on Times Square, still in his army uniform, "a long, dark room filled with soldiers, marines, sailors, and men who wanted to pick them up, not realizing that the young were there—the world was innocent then—not to hustle but to meet one another…" Vidal is also speaking directly when "V" talks about going to the Hotel Saumon brothel in Paris, where he has sex with a married engineering student from Grenoble, who he later—as Vidal did—sees on the street with his pregnant wife pushing a baby carriage. His friend Eric asks if he really likes brothels. "It saves time," V replies, "deliberately callous," adding, "Each party to the transaction knows what's expected of him. One takes money, one takes pleasure. It's the most civilized of human institutions."

In real life, Vidal also liked the Parisian brothel, that Proust had frequented and where clients selected the young men they liked through holes in the wall. In *Palimpsest*, Vidal remembers the brothel's manager, Said, as looking like an "evil djinn in the *Arabian Nights*" but was gentle and amiable. Said recalled Proust sitting where Vidal sat "in a great fur coat. Even on a hot day like this, he was always cold." The "boys" who serviced clients were "polite and rather shy; and they urgently needed money." Vidal suspected they didn't subscribe to divisions of straight or gay. One day Vidal recognized one of his favorite young men crossing the Pont Neuf with a woman, walking with a baby carriage. The two men smiled at one another and moved on: Vidal loved the category-shattering view of sexuality crystallized by that moment.

Of *The City and the Pillar*, Vidal remarks in *Two Sisters* that it "did wonders for belly-rubbing, while *A Streetcar Named Desire* made nymphomania sympathetic." *The City and the Pillar* is about "as shocking as a Galsworthy novel," Vidal writes. "But then I was not 'using' sex to make an effect as much as demonstrating sex of a certain kind to establish its naturalness in the face of a tribal taboo, a taboo which serenely continues to this day in the land of the free." When the rewritten book was published a few years ago, "I was startled to find that the popular press was quite as horrified by the subject as it was twenty years ago." The narrator says, "Amen to a Nathaniel Hawthorne quote: 'The United States are fit for many purposes but not to live in.'"

Considering the novel's brother-sister lovers, Vidal again emphasizes his lack of belief in any labels. He has "never had a jealous nature in sexual matters. I have always preferred many partners in various combinations and believed that the world would be considerably happier if others had freed themselves, as I have, of the tribal injunction that it is each man's fate to be paired for life with one woman in order to provide hewers of wood and tillers of soil."

In a 1974 interview Vidal said of the novel, "You wonder who is who and what is what. It would be unnatural if people didn't. After all it is a memoir as well as a novel. But mainly it is a study in vanity and our attempts to conquer death through construction or through destruction." In his diaries Kenneth Tynan said *Two Sisters* reflected something essential about Vidal's literary steel: "What superb and seamless armor he wears, as befits one to whom life is a permanent battle for (social and intellectual) supremacy. It is of course a battle that cannot be won by anyone who is incapable of surrender. And Gore could never surrender (i.e., expose) himself freely to anyone. All the same, the necessity to stay on top keeps him writing."

Jorg Behrendt's scholarly study *Homosexuality in the Work of Gore Vidal* concludes "all the major homosexual characters" in his novels exhibit "severe instability, insecurity and lack of identity." Vidal, says Behrendt, "is very much a child of his time who just cannot perceive of homosexuality as something 'normal,' although he himself has made the normality of homosexuality a major topic of his lifelong 'teaching' and writing." Besides *The City and the Pillar, The Judgment of Paris* is—for Behrendt—"most concerned with the naturalness of homosexuality."

Its straight hero, Philip Warren, tours through postwar Europe encountering all kinds of homosexuals and aspects of homosexual life. "Businessmen from Kansas City, good Rotarians all, embraced bored young sailors on the streets at night," Vidal writes, also noting the "Algerian boys at those bordellos which catered to such pleasures. College boys, young veterans...ran amok in the bars and urinals in search of one another...as they tried to love one another in this airy summer city." A hustler "talked a great deal, stating, as far as Philip could tell, that all Americans, English and Germans liked Italian boys, and even Italian boys, though they didn't make too great a thing of it, liked Italian boys."

Vidal, then, wasn't hiding away in his work—quite the opposite. One reviewer highlighted a passage where Vidal writes about the power of writing and reading about sex: "Now, part of the pleasure one gets from reading novels is the inevitable moment when the hero beds the heroine or, in certain advanced and decadent works, the hero beds another hero in an infernal glow of impropriety. The mechanical side of the operation is of intense interest to everyone. Partly, of course, because so few of us get entirely what we want when it comes to this sort of thing and, too, there is something remarkably exciting about the sex lives of fictional characters...one feels far more clearly engaged than one does in life where the whole thing is often confused and clumsy. Also, there is a formidable amount of voyeurism in us all and literature, even better than pornographic pictures, provides us at its best with an excitation occasionally more poignant than the real thing."

Sex, sexual gossip and sexuality also featured in Vidal's relationships with his writer friends and peers. In *Palimpsest*, he recalls a letter from Paul Bowles's wife Jane, humorously referencing her lesbian affairs: "Word has come to me that Taormina is full of lesbians. Since they all come by ship through the Straits of Gibraltar, they pass right under my window here in Tangier, so you'd think that perhaps a few—well, even one— might just stop off and pay me a courtesy call." He and Bowles never shared a room, notes Vidal: "I never go to bed with friends, much less anyone older than I."

"Truman, Gore and Tennessee were as famous then as they ever would be because they were young, and to be young was an American thing—still is," Ned Rorem writes in his memoirs. Vidal "was the least stunning (so far as 'the madness of art' is concerned), but the least difficult to talk to—he could follow a subject to conclusion that was generally illuminating (like Paul Goodman, he revealed the brightness of the obvious—of what was always under the eye but too close to see), and cared for human rights beyond his own needs."

Vidal, like many a gay man, hovered around many social sets: WASP, gay, intrinsically establishment and yet truculent, committed radical. He feasted with royalty and knew the bars on the wrong side of town. He was part of a generationally ranging gay literary milieu that embraced Tennessee Williams and Allen Ginsberg. The shared influences, sexual and professional connections, friendships and feuds among the gay writers of the fifties and sixties of which he was a key figure—Beats and non-Beats—were many and intriguing, as detailed in Christopher Bram's book, *Eminent Outlaws*.

"There was a picture of Isherwood next to his bed," says Juan Bastos, a painter commissioned by the *Gay and Lesbian Review* to do Vidal's portrait in 2006. "I said it was a nice picture and Gore said they were good friends. I asked what he was like. 'Pall Mall,' said

Gore. I assumed he was talking about cigarettes, but he meant gentleman clubs, and he was referring to Isherwood's class. I asked how he met Isherwood and he said, "We famous people, we just meet." In *Palimpsest*, Vidal recalls he and Isherwood playing with the notion of knowing the destinies of men they had just met, and addressing the men accordingly: "Sorry, I have no time to waste on you. Next summer you'll be dead...in a car accident, and by the time I'm sixty-five, I'll have forgotten your name."

The range—peaks, troughs and all—of Vidal's relationship with Isherwood is sketched intimately in Isherwood's diaries from their first meeting in Paris on April 25, 1948, when Vidal, "a big husky boy with fair wavy hair and a funny, rather attractive face" reminding Isherwood of a teddy bear, approached him in the famous intellectuals' and artists' café, Les Deux Magots. "He asks questions like, 'What did Frederick the Great do in bed?' But he's also a pretty shrewd operator—or would like to be," writes Isherwood. "He wanted advice on 'how to manage my career.' He is very jealous of Truman, but determined not to quarrel with him because he feels when a group of writers sticks together it's better business for all of them...What I respect most about him is his courage. I do think he has that—though it is mingled, as in many much greater heroes, with a desire for self-advertisement."

A few days later Vidal asked Isherwood to meet him in his hotel room. A young man dashed out of the room as Isherwood approached, misunderstanding Vidal's *"mon ami vient"* as a warning of the approach of an enraged lover. Vidal stayed in bed in his underwear. When he went to the bathroom Isherwood noted he had sexy legs. They flirted through breakfast, but nothing happened. By 1955, friendship long established, Isherwood was frustrated with Vidal's self-obsession. "Lunch with Gore. I guess he's still wondering what I think of *Messiah*, his novel. Well, I don't. I'm bored and stuck fast. He asks quite often about my journal and talks apprehensively about the famous one Anaïs Nin is keeping...in which he believes he figures most unfavorably. I believe he really thinks about 'posterity' and its 'verdict'—just like a nineteenth century writer! And I don't know whether to admire this, or feel touched by it, or just regard him as a conceited idiot." This is possibly acutely correct, but intriguing as later in his life Vidal scorned the notion of legacy.

In 1958, Isherwood noted that Vidal's favorite quotation is "I am the Duchess of Malfi still." He saw himself, writes Isherwood, "as the ex-champ, out of condition and paunchy, who still has fight in him. And all the time this rather disconcerting literary ambition: he thinks of himself as a writer of quality—a neglected writer, because readers are turning from his kind of quality to the meanderings of Jack Kerouac…Gore regards me, also, as a neglected writer of quality, so he feels a bond between us."

Vidal admired John F. Kennedy's "ruthless sex life," Isherwood writes in 1960. "As for himself, he claims that he now feels no sentiment whatever—nothing but lust. He can't imagine kissing anyone. The way he has to have these sex dates set up is certainly compulsive. He talks of himself as a failed writer. But there's a questioning look in his eye as he tells me this. I protest, quite sincerely, with praise for *The Best Man*. But I think I know what he means. First he wants to be a novelist, not a playwright. Then he wants to write fantasy, not realism. He feels he lacks imagination. And I think he does."

In their correspondence there is, inevitably, greater felicity between the men. Isherwood wryly apologizes to Vidal for "leaving in all of the homosexual aggression, it seems necessary for my character," when he published *A Single Man*. When Vidal published *Myra Breckinridge* in 1967, Isherwood wrote to him, "My dear Gore, I have read *Myra* twice and in my opinion it's your very best satirical work. It's wildly funny and wildly sensible. Even when I was laughing most I was overcome by your wisdom and seriousness…all the more honored that you're dedicating it to me." Vidal said he and Isherwood hadn't had much connection in the 1970s and '80s. "Friendship with him was always a one-way street; and I tire rapidly," he wrote to one friend, quoted in Kaplan's biography, perhaps because of what Isherwood had said about him in his diaries. "Also, he was not the same person I first knew—to the extent I knew him at all!" But he admired Vidal too, writing to another friend: "I wonder if any other living writer is going to keep at it as ferociously, unremittingly as Vidal?"

In March 1971, Isherwood notes in his diary that Vidal thought the novel, as a form, was dead; Isherwood wondered if it was because "one couldn't become a nationally known personality just by writing novels. Gore, like Mailer, has gotten around this difficulty by becoming a journalist and a TV interviewee." But their friendship continued, and in later years affection seems to have superseded scratchiness and condescension. Vidal ordered Dom Perignon for Isherwood and Don Bachardy's twentieth anniversary in 1973. In 1976 Vidal wrote movingly of Isherwood, reviewing Isherwood's memoir, *Christopher and His Kind*, in the *New York Review of Books*. He notes that Isherwood has become "a militant spokesman of Gay Liberation. If his defense of Christopher's kind is sometimes shrill...well, there is a good deal to be shrill about in a society so deeply and so mindlessly homophobic." Noting Isherwood's refusal to countenance killing a Nazi, Vidal writes: "That is the voice of humanism in a bad time, and one can only hope that thanks to Christopher's life and work, his true kind will increase even as they refuse, so wisely, to multiply."

At the end of the same year, Isherwood called the line of many young men waiting for a signing outside the gay Oscar Wilde Memorial Bookshop in New York's Greenwich Village, "my tribe...and I loved them." Vidal said, "They're beginning to believe that Christopher Street was named after you." One wonders if he was envious of this hero-worship; the very definite badge of sexual identification Isherwood wore and the adoration and respect of his readers that flowed from it. At the end of that year, Isherwood recorded Vidal being interviewed by a "reactionary character" who suggested the cat-o-nine-tails be brought back as punishment for homosexuals. Did Vidal agree? "Certainly I do. But only for consenting adults" was Vidal's response. "At such moments Gore is in the class of Oscar Wilde," writes Isherwood.

Vidal would later feel betrayed by Isherwood's observations of him in his diaries, but they shared a moving moment as Isherwood lay dying at home in 1986. Jack Larson recalls, "He had cancer of the prostate, which spread to his spine. It was a long death, very painful, but that's the way Christopher wanted it, without morphine. Sometimes Chris was awake, sometimes in a coma.

Howard and Gore came to visit and found him in this state. They thought he was unconscious, in pain, not a good sight."

Vidal wrote later that he had sat at Isherwood's bedside "and kept up a stream of chatter like a radio switched on. He listened to me, rather as one does to a radio while thinking of other matters. He had long made his peace with England and the English. But I had just come from London with numerous complaints of English fecklessness—what would happen when the North Sea oil was gone? They have no plans! I cried. It's just like the grasshopper and the ant, and they are hopeless grasshoppers, a nation of grasshoppers. The eyes opened on that. At last, I had his full focused attention, and he spoke his last complete sentence to me—in the form of a rhetorical question, needless to say. Not for nothing had he swum with swamis yet kept that magic touch. "So," he demanded, "what is wrong with grasshoppers?"'

In contrast to the bedrock of affection between Vidal and Isherwood was the poison belying Vidal's relationship with Truman Capote, who he had first met at a party at Anaïs Nin's apartment in 1945. Capote and Vidal were first thrown into competition with each other in 1947 over a Guggenheim Fellowship neither author got. In *Palimpsest*, Vidal mentions his British publisher John Lehmann writing that he had failed to sign up Capote, so "decided to take a chance on Gore Vidal, whose homosexual novel *The City and the Pillar* has just caused a considerable stir." Already then, Vidal was rankled that even to his publisher he was second choice to Capote. "Thank God we're not intellectuals," Capote once said to Vidal, who replied, "Speak for yourself." But then Vidal also liked to play dumb himself sometimes, to "give the impression that I was a professional tennis player turned hustler."

In Paris in 1948, Fred Kaplan wrote, Capote boasted to Vidal about receiving an amethyst ring from André Gide and all the fabulous people he knew. Capote may have gotten the amethyst ring, but Gide gave Vidal a treasure, a copy of his gay classic, *Corydon*, inscribed "avec sympathie." Gide was "fascinated" by Kinsey's work, Vidal reports in *Palimpsest*, and showed Vidal a book sent from a vicar in the English countryside with drawings featuring "beautifully rendered tableaux of naked schoolboys indulging in every sort of sexual act."

"The instant lie was Truman's art form," Vidal claimed. In *Palimpsest* he lists a few, like Capote claiming to know Eleanor Roosevelt "intimately" and being with her and Marlene Dietrich, who "of course she was in love with," when news of Franklin Roosevelt's death broke. Capote also claimed an improbable affair with Albert Camus. Elinor Pruder recalls: "Gore would ask, 'Are you going to see your friend Truman again?' I don't know if it was jealousy or animosity." Capote told Felice Picano in 1982 that Vidal was "the most disappointed woman in America." Why? Picano asked. "Oh, she thought she'd be president. She wanted to be president. She thought it was owed to her."

Vidal had taken Capote to the Everard Baths, Vidal told *Fag Rag* in 1974 and Capote had said he didn't like it; Vidal added Capote had fallen "tragically" in love with an air conditioning repairman, then finished off the sly insults with: "I can't read him because I'm diabetic." He particularly objected to Capote camping it up for laughs as an "effeminate buffoon," which would culminate in 1976 Vidal suing (and Capote counter-suing) over Capote's claim that Vidal had been bodily thrown out of the White House the night of his contretemps with Robert Kennedy.

At a 1978 supper in Rome, Tom Powers recalls Vidal mimicking Capote, "describing Jackie Kennedy screwing a big Negro chauffeur while her children whimpered in the back seat. 'Not a word of it true, mind you,' Vidal said. 'He just can't help himself; he has to tell lies. Which is why I'm suing him for libel. I don't like it; I believe in the first amendment. But there has to be a limit. Some lies are just too big to swallow.'" The case was resolved, with a written apology from Capote, in 1983. "Capote, I truly loathed," Vidal told *The Independent* in 2008. "The way you might loathe an animal. A filthy animal that has found its way into the house."

Capote's death in 1984, Vidal wrote to Paul Bowles, was a "good career move. T will now be the most famous American writer of the last half of the twentieth century. No one will ever read a book of his again, but no one who can read will be able to avoid the thousands of books his life will inspire. Since he has told the most extraordinary lies about every famous person of our time, the hacks will have a field-day recording the sorts of lies they usually make up. T's affair with Camus, T's help in getting Marilyn aborted, T's blow job of Pres. Kennedy…Well, he is what this vulgar, tinny age requires. RIP." Asked in 2000 about Capote, Vidal said, "I make no conscious effort to create a persona—that, whatever it was, I was born with. What success I've had as a public figure, as a speaker, was learned very early," when Vidal understood how "to talk to a million people as though it was one person. [President] Clinton is a master of it." The larger the audience the more intimate it can feel, he says. As for Capote, "it wasn't the effeminacy" that bothered Vidal, "it was the lying, which was his fault."

Their sexuality may have linked these writers, but this connection paled next to Vidal's competitiveness. When E.M. Forster died in 1970, Vidal told Christopher Isherwood: "Well, we've all moved up one rung higher." Jack Larson recalls several dinners at Isherwood's house at Santa Monica Canyon. At one in the mid-1960s for Paul Bowles, Vidal was complaining that he had been speaking on college campuses, but the students weren't "that into him, they were only interested in Allen Ginsberg, Kerouac, the Beatniks. This irritated Gore very much and he got more and bitter as he got very, very drunk as he was wont to do. He was on his high horse about it. He was attacking the Beats as these 'near-illiterates' and that young people were so stupid that they worshipped 'these people.'"

After dinner, as Vidal became more bitter and sardonic, Paul Bowles challenged him, Larson tells me. "Gore, when there's a national election you're all over the television pontificating about it, when you write a novel it becomes a bestseller, every movie you do becomes a great success, if you write a play it becomes a Broadway hit, you're as famous as famous can be—what else can you want that's making you so unhappy?" Vidal, "who was definitely quite drunk, thought for quite a while." The group "sat in silence for two minutes" as Bowles's question hung in the air. Vidal finally replied, "Well, I'll tell you. I want crowds to follow me wherever I go. For instance at this very moment there would be a crowd on top of the [Malibu] Palisades, a throng, waiting for me to make my exit from this house tonight and they would applaud my exit as I went." Vidal wasn't joking: indeed in *Palimpsest* he remembers after his sister's wedding waving to "nonexistent multitudes" from their limousine.

As Larson was driving Paul Bowles back to his hotel, he said he wasn't sure what Vidal meant by the crowds massing on the Palisades. "Paul said, 'He wants to be president of the United States like John F. Kennedy.' When Kennedy was in Los Angeles, his sister had a beach house in Malibu and there were famous pictures of crowds lining the Palisades."

Of all Vidal's relationships with other writers, none was as steamy and intimate as his one-night stand with Jack Kerouac, in New York in 1953. Vidal told Allen Ginsberg in 1994 that he and Kerouac had—before that evening—first met at the Metropolitan Opera, Vidal the guest of a writer who had paid Kerouac and Neal Cassady for sex. Vidal recalls the heat from Kerouac's muscular body in the opera box. "We were also coming on to each other like two pieces of trade—yes, I was attracted." Ginsberg told Vidal he blew Kerouac "every now and then…Jack liked company in bed, but he wasn't that keen on the sex part—with men. He blew me once to see what it was like. He didn't like it."

On the night Vidal and Kerouac slept together, Vidal and William Burroughs, who Vidal said was "upper class with a tight sphincter," went out for the evening, first to the San Remo cafe in Greenwich Village, then bar-hopping with Kerouac, who was drunk, high or both. He was both adulatory and rude to Vidal. Burroughs, wrote Vidal in *Palimpsest*, had written to Kerouac the year before asking, "Is Gore Vidal queer or not? Judging from the picture of him that adorns his latest opus I would be interested in making his acquaintance. Always glad to meet a literary gent in any case, and if the man of letters is young and pretty and possibly available my interest understandably increases."

That night, probably sensing the attraction between the men, Burroughs bid them goodnight after they'd had a drink in a lesbian hangout called Tony Pastor's. Kerouac, who Vidal described as a "prole from

Lowell," suggested he and Vidal get a room "around here." Vidal later wrote he was cautious, not wanting to have sex with someone drunk or older; he was twenty-eight, Kerouac thirty-one. From the age of thirty on, Vidal said, a man or woman was "a corpse." Vidal proudly declared he did nothing to please his sexual partners and when he became too old himself "for these attentions from the young, I paid, gladly, thus relieving myself of having to please anyone in any way."

But he crossed his "shadow line" for Kerouac, clearly attracted to him. At the Chelsea Hotel they signed their real names in the register, with Vidal mulling that the entries would be notorious one day. In Vidal's account, they showered together, Kerouac uncircumcised, Vidal seeing "for an instant, not the dark, slackly muscled Jack but blond Jimmie [Trimble], only Jimmie was altogether more serious and grown-up at fourteen than Jack." Kerouac gave Vidal a blow-job, "a pro forma affair, which I put a quick stop to." They rubbed bellies for a little while. Vidal "flipped him over," reminded suddenly of the heavier guy in the Seattle bar many years before when Vidal was in the army, who put him off the idea of getting fucked after being rough with him. Was he, in flipping Kerouac over, "getting his own back on Jack's back," Vidal wondered.

In *Palimpsest*, Vidal writes that he told Ginsberg of his night with Kerouac, "I fucked him." "'I don't think, said Allen thoughtfully, 'that he would have liked that.'" Vidal remembered Kerouac staring at him for a moment, "forehead half-covered with sweaty dark curls—then he sighed as his head dropped back on the pillow." The rosy neon from the window gave the room a "mildly infernal glow," Vidal told Fred Kaplan. The next day Vidal gave Kerouac a dollar for his subway fare and told him he owed him a dollar. Kerouac later boasted, "I blew Gore Vidal."

Vidal said Kerouac had regaled the clientele of the San Remo bar with the tale, including someone from the advertisers of a TV show Vidal had just started working on. Later Kerouac recorded the event in his 1958 novella *The Subterraneans*, but left out the sex, Ginsberg tells Vidal in *Palimpsest*, because of his mother who was a "monster." She hated Ginsberg because "I was a fag. Worse, I was a Jew, too," Ginsberg said. Vidal said what remained "irresistible" about Kerouac was the sweetness of his character, but notes—how ironic given his own later decline—Kerouac's unattractive ranting when he became a severe alcoholic. Vidal's dollar loan to Kerouac remained unpaid.

The Subterraneans was published before Vidal related the explicitly sexual version of their night together in *Two Sisters*. "He started all this business about us," Vidal said of Kerouac who, frightened Vidal would sue him for libel when The Subterraneans was published, sent a mollifying letter to Vidal's agent, Vidal revealed later. "Then he was furious with me for *Two Sisters*." Vidal used *Two Sisters* to lightly chastise Kerouac for his convenient amnesia after their sexual encounter at the Chelsea Hotel, which is intriguing. Far from being in retreat from his sexuality, Vidal in the novel outs another writer, revealing how their gay sexual encounter took place. "I have usually found that whenever I read about an occasion where I was present, the report (except once) never tallies with my own. The once was Jack Kerouac's *The Subterraneans* in which he describes with...astonishing accuracy an evening he spent with William Burroughs and me. Everything is perfectly recalled until the crucial moment when Jack and I went to bed together at the Chelsea Hotel and, as he told me later, disingenuously, 'I forgot.' I said he had not. 'Well, maybe I wanted to.' So much for the tell-it-like-it-is school."

Later Norman Mailer said Vidal had fucked Kerouac and destroyed his masculinity. "His psychic balance was more homo than heteroerotic," Vidal said of Kerouac. "He was far more attracted to boys than to girls." Their encounter, like the sex he had with "straight" Italian hustlers, appositely fit Vidal's own sexual world view. Here, one of literature's most famous gay hook-ups took place between two men, Vidal and Kerouac, whose own sexualities were of no fixed abode. Kerouac was three times married with one daughter, Vidal gay but defiantly un-self defined. But their evening together was memorable enough for both men to set it down—contested accounts, still wreathed in mystery—in writing. Later in life Vidal met a young man wearing Kerouac's image on a T-shirt. "I am in love with him," the man said. "So was I," Vidal replied, to his own surprise. "For a few minutes, anyway."

Chapter Eleven

Hollywood Radical

"If there was a social whirl, you can be sure I would not be part of it," Gore Vidal lied brazenly to me in 2009 about his Hollywood life, which was in fact thrumming with sex with hustlers, stars and parties with Paul Newman and Joanne Woodward at their Malibu home. He did a fabulous impression of Katharine Hepburn complaining about playing the matriarch in *Suddenly, Last Summer*, which he adapted with Tennessee Williams from Williams's novel. "I hate this script," he recalls Hepburn saying. "I'm far too healthy a person to know people like this." Vidal laughed in the retelling. "She had Parkinson's. She shook like a leper in the wind."

Vidal had decamped to Hollywood in the 1950s to write TV dramas and mystery novels, after his first flush of fame and critical backlash with *The City and the Pillar*. He went "into television because I was failure as a novelist," he noted balefully later in life. "Everybody has been convinced of that."

The director Curtis Harrington met Vidal in 1955, while Vidal was working on a television adaptation of *A Farewell to Arms*. "He says he has to rewrite most of the male lead's lines because the actor playing the part is so stupid he can only say the simplest things...He wants very much to make a screen adaptation of *The Turn of the Screw*, but so far no one is interested."

Vidal told Harrington he expected to make $50,000 per picture, that it "is so easy to write television scripts and plays and movies," Harrington writes. "He remains as I remember him: pompous for his age, properly conceited, cynically bored. He confided to me that he has not met anyone with whom he could conceive of having an emotional relationship with for the past five years. At one point he snorted and exclaimed, 'Human relationships are utterly hopeless.'"

Harrington had just read the "last words" of André Maurois, which he quotes: "I should like to say first of all that love has been the great concern of my life. For me, happiness consists above all in a perfect understanding with another human being in whose presence one can at last lay down that armor of constraint, of ready-made thoughts that one always has to wear in the company of other people." Harrington says, "These words would mean little to Gore: he simply could not accept them; but I can and do and pray to God to be able to continue to do so."

At work Vidal experienced the homophobia of censorious, McCarthy and Hays-era Hollywood firsthand around the production of *Suddenly, Last Summer* in which a gay man uses his sister as bait to pick up young men and is eaten alive by a group of those men he pursued. "As long as you make money for the studio or network you're a hero," Vidal told Donald Weise. "Your private life doesn't matter." The McCarthy investigations and hearings he remembered as affecting any "do-gooding actors who signed petitions for starving Armenians" who were subsequently blacklisted.

"It was my work, the screenplay," Vidal told the producers of *The Celluloid Closet* of working on the film. In the transcript of their interview with Vidal, he reveals, "I've never seen such a time in my life with censorship, the Legion of Decency, headed by this sort of shark-like Jesuit priest...I must have had five meetings with him. 'You can't say this, you can't say that.' By the time we started to cut it, it was making no sense at all. Did Sebastian like boys or not? It was trying to get anything through."

Vidal ran for Congress in 1960, the year after *Suddenly, Last Summer* was released. "I was speeding, a police guy pulled me over, he's a good Democrat. He recognized me, he was going to vote for me. And he said, 'Say, I saw that picture you wrote, *Suddenly, Last Summer*.' We had a big argument about it, the patrolman. 'Was that guy queer?' I said, 'Yeah.' He said, 'Yeah, I wouldn't have bet on that one.' Can you imagine a picture made nowadays in which the key to the entire thing is that Sebastian, usually accompanied by his mother, is now accompanied by his cousin, searching for boys? Using them as bait...It's like working under the Kremlin...Like writing for *Pravda*. You did learn how to write between the lines, [or] a photograph between the lines, you do it with a look or something or there'd be a take on Hepburn's face as Elizabeth Taylor would be telling her, getting closer to the truth, which the Legion of Decency wouldn't dare let us say."

Vidal would again have hated the plaudits, just as he would have hated been hailed as a godfather of modern gay-themed literature, but in Hollywood he was a radicalizing influence by stealth, default and sometimes design. America's rulers "disapprove of faggotry in every form and they continue to do so to this day," Vidal told *The Celluloid Closet* producers, although less virulently in modern times than before. W.H. Auden, he recalled, was supposed to be on cover of *Time* in late 1940s until it was made known he was a "fairy" and the cover was cancelled. Vidal also encapsulated the *New York Times* review of *Suddenly, Last Summer* as, "If you like incest, rape, sodomy, cannibalism, degeneracy, this is the movie for you, this sickening picture," meant that "Everybody in the country went to see it."

For Vidal, "Theater is always half a generation behind the novel. And the movies are half a generation behind the theater...*The City and the Pillar,* books like that, were all being done in the 1940s, early '50s. You didn't see much reflection of that until the late '50s and early '60s in the movies...Slimy stuff, like exercising *droit du seigneur* over young actors, aimed at gay playwrights...pure McCarthyism...ended up really in silencing the faggot writers, one by one."

Vidal, unsurprisingly, wasn't to be silenced. In Hollywood, Vidal's most famous gay-radical act was to rewrite a scene in *Ben-Hur* to suggest a gay relationship between Charlton Heston's title character and Stephen Boyd as Messala. With sexuality, Vidal says in *The Celluloid Closet*, "You just couldn't use the word. What we did get expert at was setting up situations to which it was perfectly clear to anybody on the right wavelength what you were doing. I did that in the much contested falling out scene between Ben-Hur and Messala, which I wrote as a love scene that goes wrong, that they had been lovers as boys. They had fallen out."

Vidal claimed that he proposed to director William Wyler that "the Jew and the Roman had been lovers at fifteen, sixteen...it will be clear that Messala is in love with Ben-Hur." Two scenes were written. Vidal was told not to say anything to Heston, "'cause Chuck will fall apart." The scenes were shot. Boyd's looks "that he gives him are just so clear. Well, that's what you had to go through in those days if you felt it was the correct thing to do," Vidal said. When looking at these movies, the viewer should sometimes be hearing "a cry for help from the creators on the other side of the camera saying, 'This is what we meant,'" said Vidal.

However, Heston, in a letter to *The Advocate* in 1996, claimed Vidal was employed "for a trial run on a script that needed work. Over three days...Vidal produced a three-page scene that director William Wyler rejected after Steve Boyd and I read it through for him. Vidal left the next day. His ludicrous claim that he somehow slipped in a scene implying a homosexual relationship between the two characters insults Willy Wyler and, I have to say, irritates the hell out of me." Vidal replied that he had written the material, Heston was being egregious. "I think we must all be charitable when it comes to Charlton Heston," Vidal said, who "has other strings to his balsa wood bow: spokesperson for the National Review and, if that were not glory enough, proud trumpet of the National Rifle Association...What is one to do with an old actor who when he works often wears two toupees, one of top of the other on the interest of verisimilitude?"

While *Ben-Hur* combined a trio of Vidal's great interests—film, history and same-sex desire—Vidal later analyzed the male body in film in a note to the activist and writer Jay Blotcher, who in 1995 was preparing a documentary, *Sword, Sandal and Context*, about the Hercules films of the 1960s. Vidal writes: "I think your theme is actually the male body as an object of beauty and desire for both sexes, and this was very late coming in a sad Jesus Christbesotted peasant nation like the US." Vidal cited *It Happened One Night*, in which Clark Gable took off his shirt to reveal no undershirt as the first occasion of such a thing in a "mainline movie." "But no one quite understood what was happening. Beauty and desirability were the province of the dame. A man could be handsome but hardly erotic. Then came Tennessee Williams with quite other notions of what the male meant. When [Marlon] Brando appeared in 1947 on stage [in *A Streetcar Named Desire* on Broadway] in a torn, sweaty T-shirt the male as erotic object exploded into the slow American consciousness."

Brando, Vidal says in his *The Celluloid Closet* transcript, "was at the height of his beauty" and "for the first time in American history the male, who had always been considered coarse, ugly, nothing" was transformed. The American male, previously "nothing but a suit with a fedora hat...a nice man, a little twinkle in his eye" had transformed in popular culture's glare into a sexualized object of desire. It might be "hard for people to believe now in the age of Calvin Klein ads," Vidal says, that those ads "could never have happened without that one performance in *A Streetcar Named Desire* where a homosexual, an adjective I don't like to use to describe people but we must here, playwright in the form of Tennessee Williams had created a sex object that was male. That had never been done before...Everybody was sexually attracted to him..." So game-changing that Vidal had to break his own rule and use "homosexual" as a word to describe someone. Praise, indeed.

For Vidal, Kinsey's finding that a third of American males "confessed to at least one homosexual act leading to orgasm meant there was a "huge audience out there. What to do?" Jay Blotcher's subject was "a part of what was done in the '50s: classical themes with bodybuilders on display...In my time in Hollywood, male beauty deeply disturbed directors and producers." The film *Advise and Consent* and Vidal's own play *The Best Man*, featuring accusations of homosexuality, were both rooted in rumors that Adlai Stevenson had "homosexual leanings" Vidal said. An unnamed English politician—most likely, his friend the Labor MP Tom Driberg—told him if Don

Murray's character in *Advise and Consent* was translated to British parliament, "ninety per cent of our Parliament would have to leave office!" They'd all had gay sex "in public school if nowhere else." Joseph McCarthy linked homosexuality and communism, Vidal said, because "it was really a way of saying they were security risks; that they could be blackmailed by evil communists."

Vidal said he had written a screenplay about Libby Holman, a torch singer who killed her husband. "She liked ladies, she liked men, he was the same, they were bisexual...And the producer, the head of the studio, both were great friends of mine." They told Vidal, "The American people will not accept that. I said, 'Well, you're never going to find out unless you try it and these are, after all, Southerners. Southerners are known for their, on the one hand going to church and getting drenched in the blood of the lamb, on the other hand being very easy going about sexual matters, particularly this sort.' Couldn't get that done. 'Change it'...They would do the picture if it were just man-woman. And jealousy of an ordinary sort."

According to Vidal, those running studios would say, "Well, look, we've got to think about the audience. We've got to think about the Church. You've gotta think about censorship..." In response, Vidal always invoked *Suddenly, Last Summer.* "It made a fortune out of being so disgusting." Vidal spoke candidly to *The Celluloid Closet*'s producers about gay Hollywood life off-screen as well. Hollywood of "the great days, the late '30s, '40s, really the Golden Age was very much a lesbian scene," said Vidal. "You really see in these photographs of [actress and photographer] Jean Howard, taken by herself, the power structure of Hollywood, which was almost entirely lesbian. Wives of studio heads like Jack Warner was one. There were the Marlene Dietrichs and the ladies in slacks. You can see them all in the photographs. For the eye knows what to look for. These are very forceful women, and the women were sort of determining what will be on the screen because most of them are married to directors or to movie stars."

Conversely, the gay male star "lived in terror," Vidal said. Clark Gable had been a hustler "for a brief period. I don't think his heart was perhaps into it, but certainly he had been into it. One of the reasons he got rid of George Cukor on *Gone With the Wind* [was because] George had twenty dollars-worth of him earlier in his career, and suddenly here Cukor is directing *Gone With the Wind* and Gable said, 'I've got to have a man's director' and got Victor Fleming who was the most macho of all the directors. They could allow one official queen like George Cukor. Everybody knew, nobody cared. However, he only did women's pictures. They thought, 'Well, queens like women...Nobody else wants to be on set all day with high-powered actresses. So we'll let George do it. As for the actors themselves, they were deeply closeted. They had to be."

He may not have wanted to have been defined as gay, but his gay-critical eye was acutely trained on Hollywood film as well as culture. Alfred Hitchcock's *Rope* (1948, its screenplay by Arthur Laurents), hailed today as a queer classic and released the same year as *The City and the Pillar* was published, was for Vidal "the sort of film that you would make if you wanted to demonstrate that faggots are evil," with a villain who is gay and Jewish, "so you have an anti-Semitic film on top of all that." On why its two villains were hardly thinly-veiled gay men, Vidal said, "There was a feeling that the fags were getting loose and that someday same-sexuality might possibly be given parity with other-sexuality, so of course let's start snaring them. This was the importance of my colleague Truman Capote. He was a great favorite on television, not because of his beauty or wit, because he was a good example to show your sensitive son. 'You will end up like that.' 'No, no, no. no. Get me married quickly, Father.' These are cautionary tales."

Recalling *Night of the Generals*, another film he contributed writing to, uncredited, Vidal said that when he suggested Dirk Bogarde as the star, producer Sam Spiegel told him, "Oh baby, baby, we can't. He's a fag." "Well," Vidal said in 1994, "if it was as bad as that in '68 [the film was released in 1967], think of what it was in '48 or '38." Vidal said one looked for "covert signals" in buddy movies like *Butch Cassidy and the Sundance Kid* (1969) and *Pat Garrett and Billy the Kid* (1973).

Vidal's friend, the filmmaker John Schlesinger, tried to get Vidal to write *Midnight Cowboy* (1969). "The only really good male to male film, sexual and absolutely upfront, was also made by Schlesinger, which was *Sunday Bloody Sunday* (1970) but that was made in England," said Vidal. "He couldn't have made that in the United States. He couldn't get anybody to play it, maybe not even to release it."

The director William Friedkin showed his controversial movie *Cruising* (1980), about a crazed gay killer, to Vidal, who recommended Friedkin cut two scenes, "particularly the last one where the nice young man, the blond man, is butchered in a toilet or whatever. I said you don't need it. It's gratuitous violence, and it establishes that to like your own sex means that you are a murderer at heart, that you're a psychopath, which we've heard in America for several hundred years now. This is not true. Why add to the fuel? You have enough excitement and melodrama going on without that." There's a faint historical irony to Vidal's sensitivity to the presentation of gay men: Isherwood had cautioned Vidal along the same lines in his critique of the original murder finale of *The City and the Pillar*. While Vidal did change that ending (a murder became an implied rape), "I did not convince Friedkin to change it and he didn't," Vidal said.

Although speaking before the likes of mainstream movies like *Brokeback Mountain* (2005) and *The Kids Are All Right* (2010), Vidal didn't believe contemporary movie-making was ready to portray gay desire openly. "I don't think Spielberg could put it in one of his toy movies which are so popular," Vidal said. "It would be interesting to see what would happen if he did...Now you're starting out in a world in which there is no information of any kind about anything other than a constant barrage—heterosexuality is not only good, it's compulsory. It goes on and on and on. Forget gay lib. That's a few cities."

If these perceptive observations showed a glimmer of Vidal as gay activist, Vidal the contrarian soon emerged to roll back the rainbow flag. "I'm not so sure that I understand what is meant in some circles that the gays are eager to have images of them as role models and so forth in the movies. Boy falls in love with boy, boy falls out of love with another boy then comes back together, the usual heterosexual plot. I suppose it would be useful but why not...be a universalist and regard the boy on the screen and the girl as perfectly adaptable? If you're a boy watching it and attracted to it, it's perfectly adaptable to you as well as the girl. That's the truth of the human condition."

Vidal's relationship to Hollywood wasn't restricted to script-writing and perceptive commentary. As he grew older—his reputation as a witty, sharp talking head on chat shows and political discussions already established in the public consciousness—Vidal began dramatizing his icy grandeur in films. In 1992, he wrote to Claire Bloom, "Beloved...I never regret anything in principle but sometimes I think what if? Answer, I'd be Sen. Pat Moynihan. What a fate! Instead, I co-star with Tim Robbins as a senator in *Bob Roberts*, now at Cannes. Good school-of-Altman movie. I am *very* moving or, as I said to Paul [Newman] & Joanne [Woodward], of the three of us, I'm the only one still acting in movies. This did not cause thighs to be slapped, ribs tickled." Vidal's longtime friend Elinor Pruder wasn't convinced: "At the end of his life he was a frustrated actor. He was in some movies and wasn't very good."

Vidal's first biographer, Walter Clemons, records in his diary of March 9, 1994: "Gore is in Hollywood, according to George [Armstrong], arguing he should have the part in a new Danny DeVito picture because 'what people don't understand about DeVito is that you have to play against his shortness. I'm tall enough to be funny with him.' Gore has said that his first ambition was to be a movie star from the moment he saw Mickey Rooney as Puck. When he appeared in Bob Roberts, he said grandly, 'All the John Houseman roles are now open to me.' And he recently played a Harvard law professor opposite Joe Pesci, as Houseman did in *The Paper Chase*."

In 1997, Vidal appeared in the science fiction film *Gattaca*. The painter Juan Bastos said to Vidal of appearing in the movie, "Oh, you met Jude Law." Vidal's response was imperious-Vidal with a dash of haughty dowager: "You mean Jude Law met *me*." Vidal wanted to talk about politics during Bastos's visit, Bastos did not and started talking about movies, "which he loved," revealing himself to be a witty, and surprisingly camp, mimic.

Vidal re-enacted small conversations featuring Jacqueline Kennedy, Greta Garbo and Bette Davis. "He would become them and sound just like them," says Bastos. "I asked him what he knew about the gossip that Cecil Beaton and Garbo had an affair. He quickly answered, 'Nonsense, I was with Garbo when she found out she was having an affair with Beaton. We went to the magazine stand where I was buying *Le Monde*, while Garbo was buying those trashy Hollywood magazines she liked so much, and that's when she found out she was having an affair with Beaton.' Then Gore's face changed, and he started mimicking Garbo perfectly. It was amazing."

Vidal and Garbo met in Klosters, Switzerland, where he and Austen wintered for five years in the 1970s. In *Palimpsest*, he remembers her dressing up in his clothes. Garbo also left the toilet seat up, Vidal recalled. She referred to herself as "he." "She also had an eye for girls," asking one woman to show her breasts, which she did. Garbo praised them. Garbo said she had never worn a bra: "I was the original women's liberation." She feared coming to Ravello because of the paparazzi, but told Vidal about a funny visit to the White House when JFK had taken her to his bedroom. "So romantic. Then he gave me a whale's tooth and we went back to Mrs. Jah-kee, who said, 'He never gave *me* a whale's tooth.'"

Bastos and Vidal also talked about Bette Davis. Bastos told him that one of his favorite movies was *The Letter*. Suddenly Vidal began re-enacting the very beginning of the movie, "with all the pauses, silences and descriptions of that first scene. Then he shouted 'Bam bam bam'—his face was transformed like Davis in the movie—while he pretended, like Davis, to look at the moon after she has shot a man on the stairs. Gore mentioned that scene as one of the best opening scenes in movies," Bastos says, smiling. "He imitated Bette Davis as brilliantly as he had done Garbo. You can imagine that I was like a kid in a candy store, having Gore Vidal do this private show for me." Bastos asked

Vidal if he had known Joan Crawford. "Joan and my mother were born in the same year in the same town. But little Lucille [LeSueur, as Crawford was named at birth] was born on the wrong side of the tracks." "Never play with that little girl," Vidal's grandmother told his mother.

Late in Vidal's life, the director Bill Condon wanted him to appear in a cameo in his 2004 biographical film *Kinsey*, about the famous sexologist Vidal himself had known, but Vidal cancelled at the last minute for reasons of health. This late flurry of big-screen cameos, whatever his acting chops, bought Vidal's relationship to Hollywood full circle. In the mid-1990s Vidal wrote to the author Muriel Spark, that he had just got "a large part" in a film, noting that in old age instead of having a bridge named after him or immortality conferred, "I have become a celluloid shadow."

Chapter Twelve

Freedom Fighter

Vidal was dexterous, and devastating, with words. The range of Vidal's writing around sexuality—much of it still unhailed and remarked upon—was derived from his passionately held radicalism that embraced equality and sexual liberation though was not centered around it. Vidal would have hated to have been seen as a one-issue writer, just as he would have hated to be seen as "gay." It was in his essays and TV appearances and ever-proliferating public feuds that Vidal's pugnacity found a focus. Vidal "loved to fight," says David Schweizer. "He wasn't hiding but he never defined himself. He never joined the gay movement, never spoke of people being out or gay rights. That outlaw stance appealed to him. He was a renegade, not a crusader."

In his essays Vidal fought the good fight, without ever saying he was a member of the tribe. But the scale of his essay writing and its depth bravely underscores his belief in equality, at a time when few others were writing and grandstanding around gay rights in such a public, high-profile way. In "Sex and the Law," published in *Partisan Review* in 1965, four years before the Stonewall Riots, Vidal wrote, "Why should homosexual acts between consenting adults be considered inimical to the public good?" Individual states have managed to make "a complete hash of things," as, some would argue, they continue to do today.

In the *New York Review of Books* in 1966, Vidal wrote that *Time* magazine had recently diagnosed homosexuality as a "pernicious sickness," yet Vidal demonstrated how homosexuality had been perceived differently in different historical eras. "What was undesirable in peace was often a virtue in war, as the Spartans recognized, inventing the buddy system at the expense of the family unit." Vidal quotes Frederick the Great to his officers: "You know where you can find your sex—in the barracks."

In the world of pre-Christian cities, Vidal writes, "it never occurred to anyone that a homosexual act was less 'natural' than a heterosexual one. It was simply a matter of taste. From Archilochus to Apuleius, this acceptance of the way people actually are is implicit in what the writers wrote. Suetonius records that of his twelve emperors, eleven went with equal ease from boys to girls and back again without Suetonius ever finding anything remarkable in their 'polymorphous perverse' behavior." Yet again, Vidal emphasized, "We are bisexual." The variety of pornography on sale "tells us most about the extraordinary variety of human sexual response."

There was no strain of political correctness or expediency in what Vidal argued. While gay rights groups pleaded—and continue to plead—homosexuality's normality and equivalence to heterosexuality, in the CBS Reports 1967 documentary, *The Homosexuals*, Vidal the radical said, "I think the so-called breaking of the moral fiber of this country is one of the healthiest things that's begun to happen." Many years before "cure therapy" became a topic taken up by gay activists, Vidal condemned Dr. David Reuben, a doctor and bestselling author who offered it to patients seeking a "cure" from being gay, who was the subject of a 1970 *New York Review of Books* profile. Vidal wrote that "to change a man's homosexual instinct is as difficult (if not impossible) as changing a man's heterosexual instinct" adding, in his dry way, that it was also "socially less desirable" as "the race currently needs no more additions." Dr. Reuben, writes Vidal, seemed to believe gays are "half a man, a travesty of a woman."

The legal and social prohibitions and inequalities in relation to his sexuality don't seem to have bothered Vidal much. "Except for Paul Bowles (blackmailed by two NYC cops, re. adolescent boy) I have never known anyone who was bothered by the police or anyone else," Vidal wrote to one friend, "saving always those masochists who walk, drunkenly usually, into fists, and joy. On the other hand, I hear a lot about police entrapment etc. Recently in LA, I proposed the deliberate entrapment of the entrappers, a few cops sent to jail should have a 'wholesome effect,' as T. Jefferson would say."

Vidal's growling impatience with homophobia in print reads as less anchored by the righteous anger of the activist than the simple ignorance it embodied when seen in relation to history, his great obsession. His unequivocally stated arguments remain fresh today. In an essay, "Sex Is Politics," for *Playboy* in 1979, Vidal writes that marriage "is the central institution whereby the owners of the world control those who do the work." Women who can support themselves and their children threaten marriage, just as much as homosexuality does, "because men who don't have wives or children to worry about are not as easily dominated as those men who do."

To divert the electorate, Vidal writes, "the unscrupulous American politician will go after those groups not regarded benignly by Old or New Testament." He ran through the homosexual relations often celebrated in the ancient world. "The oldest of religious texts tells of the love between two men, Gilgamesh and Enkidu. When Enkidu died, Gilgamesh challenged death itself in order to bring his lover back to life. In *The Iliad*, Gilgamesh's rage is echoed by Achilles when his lover Patroclus dies before the walls of Troy. So intense was the love between the heroes David and Jonathan that David noted in his obituary of Jonathan: 'Thy love to me was wonderful, passing the love of women.'" Also in the Old Testament, the love that Ruth felt for Naomi "was of a sort that today might well end in their joint ownership of a ceramics kiln at Laguna Beach."

Vidal again emphasized the theoretical knot that so many gays, activists and not, disagree with him on: "There is no such thing as a homosexual person, any more than there is such a thing as a heterosexual person. The words are adjectives describing sexual acts, not people. Those sexual acts are entirely natural; if they were not, no one would perform them." Whatever Vidal felt about his own sexuality, whatever he did in bed, intellectually he would never waver from this.

Sodom was destroyed not because its inhabitants were, as Vidal writes, "homosexualists," but "because a number of local men wanted to gang rape a pair of male angels who were guests of the town." The irrational rage of homophobes, he says, "has triggered an opposing rage. Gay militants now assert that there is something called 'gay sensibility,' the outward and visible sign of a new kind of human being. Thus madness begets madness." Vidal did not recognize a "gay sensibility" or "gay" anything that had a power or uniqueness of its own. The "homosexualist (sometimes known as gay, fag, queer etc)...does not exist. The human race is divided into male and female. Many human beings enjoy sexual relations with their own sex, many don't; many respond to both. This plurality is the fact of our nature and not worth fretting about." There was hysteria around it because "the owners of the country (buttressed by a religion they have shrewdly adapted for their own ends) regard the family as their last means of control over those who work and consume."

Vidal's most famous gay-themed essay, "Pink Triangle and Yellow Star," was written for *The Nation* in 1981 in response to "The Boys on the Beach," an article in *Commentary* magazine by Midge Decter, the writer and wife of editor Norman Podhoretz, who wondered why gay men had become so militant when the ones she fondly remembered "were characterized by nothing so much as a sweet, vain, pouting girlish attention to the youth and beauty of their bodies."

As the title of his essay suggests, Vidal drew a persuasive and firm line between the persecution of Jews by the Nazis, the codification and stereotyping that stirred hatred so hideously and murderously in the 1930s and '40s, and the stereotyping, codification and contempt Decter deployed in her essay towards gays, against a broader context of wider homophobia. He equates this new Manhattan "ruling class" Decter and her ilk embody, aligning itself to corporate America, akin to Nazi-embracing Jews like Max Naumann.

Vidal derides her narrowness. "Decter knows that there have always been homosexual teachers, and she thinks that they should keep quiet about it." Having read "several thousand words into her tirade," Vidal realized that Decter "does not know what homosexuality is." Decter worried what influence openly gay people would have on vulnerable straight people, and classified them as effeminate and swishy, and in addition hated themselves so much that they invited murder or committed suicide; or as Decter put it, "What is undeniable is the increasing longing among the homosexuals to do away with themselves—if not in the actual physical sense then at least spiritually—a longing whose chief emblem, among others, is the leather bars."

Surely, Vidal writes dryly, Decter would be happy about this, but then noted the "shrill, fag-baiting" Decter wouldn't be happy with anything "same-sexers" do—"if they get married," he writes of her vision, "their wives will drink...if they populate the arts, heterosexuals will have to protect themselves against propaganda and attack, if they work in fashion they will only employ heterosexuals who put out for them." Vidal sums up Decter's argument thus: "Since homosexualists choose to be the way they are out of idle hatefulness, it has been a mistake to allow them to come out of the closet to the extent that they have, but now that they are out (which most are not), they will have no choice but to face up to their essential hatefulness and abnormality and so be driven to kill themselves with promiscuity, drugs, S-M and suicide." Decter, he says, is a "virtuoso of hate, and thus do pogroms begin."

If Decter was an extreme example, Vidal more generally perceived Judaism in opposition to homosexuality. At one supper in 1978, recalls the author Tom Powers, Vidal argued vigorously that a strain of "Jewish Puritanism" informed Henry James's biographer Leon Edel's characterizing of his subject as "a kind of sexual neuter." Powers says Vidal insisted that Edel "refused to admit his hero got into bed with men. It was a kind of conspiracy. James, Walt Whitman, even Proust—they were figures of a different age, spoke in a way which suggests sex to us, lived in a world of healthy, masculine intimacy, but great writers do not go to bed with boys. Jews are never homosexuals, 'except for those who are', and Jewish intellectuals will not concede that their heroes might do something they themselves would not do. Vidal was absolutely certain of this: Jewish Puritanism had blinded Edel and turned a scholar into a suppressor of evidence."

Vidal retold a story related to him by John Lehmann and Stephen Spender, who had been told by the novelist Hugh Walpole that he had tried to seduce Henry James, with James renouncing Walpole, naked in bed; James saying, "This cannot be." Vidal insisted James was gay. "The giveaway is a description of Minnie Temple's [James's cousin] brother naked. He was serving as an artist's model when James happened by and his description of the late afternoon sun, the beauty of the boy—and he certainly does seem to have been something quite extraordinary—the whole feel and air of it...Well! It just can't come from anything else. When I read that I knew." The description of Minnie Temple's brother left no room for doubt for Vidal, says Powers. "Henry James got into bed with boys and *fucked*."

"Fuck," recalled Powers, was "a word Vidal uses a good deal. He can be courtly in his way, but every few minutes—I mean that literally; twenty minutes would be a long stretch without some such word—he feels the impulse and finds the occasion to refer to fucking, and he puts a lot of mouth into the word. He does not shirk its clear enunciation, he puts his teeth right down over his lower lip to put force into the initial and fires it out— 'ffffuck!' Clearly, he likes to say it. He likes being straightforward, and he likes to offend the proprieties of academia, which he puts right up there next to Jewish Puritanism as an enemy of homoeroticism, but mainly he likes thinking about sex and he wants to get it into the conversation. He's like a fly fisherman, flicking out the bait with steady optimism, convinced by experience of one thing at least—if you don't flick the bait out, you won't ever take anything home. So he flicks out a fuck every little while, from pure habit by this time, on the off-chance something will bite. He likes talking, but he likes sex more, and he never strays too far away."

Vidal told Powers that the novelist Elsa Morante, author most famously of *La storia* (History, 1974), once had a young, blond English lover who looked a lot like the actor James Fox. "He drank too much," Vidal said. "But very handsome. I was ffffucking him at the same time. He'd spend a week with her until he couldn't stand it any longer and then he'd come back for a week with Howard and me. Eventually, he committed suicide. It had nothing to do with us. Drink and drugs...So Morante and I were not exactly friends, but in between fucking this boy we sent each other polite little messages."

It was, says Powers, "a characteristic Vidal story: violent, un-expected, a bit pugnacious, interesting, and at heart a kind of ad-justment of the wheel to bring the conversation back around to sex. After all, if you don't flick out the bait, you'll never take any-thing home. But the 'fffs' are drawn out too richly to be explained by that alone. Vidal may fuck boys but by God he fffucks and Henry James did too. Vidal is not just convinced that James liked boys. He's convinced he fucked them." Powers, listening to this point "hammered home the third time," thought how much this meant to Vidal, "and how perfectly his own certitudes seem to mirror those of the Jewish puritans. Perhaps Edel is happier with a James who is repressed, but there is no question Vidal is upset by the very idea of abstinence. James would not restrain himself, any more than Vidal does. No sad longing in the loneliness of middle age. No, no—he was just like Vidal, he flicked out the bait, he took the catch home, he got into bed and he *fucked*."

If Powers is right, there remains an irony in Vidal freely casting James as a homosexual and homosexual writer, whereas he strenuously resisted any such definitions being applied to himself, even though in essays he wrote consistently thoughtfully about sex and sexuality. The brilliant, dry "The Birds and the Bees," first pub-lished in *The Nation* in 1991, was a belated corrective, Vidal said. Until its composition he had "never really explained sex," beyond stating that "homosexual" and "heterosexual" were "dumb neolo-gisms" that "describe acts but never people." Vidal claims there is no point to humans, bar "proliferation and survival"; the concept of love was invented by "some artist who found depressing the dull mechanics of our mindless mission to be fruitful and multiply."

Sexual taboos were created to keep the population "in line," though these dos and don'ts have created, among other things, "asthma and rape." Everything the Bible said, including about sex, was wrong, says Vidal. Men and women do not thrive in closed relationships, because "he is designed to make as many babies as possible with as many different women as he can get his hands on, while she is designed to take time off from her busy schedule as astronaut and role model to lay an egg and bring up the result." Given the grave implications of overpopulation, "those who would outlaw abortion, contraception and same-sex while extolling the family and breeding are themselves the active agents of the destruction of our species."

Gay men—not that Vidal calls them that, of course—should be encouraged "when he wants to shoot with another shootist...in an activity that will not add another consumer to the population. The woman who decides not to lay that egg should be encouraged, if so minded, to mate with another woman. As it is, a considerable portion of the population, despite horrendous persecution, does just that, and they should be considered benefactors by everyone, while the breeders must be discouraged though, of course, not persecuted." For Vidal, homosexuality was the most socially responsible sexuality.

Vidal references a recent book, which reports that seventeen percent of men and eleven percent of women have had "same sex," which struck Vidal as "low—even mendacious...I don't think the folks have changed all that much since 1948, when thirty-seven percent of the men told Dr. Kinsey that they had messed around in those years." People in this most extreme era of AIDS, when Vidal wrote the essay, may be nervous about sex, he says, but not when they're young. In the prewar Southern town of Washington, D.C., where Vidal grew up, "it was common for boys to have sex with one another. It was called 'messing around,' and it was no big deal. If the boy became a man who kept on messing around, it was thought a bit queer—sexual exclusivity is odd and suggests obsession—but no big deal as long as he kept it quiet."

So if you choose to sleep with your own sex exclusively, for Vidal this is "obsession," rather than simply your sexual choice. To choose to sleep with one sex is deficient, to be suspected, because for Vidal homosexuality was restrictive, implausible. But I wonder if Vidal wasn't also writing from a nostalgic, bruised heart: his two experiences of all-consuming same-sex desire, recorded at least, were with Jimmie Trimble and Harold Lang. With both men—Trimble most profoundly—Vidal had been left deeply affected. Trimble had become Vidal's own lifelong obsession. With Austen he had warded off such intense feelings, a recognition of a consuming attachment, though after Austen's death Vidal acknowledged the depth of his devastation and grief—and, by extension, admitted the depth of the relationship itself.

Women, he said, were more "candid" today about their desire for one another, although lesbian desire for Vidal is connected to men, rather than women—"egg-layers," as Vidal described them—desiring one another for themselves. As Vidal puts it, "A pair of egg-layers will have more in common (including a common genetic programming for nurturing) than they will ever have with a shootist, who wants to move on the second he's done his planting—no nurturing for him, no warm, mature, caring relationship. He isn't built for it. His teats may have a perky charm but they are not connected to a dairy."

Vidal did not believe that heterosexuals outnumber homosexuals. "The percentage of the population that is deeply enthusiastic about other-sex is probably not much larger than those exclusively devoted to same-sex—something like ten percent in either case. The remaining eighty percent does this, does that, does nothing; settles into an acceptable if dull social role where the husband dreams of Barbara Bush while pounding the old wife, who lies there, eyes shut, dreaming of Barbara too." The "whole thing is a perfect mess," Vidal writes.

Away from the page, Vidal was also publicly and privately active around gay rights, especially in the early years of the modern movement. The first contemporary US gay rights campaigning group, the Mattachine Society, founded in 1950, approached Vidal in a letter dated August 12, 1969, just over a month after the Stonewall Riots, asking for a donation. Madolin Cervantes, the chairman of the Village Shelter Fund and later treasurer of the organization, said the Mattachine was seeking money for a project for lesbian and gay youth. Her letter bracingly outs him, as well as seeking his money. "I don't think it is any secret to anyone that you are gay—most people seem to take it for granted—and it is on this basis that this appeal is being made to you, to help us lend a helping hand to your less fortunate brothers (or should I say 'sisters')." Vidal was supportive of the organization. A 1971 letter from the Mattachine includes their new letterhead with a "thank you very much for allowing us to put your name to it," Vidal's name listed alongside the likes of Evelyn Hooker, Allen Ginsberg and Christopher Isherwood. Vidal even kept the letter, dated February 20, 1977, informing all members of the winding down of the organization.

On May 16, 1972, Bruce Voeller, then chairman of the state and federal government committee of the Gay Activists Alliance, wrote to Vidal thanking him for appearing at a Gay Unity Rally on Christopher Street, though "ugly beatings followed." Voeller writes, "To have you and Congressman Koch come and indicate your solidarity with our demand of our rights as human beings was heartening." Like Vidal, Ed Koch—later to become New York Mayor and widely rumored to be gay—never came out. Indeed, his private life is clouded in much more mystery than Vidal's. Koch once said, "There were lots of people who believed I was gay, and voted for me, and lots of people who didn't believe I was gay who voted for me. Most people didn't care, and my attitude was, f*** 'em."

In 1980 the Gay Community Center of Philadelphia Building Fund asked Vidal to appear at a fundraising evening; he was also invited to write for an anthology called Gay and Growing, edited by Betty Berzon and Don Clark, featuring "personal stories from successful lives...what it means to be gay and maintaining a positive personal identity." Sexual rights was also on Vidal's agenda on a tour of American college campuses in autumn 1974, or as he put it to his cousin Louis Auchincloss: "three months of lecturing, whistle-stopping with splendid large crowds of masochists, lusting for my whip!...But to a good end, I like to think. The people-out-there, by the way, are a good deal more thoughtful than their rulers; they also know that they are being most beautifully and perfectly fucked."

Vidal's commitment to equality crossed the Atlantic. He was good friends with senior Labour MP Tom Driberg, describing him in *Palimpsest* as a "sort of stout Dracula...forever being caught in lavatories with rough youths." He had urged Driberg in the 1960s to get his Labour Party colleagues signed up to homosexual law reform in the wake of the Wolfenden report recommending decriminalization, which would come in 1967. Vidal wrote, "I am troubled by what seems to be a new Puritanism rising in England, fully blessed by socialism, which does like nothing better than to involve itself in private lives under the guise of 'morality' and the good life, not realizing that the 'morality' is Mosaic in origin and beautifully antipathetic to the good life."

Vidal asked Labour leader Hugh Gaitskell if Driberg would ever have a place in his future Cabinet. Gaitskell, who died before achieving Prime Ministerial office, said, "How can we? He's bound to be arrested in some loo." Driberg worked on his memoirs at La Rondinaia, Vidal recommending he be honest about his homosexuality but hold back on the juiciest details, such as giving former British Foreign Secretary Ernest Bevin a blow job. Driberg died before completing the book.

In 1976, Vidal wrote to the New Statesman magazine objecting to the historian A.J.P. Taylor's obituary of Driberg, which was, says Vidal, "both condescending and inaccurate." Taylor had written, "Tom was also homosexual, flagrant and unashamed." Vidal admonished Taylor thus: "I was not aware that homosexuality was something to be ashamed of. Certainly Taylor would not write of Lloyd George that he was 'heterosexual, flagrant and unashamed.' I daresay Taylor meant 'compulsive' or 'promiscuous'; even so, shame hardly enters in."

Vidal wasn't just hiding in open sight, he was campaigning and agitating for gay equality. In 1974, he allowed himself to be interviewed by John Mitzel and Steven Abbott for *Fag Rag* magazine, saying to a friend that he didn't see "much point" to "fag-mags—at least for those of us who can write elsewhere and say the same sort of thing. It is the dream of all these papers that the L.A. Chief of Police will become addicted to their style and, finally…realize with a sudden blaze that Fags are not only GOOD but BETTER." This revealed Vidal's lacerating priggery: a gay man scorning the notion the police should treat gay men and women equally, not better; it was an era when a gay writer of Vidal's standing might be expected to question or confront police homophobia and their lack of engagement with anti-gay crime—but again he was content to mock and disparage "fags."

But then, at the same time, a more sober Vidal noted, "I think it's always true that things begin to liberalize, revolutionize. Once there is an atmosphere for change, change increases exponentially." He didn't think "the gay liberation movement is particularly strong. I don't think it's touched ninety-nine percent of the people. You can go into any small town in America and the attitudes of the people there are no different from what they were in 1900."

Vidal allowed an interview with him to be published in a *Gay Sunshine* anthology and in 1985 he donated money to the campaign to fund London's gay bookstore Gay's the Word's legal campaign against Customs and Excise, who had seized 2,250 books in a raid, charging its owners with conspiracy to import indecent books. One of the books seized was Vidal's 1956 story collection, *A Thirsty Evil*, which Gay Sunshine Press had republished. Customs and Excise assumed that any imported title, including works by Kate Millet and Tennessee Williams, were pornographic. The case was eventually dropped.

Vidal's gay radicalism remained consistent into his old age. Speaking to his onetime publisher Donald Weise, Vidal said he had "toyed with the idea of violence, particularly in smaller communities," which was on his mind after the murder of Matthew Shepard, the twenty-one-year-old University of Wyoming student, tortured and murdered by Aaron McKinney and Russell Henderson in 1998. Shepard had been tied to a fence in a remote rural area and left to die. "If those two boys in

Wyoming were found beaten up in Wyoming one day I would applaud," said Vidal referring to Shepard's murderers, "and everybody would see the causal link between their being beaten up and the one they killed. They respect violence. I think they expect it." On the practice of outing, he was the more moderate, perhaps inevitably given his own dislike of labels and public declarations: "It's the hypocrites we all want to out," he said in 2000. "No one wants Rock Hudson to be a faggot." Although, one would have thought, the fact that Hudson had been gay allowed the two men to get together sexually fifty years previously.

It was television, which became a mass medium in the late '50s and early '60s, that really made Vidal famous. He relished becoming a personality. "My entire life is now devoted to appearing on television: a pleasant alternative to real life," Fred Kaplan quotes him quipping to friends. It was television that provided a still-notorious, defining incident remembered by Christopher Bram, as well as many gay men of that generation who saw and remember it, as "a really startling, memorable" moment. It occurred on August 28, 1968 in a televised ABC debate between Vidal and the conservative William F. Buckley.

The two had been set up as irascible political opposites, Buckley for the right, Vidal, the left. As they debated the police's violent crackdown on protesters at that year's Democrat National Convention in Chicago, Vidal described Buckley as "Hitler without the charm." Buckley compared the anti-Vietnam war demonstrators to Nazis. "As far as I'm concerned," Vidal told him, "the only pro- or crypto-Nazi I can think of is yourself." Buckley replied, "Now listen, you queer. Stop calling me a crypto-Nazi or I'll sock you in your goddamn face and you'll stay plastered." The moderator stepped in and asked that they not call each other names. Buckley added: "Let the author of *Myra Breckinridge* go back to his pornography and stop making allusions of Nazism," Buckley shouted.

Long before the confrontation, Kaplan reveals that Buckley had composed a telegram to a TV presenter that he never sent after another on-screen confrontation with Vidal. "Please inform

Gore Vidal that neither I nor my family is disposed to receive lessons in morality from a pink queer. If he wishes to challenge that designation, inform him that I shall fight by the laws of the Marquis of Queensberry." After Buckley's flare-up, Vidal said, "I don't know what I did to deserve it. I always treated Mr. Buckley like the great lady that he is." After the debate Buckley was commissioned by *Esquire* to write an article and Vidal to respond to it. Buckley sued Vidal for libel, Vidal countersued. The case went on for three years and was abruptly, mysteriously terminated.

It was the first time "queer" had been said on TV in such a context. Richard Harrison says of Vidal's consistent contrarianism, "You say right hand, he says left. He told me, 'I'm not really a Democrat. When someone calls me a fag I know I've won.' For him it showed Buckley's weakness. Right away it gave him more power. He didn't say to Buckley, 'You're a weak-looking fella...He'd never do that, he didn't attack like that. He loved when they attacked him because he stayed above it all. Their attacks made him look better. He never felt insulted or embarrassed. He loved it. He thought it was great."

The matter still won't rest. His half-sister Nina Straight reveals that "Gore was terrified" that "material Buckley had on him would come out." What material, I ask. His sex life? The hustlers? "It's more complicated than that," says Straight, "you're able to think of the spectrum." Sadomasochism? "It had to do with sex, it was definitely more detailed than calling Gore a fag. Gore didn't want these records to come out. He was very upset, terrified, about the material." So the one million dollar legal debt Vidal ran up was somehow connected to ensuring the secret didn't come out? "Yes, it's very sad," says Straight. Burr Steers, her son, clarifies that his mother lent Vidal the money to fight the legal battle by paying his fees to Edward Weisl, the lawyer she recommended he engage. "My mother expected Gore to pay her back, but he never did."

I ask Straight, was Vidal right to be afraid of Buckley, did she know the details of what Buckley held on Vidal. "I can guess what they are. Jerry Sandusky acts," she says. Buckley claimed to have evidence that Vidal was having sex with underage males, I ask? Straight nods. "It would be hypothetical but you can cover that range, yes." I ask if I would be wrong to take from this that she is suggesting Vidal thought Buckley had incriminating evidence Vidal had sex with underage men. "No, you would not be incorrect in taking that from what I've said," replies Straight. When I subsequently asked for further detail from Straight, she declined to comment.

In *Palimpsest* Vidal claimed he was "attracted to adolescent males"—"like most men." It's one of Vidal's most curious sweeping statements: it's not true, of all men that he cites, or indeed of gay men if he was just referring to them; and even if he was it's still even more curious for someone who professed an enduring belief in unfixed sexuality.

Burr Steers tells me, "I know Buckley had a file on him that Gore feared. 'The file,' as he called it, was something he was afraid of. Buckley definitely had something over him. It would make sense if that material was about him having underage sex. Gore spent a lot of time in Bangkok, after all. My mother's younger brother [and Jacqueline Kennedy's half-brother] Jamie Auchincloss was caught with child pornography and was sent to jail, and Gore would not condemn him. [Auchincloss was jailed in 2011 on child pornography charges.] Gore also had a very weird take on the abuse perpetrated by Catholic priests—he would say that the young guys involved were hustlers who were sending signals. Gore was so twisted up about sex, there was a big difference between the public image he crafted and what he was about in reality."

Does Steers know if his uncle had sex with underage men? "I don't know for sure and I don't want to know. But look, the love of his life was Jimmie Trimble, stuck forever as a teenage boy, a Peter Pan. The photo he carried around of Howard in his wallet wasn't of Howard as an adult, but Howard as a teenager."

In 1978, Vidal spoke at a fundraising event for the Boston-Boise Committee, set up to counter the anti-gay reaction—"a witch-hunt of Salem-esque intensity," Vidal wrote in 2006—stoked by the case of a group of Boston men, all married with children and grandchildren, indicted for having sex with legally underage men. "Not one" of the young victims "was a child," said Vidal.

The Committee, wrote the author Bruce Benderson in a subsequent book, *Sex and Isolation: And Other Essays*, "eventually sponsored a conference on man-boy love and the age of consent. An Episcopal Bishop, some social workers, and a psychiatrist participated in this conference, a caucus of which led to the founding of the North American Man/Boy Love Association [NAMBLA]. At the time, the most salient features of this now-maligned organization were neo-Marxist, and at different times its members have protested against corporal punishment, the draft, compulsory schooling, and intervention in El Salvador. NAMBLA members, though some may be naive utopianists, have also endorsed the right of even young children to serve on juries, vote, hold office, and make their own living arrangements. Though currently the most publicized feature of this organization is its insistence on legalizing intergenerational sex, over the years it has also been concerned with radical children's liberation, and some percentage of the activities of members is devoted to literary and theoretical analyses of American culture's treatment of youth—as in the writings of Paul Goodman."

Originally, Benderson says, the organization was "closer to the political and cultural views of a person like Vidal: it was about children's rights more than it was about the right to have sex with children." But this early theoretical framework is incidental to most observers today. NAMBLA is, to the minds of many, a sinister, beyond-the-pale organization, rightly detached from the cause of mainstream gay equality as it argues for legalizing sex between adults and children.

The Boston-Boise fundraiser "was not a NAMBLA meeting, although subsequently NAMBLA was formed to defend against similar witch-hunts," a NAMBLA spokesman told me. Bruce Benderson disagrees: "In my estimation it was at the basis of the founding of NAMBLA." Various right-wing, anti-Vidal screeds frothed online after Vidal's death that his appearance at the 1978 fundraising event showed that he "supported the rape of kids by gay child molesters"—and worse. Burr Steers cautions that his uncle's appearance at the event should not be read as (if it ever was) personally motivated: "It would be entirely in keeping with his politics to take a radical, contrarian stand on that."

I asked the NAMBLA spokesman a series of questions: Did Vidal have any other connection with the organization? Was he a member? Did he correspond with NAMBLA? Did the spokesman know if any members met or knew him personally? Did he ever vocalize his support for NAMBLA directly—either publicly or in correspondence with the organization or any of its members? The spokesman would not disclose any further information.

Vidal's longtime friend Scotty Bowers never heard Vidal express a sexual interest in underage men. "Hell no. The guys I fixed him up with early on were his own age, and later in his life were in their twenties and thirties, never younger or illegal," Bowers says. "The guys I saw him and Howard cruise in Italy were in their twenties." David Schweizer concurs. "I personally only witnessed a procession of very handsome young men in their twenties, no children as far as I knew. He liked that some-what manly athletic type descending from his crush of yore [Jimmie Trimble] in his early days, methinks."

A friend who knew Vidal for twenty years says he would "occasionally comment, jokingly" about attractive adolescents and teenagers, "but nothing out of the ordinary. Most of the time the comments and his cruising were about sexy men in their twenties." In Italy, Vidal took this friend to the Archaeological Museum in Paestum, about fifty three miles south east of Naples, where he enjoyed one particular ancient painting of an adolescent diver. Vidal, says the friend, also "appreciated" the tradition of the Capri and the Amalfi Coast exemplified by the writer Norman Douglas, the British expat who lived on Capri and had sex with underage, typically ex-pat boys.

Vidal once shocked a guest at Ravello, this longtime friend says, by announcing: "You know I'm a pederast." The friend isn't sure if Vidal had sex with underage boys—"and it's worth remembering the age of consent is relative, depending on where you are in the world"—but thinks Vidal "just liked to shock people he thought were square. He was also brutally honest: a lot of older guys are attracted to younger men. And yes, he did go to Thailand every year, and he was definitely having sex with male prostitutes there, and they weren't older male prostitutes. Someone I know ran into him at a hotel, and Vidal told him: 'I'm here trying to get AIDS'—the ultimate expression of his mordant sense of humor." Vidal, says the friend, also "seriously thought Buckley was himself gay."

After approaching Vidal in regards a magazine story he was working on, the journalist, broadcaster and activist Michelangelo Signorile recalls Vidal raising the possibility of Buckley "perhaps being gay and closeted himself." Vidal had reviewed Signorile's 1993 book, *Queer in America*, for the *Village Voice* "and so knew about—and was fascinated by—my role in the 'outing' debate and knew that I'd revealed the sexual orientation of hypocritical figures in my role as a journalist," Signorile tells me. "He told me that Buckley used to spend summers in Mykonos, which has always been a gay destination, especially in summer. Vidal told me there were rumors of Buckley's involvement with at least one particular man, and perhaps others, and that there were people there who could help track it down. But I'm not sure whether he'd not given me any leads or if he did but they were too vague—it was a long time ago—but it wasn't anything I pursued."

The novelist Edmund White says Vidal was "unpleasant, very clever and argumentative," but William F. Buckley was "revolting. Later he wanted HIV-positive people to branded on their ass" or as Buckley wrote in the *New York Times* in 1986, "Everyone detected with AIDS should be tattooed in the upper forearm, to protect common-needle users, and on the buttocks, to prevent the victimization of other homosexuals." If you look closely at the footage of the 1968 TV contretemps between Buckley and Vidal, his son Christopher wrote in the New Republic after Vidal died, "you'll see WFB [Buckley] trying to rise out of his chair at the moment of maximum heat. If you look very closely, you'll see him physically straining, but something hold-ing him back. A few days before, he was sailing in Long Island Sound when a Coast Guard cutter zoomed past his sailboat, knocking him to the deck, breaking his collarbone. During the Chicago debates, he was wearing a clavicle brace. It's possible that the brace prevented the moment from being truly iconic."

When Buckley died in 2008, Christopher recalled after Vidal's death, "I found in his study, more cluttered than King Tut's tomb, a file cabinet bursting to the seams, labeled 'Vidal Legal.' Into the dumpster it went, and I still remember the sigh of relief upon heaving it in. WFB's body was still warm (I ex-aggerate only slightly) when Vidal rendered his obsequies: 'RIP WFB—in hell.' It was a thorny wreath indeed that he laid on the grave: 'a world-class liar,' 'a hysterical queen.'" Christopher Buckley declined to comment for this book.

Buckley wasn't Vidal's only famous feud. Another began with former buddy Norman Mailer in 1968 when Vidal saw him con-sorting with Buckley. In July 1971 in the *New York Review of Books* Vidal wrote a condemnation of an article Mailer wrote for *Harper's* magazine which Vidal thought was offensively anti-female (characterizing women as birth vessels) while linking homosexuality to evil. In November 1971, in a dressing room of *The Dick Cavett Show,* Mailer, drunk, head-butted Vidal before they were about to appear and Vidal punched him in the stom-ach—then on camera Mailer approached Vidal as if to hit him.

Mailer, boorish on the show, demanded Vidal tell everyone what he had done to Jack Kerouac (alluding to their sexual en-counter). He asked the audience if they were crazy or he was and got the unanimous answer: "You are." In 1970, in his novel *Two Sisters*, the narrator V mulls of Mailer that "one senses that beneath the mask he elects to wear there is a nice Jewish boy (his own phrase) playing desperately at being a Goyisher slob, and hoping that his liver—not to mention nerves—will survive the strain."

Both men's animosity percolated until a party in 1977 at the home of writer Lally Weymouth. After swapping an insult or two,

Fred Kaplan reports, Mailer threw his drink over Vidal, then attempted to punch him but forgot he was holding his glass, which cut Vidal's lip. They then gripped one another, scuffling. Mailer then challenged Vidal to fight him outside. His partner Austen said he'd take Vidal's place. Mailer told Austen his fourteen-year-old son could beat him up. Mailer wrote to reconcile with Vidal in 1985, suggesting the imminence of death as they aged ("the same sinking ship") made old feuds absurd.

A revived friendship began, though Vidal told Kaplan: "Norman is homophobic." And Mailer told Kaplan, "No, I've never been irked or bothered by Gore's homosexuality. Gore has always treated his homosexuality as a rather interesting quirk caused by—whatever. As a homosexual, he's very much a man. He insists on that and he acts that way. In sex, he does it...No one does anything to him. So he's just as much a male as any 'convict,' so to speak, any strong male. That's never entered into our feuding."

One sharp piece of criticism Mailer made of Vidal-as-a-novelist in the 1950s may still resonate with those critics who feel Vidal's fiction was unsuccessful: "I cannot resist suggesting that he is in need of a wound, which would turn the prides of his detachment into new perception." Of course, Vidal had wounds; he had simply chosen to cauterize them to protect himself and constructed a suit of armor for his role as a public figure. This inviolable persona wouldn't brook the kind of vulnerability and openness Mailer was suggesting would benefit Vidal as a novelist.

One of the more curious demi-feuds Vidal began was with the gay novelist John Rechy. "People assumed we were friends," Rechy tells me. "They were surprised that we never met, even though we lived within almost jumping distance of one another." When Rechy's bestselling hustling-themed novel *City of Night* was published in 1963 it was the subject of a vicious, homophobic takedown by Alfred Chester, himself gay, in the *New York Review of Books* under the headline "Fruit Salad," in which, "apart from column after column of vitriol," recalls Rechy,

Chester wondered if the author existed.

The magazine was at the time edited by Vidal's friend Barbara Epstein, who declined Rechy's request for a right of reply. Vidal later wrote that, "I could have gone on to write John Rechy novels, but I chose not to," which Rechy found "pretty nasty, bitchy, gratuitously so." In another piece Vidal said the kind of critic he most admired was the kind exemplified by Chester in his review of *City of Night,* which he said was "grossly unfair but entirely true."

Here was Vidal going after another gay writer siding with a gay and homophobic reviewer, even though he had smarted for many years himself after similar treatment from the *New York Times.* His words "incensed" Rechy, who had respected Vidal and which was why he found the words extra-galling. Rechy wrote him an "elegant, not insulting letter" asking why he had praised "such a vile review when he had been the object of the same."

Rechy didn't expect to hear back, but Vidal responded in a "really long, brilliantly hilarious" letter that was "as close as Vidal ever came to apologizing. I must know that he admired very highly *City of Night.* Well, no, I did not. He particularly admired the chapter where the two hustlers kind of connect, but it's not possible because they're too afraid of being gay. He had heard, he wrote, that Alfred Chester was a real monster, but he had a certain, gratuitously nasty wit that he admired sometimes. Vidal said he didn't know what happened: he had fallen under the spell of the demon Chester and therefore wrote what he wrote."

Rechy knew he had gotten to Vidal with his "very honest presentation" because Vidal continued, fulsomely, that an "outstanding Italian critic he knew told him how good *City of Night* was." Rechy had asked hadn't Vidal been appalled by the "Fruit Salad" headline, and Vidal said he couldn't remember it. "I have tamed them and no longer write for them," he said, addressing Rechy's charge that the *New York Review of Books* was notoriously homophobic. "That was hilarious," says Rechy today. "He was in every goddamn issue after that." Still, Rechy replied to the letter and suggested they have dinner together.

Then began a set of near-meetings between the two men. Vidal first did a "double-take" when he saw Rechy at a book awards ceremony in Los Angeles where "everyone ignored Vidal in that way people do when someone is very famous and they're not." Rechy was in his hustling outfit: Levis, leather jacket—he still has the battered, black one he wore as a hustler in the '50s—and very tight cowboy-style shirt "that I used to be able to pop the buttons off with my chest, without touching them." One day, out of the blue, a mutual acquaintance, phoned at eleven o'clock in the morning and said Vidal wondered if Rechy would like to have lunch that day. "I thought, this is like a summons from…I didn't say the Queen. I may have had better days, but I'm not one to be 'had' for lunch. I said to tell him that no, I wasn't available."

More time passed, then one evening at Vidal's favorite restaurant, Musso and Frank, three years ago Rechy was dining with friends. Vidal entered "looking in bad shape." Rechy asked the waiter to ask Vidal "and the gentleman helping him if they would like a drink as a small indication of my great admiration for his courage and elegance that were unassailable." The waiter, flustered, returned and said that "Mr. Vidal would welcome you joining him." Rechy's dining companion, from *The New Yorker*, begged him, "Oh please, I'd love to see this." But Rechy declined. "I'm not going to respond to another one of his summonses, absolutely not. I asked the waiter to please tell Mr. Vidal that, in the intimation of Elvis Presley, I had just left the restaurant."

Rechy was amused that some of Vidal's obituary writers quoted his review of *Live From Golgotha*, "If God exists and Jesus is his son, then Gore Vidal is going to Hell," but remains intrigued at the original root of Vidal's antipathy towards him. "Maybe because my books are very 'out there,' maybe the discomfort was with someone who was not uncomfortable with being gay, at all." Of course, the biggest irony was that Vidal used hustlers himself, when he was sneering at this novel about a hustler. "I know that was a discomfort for a lot of people: someone who had actually hustled and sold his body on the streets and written about it unabashedly." Vidal and others were writing "from the point of the desirer, I was writing from the point of the 'desire-ee.'"

Rechy thinks critics like Vidal were so rattled because "in the arenas that people like Vidal use hustlers it is because the hustlers are attractive because they are not too literate. I experienced that myself. At the beginning of my hustling career I once lost a contact, a nice guy, by picking up a book on his table by Colette and rifling through it. The man said, 'Do you read Colette?' I said, 'Yes, she's a good writer.' Boom, I got five bucks at the end of it—he had realized maybe that the person he was paying for sex was not so dumb after all. The desire in that situation, how it operates, is based strictly on appearance and fantasy—and the identity of the hustler and everything that goes with that is wiped away the moment you reveal the unforgivable, that the hustler is intelligent. Perhaps Mr. Vidal felt a trace of that with me, I don't know."

Rechy might be right. In *Palimpsest*, Vidal quotes Tennessee Williams approvingly, saying, "It is most disturbing to think that the head beside you on the pillow might be thinking too." The Bird, says Vidal, "had a gift for selecting fine bodies attached to heads usually filled with the bright confetti of lunacy." Once, after his 1967 novel Numbers was published, Rechy was hanging around Griffith Park, where he picked up clients, and a guy said, "You're that guy who wrote that book, aren't you? John Rechy? I don't think that's his real name, because nobody would write a book like that under his real name." Rechy had to smile: he was the writer, who had written about his own experiences, and now a john was telling him someone else had to have written about him and his experiences, because someone like John Rechy could never have written such a thing. "I told him who I was and he was startled and suddenly there was no attraction at all." Rechy's clients wanted him to be "a character, the less intelligent, the more desirable. The role I played was the one people wanted: young and sexy."

Certainly that's what Vidal's great friend Christopher Isherwood wanted when he sent "spies" to look for Rechy "and found me hustling." Isherwood invited Rechy over, but when Isherwood made a move Rechy asked him to leave him alone. Isherwood offered Rechy his guest room, and then tried to climb into bed alongside him. "Eugh no, I can't," said Rechy. "Just go and leave," snapped Isherwood. By a gas station, a john picked him up, "so I made ten bucks: such an irony."

Rechy notes that in the world of the john and hustler, Vidal's sexual world, there is "a lot of ugliness. Some people [like Vidal] felt superiority towards the hustler and yet desire was the common denominator. I often compare it to a battle in which both sides are finally wounded." Rechy has "great empathy for the hustlers who hustled alongside me who didn't write books or live in the Hollywood hills. What happened to them? The people who picked them up have other lives, and there will always be a fresh crew of young hustlers." How did he come to terms with feeling, when he did, of being used and abused? "I have a giant ego," he says with a laugh. "I used to think, 'You're not getting *me*.' I knew that carnivorous world."

Rechy was finally honest about who he was with his partner Michael, who has been with for almost thirty years; when they met Rechy was cruising for business on Santa Monica Boulevard and Michael was lost. The last time Rechy hustled was when he was fifty-seven (he is eighty-two at the time of writing) "and I returned the money, it just seemed inappropriate."

As more open times shifted into view, the post-Stonewall generation of gay writers tried to connect with Vidal. In 1985, the author Felice Picano, then running the Gay Presses of New York, heard *Myra Breckinridge* was out of print. He proposed to Vidal, "not expecting an answer," that the Presses republish it. Vidal replied ("Caro Felice...") that Vintage was looking to republish *Myra* and *Myron* together. "Thereafter followed a bunch of very late at night transatlantic phone calls from him, virtually none about the book," says Picano. "It ended up with him using our offer to get Vintage to do what he wanted. The phone calls were I believe drunken, and were on all kinds of topics, including how stupid America and Americans were and how fat American boys' asses were. I thought they were fine enough at the time."

Picano sent Vidal galleys of his first memoir, *Ambidextrous: The Secret Lives of Children*, hoping for a blurb. None arrived: "The book might have been too much for him as it detailed me and my pals using model airplane glue as drugs and having bi-sex when we were eleven-to-fourteen years old." Vidal wrote back saying, "The only interesting childhood memoir would be of someone like Svetlana Alueyevna, because she was Stalin's daughter." However, several years later Vidal wrote *Palimpsest*, which Picano "thought kind of copied my book. I was never really convinced of the romantic love affair with Jimmie Trimble."

Yet Vidal's gay literary knowledge was acute: he pointed Picano "towards a book he thought we should publish, *The Young and the Evil* by Charles Henri Ford and Parker Tyler, the first really 'gay' novel, published [before *The City and the Pillar*] in 1933. I met Charles who became the gay 'mother' I never had, and Gore was responsible for that."

Picano got the impression Vidal "was repelled by America and was looking for excuses not to come back. I told him about the gay cultural scene of the West Village at that time—we were publishing plays by Harvey Fierstein—and he seemed ambivalent. 'If you come here, I'll introduce these people to you,' I said. He didn't seem enthusiastic, but he didn't mind the idea of *Myra* being published by a gay imprint. I sensed he was drinking during the calls: he would change subject suddenly. He would say how big and beefy Americans were compared to the slim-hipped gay Maurizios of Italy. I told him that was nonsense. In L.A. and New York there were lots of those kinds of men too. I asked him where he was being put when he was in America: Indiana?"

The novelist David Leavitt, whose novels and short stories ushered in a new era of gay literary visibility in the late 1980s and '90s, met Vidal at a 2003 event in honor of *The City and the Pillar*. Leavitt says: "It feels like an artifact now (alongside James Merrill's *The Seraglio*), rather than E.M. Forster's *Maurice*, which feels timeless, But Vidal is a huge hero to me. He comes from a time where being known as a 'gay writer' could leave you marginalized in a side category of special pleading. He was never known as that. He didn't want to be labeled. It meant he could get on to a TV show and confront Buckley."

Vidal was scornful of contemporary gay commentators and firebrands, assuming the limelight in his place. In a note to Sean Strub, he decried Right-leaning columnist and author Andrew Sullivan as "too stupid by half and too opportunistic by one whole..." But he also recognized a kinship with Sullivan, both of them outside the gay activism mainstream and berated for being so. "Larry [Kramer] goes on with him as he did with me—are we expected to fulfill messianic prophecies and restore our people to their rightful home, Sodom, now occupied by Jewish hets?" But Vidal hadn't finished with Sullivan, who "should go back to England where social inferiority is never not put exquisitely to the test."

Some gay writers scorn Vidal in return. Bruce Benderson thinks he was "very ambitious because of his narcissism. I felt he was very in love with his aristocratic heritage, even though it was not as aristocratic as he'd like us to believe. I didn't trust his crusades for objectivity, truth and justice. By pretending he was this uncategorizable bisexual he wasn't being very honest about his homosexuality. OK, he believed in gay acts, not gay people, but part of the reason he developed that theory was because he was half in the closet himself. He didn't want to be thought of as a miserable fag with nothing interesting to say."

For Benderson, Vidal professionally inhabited "an elite community where homosexuality was something not everyone accepted. I think he was like a fake provocateur, dying to be part of that blue-chip background and more but at the same time expressing contempt for it." Benderson, theoretically, agrees with Vidal's contention that one's homosexuality is "petty, like liking chocolate ice cream, and those that build an identity around it are very silly people. There is no such thing as a gay sensibility today." But, according to Benderson, Vidal used these "laudable cultural politics to get ahead and protect himself. I think he was boring, pretentious and shallow. I disliked him most for the society he inhabited, while poking fun at it—like trying to have his cake and eat it. I prefer John Rechy and William Burroughs." His imperially voiced and projected hauteur made Vidal a hypocrite, says Benderson. "He was incredibly grand. It's ironic, in a dark way, that this person, so interested in democracy, multiplicity and the evil effects of power, behaved like he was the Queen of Romania."

Christopher Bram disagrees, praising Vidal's writing. "We regularly hear that Vidal was a great essayist and a terrible novelist and there's no denying that the essay was his strength," Bram says. "But he wrote some excellent novels. *Julian, Myra Breckinridge* and *Burr* are all strong. *Myra* is more about voice than story, but it's a remarkable voice and great fun as well as wonderfully subversive. *Julian* is a literary entertainment worthy of comparison with *I, Claudius* and *Memoirs of Hadrian. Burr* is brilliant, a witty look at American history told in two different voices, old Aaron Burr and young Charlie Schuyler. Both suggest different aspects of Vidal, young and old selves arguing with each other. Yet the real subject is the Founding Fathers and they are brought fully to life, especially Washington and Jefferson. The book is beautifully crafted. The scene where Burr rows Charlie across the Hudson to Weehawken and reenacts the duel with Alexander Hamilton is unforgettably good."

These books all use "Vidal's first-person egotism" to tell their stories, concedes Bram, "but there's nothing wrong with that. The other books are more hit or miss. *The City and the Pillar* is postwar pulp fiction with some good snapshots of contemporary gay life. *Lincoln* has its fans but I think it drowns in talk: a dozen different figures talk about Lincoln while the man himself remains a mystery at the center—deliberately so. Experimental novels like *Duluth* fail, as most experiments do. And most of Vidal's 'Narratives of Empire' books [a heptalogy of historical novels, published between 1973 and 2000; *1876, Empire, Hollywood* among them] are pleasant time-killers, little more. But the man wrote three terrific novels, which is nothing to sneeze at."

One passionate, flinty, confrontational encounter embraces the panoply of gay responses to Vidal: suspicion, anger, celebration, respect and bafflement. In 1992 the playwright, author and activist Larry Kramer interviewed Vidal for *QW* magazine. It is hard, on the surface, to imagine two more different people facing each other as interviewer and subject: Kramer, out, angry, campaigning, furious at the iniquities endured by gay men and those who had died so painfully of AIDS in the face of government indifference and inaction; and Vidal, of undeclared definitive sexuality, no overt freedom fighting for "the cause" to his name, and one who barely mentioned AIDS.

In Sean Strub's forthcoming memoir, he recalls seeing Vidal a few weeks after Kramer had given a speech claiming correspondence between Abraham Lincoln and his one-time bedmate Joshua Speed was evidence of Lincoln's likely homosexuality. Vidal had written a historical novel about Lincoln. "No one will take it seriously now, no matter how convincing the case," Vidal told Strub, "because Kramer's made Lincoln's homosexuality the claim of gay activists with an agenda, rather than the scholarship of serious historians. It will take another generation before this is recognized." Vidal said Lincoln's predecessor, President James Buchanan, the country's only bachelor President, was homosexual; he had lived for fifteen years with William Rufus Devane King, Vice President under Franklin Pierce, Buchanan's predecessor. When Strub noted the span of three consecutive presidencies, Vidal's eyes lit up. "Yes, a cabal!" he said.

Despite their personal and political differences, what an interview Kramer elicits from Vidal, mixing warmth and rancor, revelation and reflection, with Kramer coming close to getting the gay measure of his quarry and Vidal inevitably resisting at every turn. In "The Sadness of Gore Vidal," Kramer begins by noting that Vidal is "one of my heroes and, like me, he's obviously very tired. Of fighting and seeing so little progress. Of raising a voice no one hears with any sufficiency. His voice rises almost automatically to sound angry—to sound the anger that he knows we expect from him...he goes on automatic anger...I identify with him completely. Who has listened to him? What has his wrath made right? The world is further away than ever from his dream. He calls me the romantic. I protest. He is as romantic as I am." Their conversation is both "great fun" and "exceedingly moving."

Kramer says he wants to talk about homosexuality, Vidal responds drily that it is a startling subject to bring up. He repeats that there is "no such thing as a homosexual person," only homosexual acts. "Is anybody one-hundred percent one thing or the other. I rather doubt it. Is anybody fifty-fifty? I rather doubt that too...What I'm preaching is: don't be ghettoized, don't be categorized. Every state tries to categorize its citizens in order to assert control of them." Kramer tells him that many gays want to be known as gay, that there's safety in numbers. "Well, I disapprove," says Vidal. He says Tennessee Williams was asked why he didn't make his characters queer and Williams had responded, "Why should I diminish my audience even more than it is?" Vidal adds he's written about homosexuality, "but it's not the center of my life." Kramer, writing in 1992 with the "culture wars" around homosexuality in full cry, says, "Well, I feel now this is the center of our lives and the center of most gay writers."

However, Vidal approves of ACT UP's campaign of civil disobedience: "I approve of successful violence, not unsuccessful." Vidal suggests: "Why don't you fuck Bush and give him AIDS? And say, 'This will happen to the next president and the next president and the next?'" Kramer says that ACT UP had "talked around a few ideas of that nature."

Kramer notes Vidal hasn't spoken much about AIDS. "I'm not a virologist," Vidal replies. "I'm not a hand-wringer. If I don't have anything useful to say, what am I to say? It's a terrible thing. Of course it is." He mentions Hugh Steers, his nephew, who by then had lived with a positive diagnosis for eight years "and that obviously brought it home dramatically for me." So write an essay "of great strength and anger" as a testament to Hugh, says Kramer—echoing Hugh's own heartfelt request to Vidal he step into the same breach. Vidal says it's better he attacks the national security state, Supreme Court and Jesus Christ. No, says Kramer, you've done all that, "we don't know how you feel on this new issue which is perhaps closer to home and much more personal." Vidal answers, "That is wrong in my view. Why get upset only when it touches you personally?" Kramer says, "I never became political *until* it touched me personally."

All Vidal says to interviewers who bring up the subject of his private life is, "Everyone is bisexual." Kramer says he's never seen a headline saying "Gore Vidal is homosexual." "Because I don't believe in it," says Vidal. "But Gore, you *are* gay," counters Kramer. "You've lived with a man for forty years or something, and everyone who knows you personally knows you're gay. And I think *you* think of yourself as gay." Vidal says he doesn't think of himself in those categories, then tells Kramer he's a "subjective and romantic writer," while Vidal is "objective and classical." Kramer tells Vidal, rightly, he is a romantic. "It takes a romantic to be so angry." Vidal says he was brought up with an "over-developed sense of justice—and not only about myself. I have a general view that this is *my* country. My family helped start it, and we've been in political life of one kind or another since the 1690s."

Kramer says he'd rather have Vidal "fighting for your heart—exploring what it means to be a gay man at age sixty five in the world today." Vidal corrects him: "Sixty seven...I never thought it was a big deal." Kramer implores Vidal, "We just want you, whole-heartedly and full blown—if you'll pardon the pun—on *our* team." Vidal says, "I *am* on your team. After all, I've been there all along." Then Vidal cuts brilliantly across the intensity of proceedings, telling Kramer: "They have very good dessert here." Kramer, still flowing in the stream of the main conversation, says he thinks Vidal is getting sharper and wiser and certainly no less angry. Vidal gruffly assents: "I'll say." Kramer supplies a warm and emphatic payoff. "And you must never stop," he tells Vidal, one freedom fighter to another.

Chapter Thirteen

Losing Howard, Losing Himself

Howard Austen was diagnosed with lung cancer in 1999. In *Point to Point Navigation*, Vidal describes the cancer recurring in his partner's brain. Vidal chartered a private plane to bring Austen back from Rome to the US for treatment. "Gore spent God knows how much money and effort to save Howard from that terrible cancer," recalls Claire Bloom. Vidal told me he wished he'd never moved back to the US from Ravello, but he did so, say his friends, for Austen who needed the best medical care available.

The couple was tentative in front of friends, talking about Austen's illness. Donald Gislason, their Ravello housesitter, remembers that Vidal asked Austen "Why did you tell him?" when Austen told Gislason he was dying of cancer. Arlyne Reingold, Austen's sister, remembers her brother "really didn't talk about dying," remaining focused on completing his treatment. "Smoking is a bummer," sighs Scotty Bowers, speaking of Austen's illness. "Every smoker I know is dead already. If Rock Hudson had not died of AIDS he would have died of smoking: he'd smoke twenty in half an hour."

Vidal was grumpy and dissatisfied, even with Austen's support and care. When Steven Abbott and his partner Jim Stephens met the couple in Ravello in 2001, Abbott says, "I remember thinking when Howard was still alive, 'They have everything you could possibly want, including a formidable literary legacy,' but Gore was so different from how he was when I first met him when he was on top of the world, fully engaged as a literary megastar. He was witty and charming then."

His writing, thinks Abbott, changed around 1990 with *Hollywood*. *The Golden Age*, published in 2000, the last of the "Narratives of Empire" novels, wasn't "a great book to cap off this chronicle. His essays continued to boost his career, and in 1998

The Smithsonian Institution became a bestseller. I could never get Gore to understand how many people loved and respected him. People saw him as a spiritual father of gay liberation, but if you ever tried to express that, he would say he didn't want to go there."

Abbott and Stephens visited Vidal one night in Los Angeles while Austen was in hospital receiving cancer treatment. "He made it clear he wanted company that night. The house was full of flowers for Howard's return the next morning. He was very distressed about Howard's condition." Abbott and Stephens returned the next day to a "joyous house" and the sight of Austen at the top of the stairs and Vidal at the bottom. "Jim and I drew a Romeo and Juliet line between them," Abbott recalls. "They didn't say 'darling' and 'I love you,' but you could see the connection between them—the love or relief or whatever it was."

However stoic he appeared, Vidal was "terrified" when Austen was dying, says Burr Steers. "People thought Gore would die sooner, but Howard was a smoker. Howard cut people short when they started reminiscing or talking about dying or saying good-bye or some flowery memory and say, 'Oh that's bullshit.' Howard was very sweet, but outwardly that tough Bronx thing was very much there."

Vidal caught, heartbreakingly, the last segment of Austen's life in the searing chapter devoted to Austen in *Point to Point Navigation*. Vidal refers to him first, finally after his death and fifty-three years together, as his partner (with a typically clenched Vidalian qualifier, "as the politically correct call it"). They were planning a cruise from Salerno to the Greek islands and Turkish coast, with Vidal doing some lectures on board. Suddenly, Vidal's depth of his feeling for Austen becomes clear as he writes about his partner's decline and death. Austen "remains permanently present in my memory," Vidal wrote, revealing Austen's succession of illnesses: peritonitis, which almost killed him, then lung cancer, an operation (Austen's last words before it: "Well, it's been great"), then the good news he was cancer-free in the lungs, then a fall coming out of the pool that signaled Austen's cancer had spread to the brain.

As Vidal left Austen's hospital room one night, Austen said, "Kiss me." Vidal wrote: "I did. On the lips, something we'd not done for fifty years." Austen rallied again and winked to Vidal who imagined the old men who sit outside Ravello's post office; when one of them dies, they all move down a place on the bench: "He was now close to the corner." Austen would hallucinate and rage: "Why is it always about you?" he said to Vidal, apropos of nothing Vidal had said, but still—oddly—deserving of the admonishment. "I don't think I want to do that again," Austen said of radiation treatment; he still smoked when his oxygen tank was turned off.

One morning Austen announced to Vidal, "At first light the angel of death, all in white, arrived with the sun." Austen sang with his nurse, a former piano prodigy, accompanying him: "Cole Porter, Sondheim, and his favorite 'Our Love Is Here to Stay' echoed through the house at the end," Vidal wrote, as well as a live recording of a Barbra Streisand concert. Vidal said they had introduced her to Beluga caviar at Paul Newman's fortieth birthday. Austen asked Vidal how old he was. Seventy-four, Vidal replied. "That's when people die, isn't it?" Vidal said that he hadn't and so far Austen hadn't. Austen, looking puzzled, said, "Didn't it go by awfully fast?" "Of course it had," writes Vidal. "We had been too happy, and the gods cannot bear the happiness of mortals."

Vidal tried to find "reasons to hope." He noted that the hospital bed Austen was ensconced in made holding hands difficult. One night after the evening news, which they often watched together, Vidal asked, "Don't you want to talk?" Austen shook his head, no: "Because there's too much to say." The men celebrated the color of what Austen was coughing up, going from green to beige. When the nurse alerted Vidal that Austen had stopped breathing on September 22, 2003, Vidal approached his partner: "The eyes were open and very clear. I'd forgotten what a beautiful gray they were—illness and medicine had regularly glazed them over; now they were bright and attentive and he was watching me, consciously, through long lashes." The optic nerves were still sending messages after the heart and lung had stopped. "So we stared at each other at the end." Vidal asked, "Can you hear me? I know you can see me." Vidal wrote that "there was no breath for speech, he now had a sort of wry wise-guy from the Bronx expression on his face, which said clearly to me who knew all his expressions, 'So this is the big fucking deal everyone goes on about.'"

Austen's nurse wept, but "the WASP glacier had closed over my head," recorded Vidal. He pulled back the sheet covering Austen to see "those clear gray eyes" once more, "but the substance of the eyeballs had collapsed and two gelatinous streaks of the sort snails make had coursed down his cheeks." In a "frustration dream" that night Vidal saw him and Austen in a side street in Rome where the entrance to their home should have been but wasn't. Austen grabbed a handful of fava beans and started shelling and eating them; the Pythagorean cult said each bean contained the soul of someone dead waiting to be reborn. Was Austen preparing for rebirth, Vidal wonders.

"Gore was really shattered when Howard died: they were very much a team," says Burr Steers. "They were as close as any married couple, it was a really tight relationship. They had a shorthand. They were connected in a fundamental way. Howard took the piss out of him. Howard was his gatekeeper. He really protected Gore. Howard was no bullshit. Gore lost a big chunk of himself when Howard died. He couldn't really function as a person on his own." Jean Stein says that as puzzling as their relationship was, "They were very caring with each other. It broke his heart when Howard died. Gore was devastated."

Steers recalls that taking Austen's ashes to bury in his plot in Washington's Rock Creek Cemetery, alongside Vidal and near Trimble, was "an intense experience. Emotionally he was unsettled, and he just got obliterated at the bar of the Willard Hotel where we were staying. It wasn't drinking like you've ever seen it. My grandmother was the same way." Vidal went to Washington with his nephew and his friends Barbara Epstein and Boaty Boatwright, who recalls, "After we put Howard's ashes into the ground we left Gore there a moment to contemplate. When he showed us Jimmie's grave he said, 'This is the other person in my life.' I remember thinking, 'He's managed to get them as close to each other as he could.' He handled his business affairs so badly and changed his will after feuding with people, but he did make the right instructions about the grave."

Susan Sarandon says Austen's death affected Vidal profoundly. "It was such a huge thing that opened up in Gore when Howard passed. He expressed to me that he missed him, and he talked of his own final days. He had never talked about it before, or shown me this emotional vulnerability. Nobody thought Howard would go first. He seemed the stronger of the two and everyone was worried about what Gore would do without him. Paul's [Newman] death [in 2008] was a big thing for him too." In Ravello, his maid and cook, Rita Calce, recalls Vidal would sit by the pool and worry about what he would do without Austen. After Austen died, he cried. Calce said he became "a different person." He drank more and felt he could not keep the house because it contained too many memories of Austen. Vidal finally sold La Rondinaia in 2005.

Arlyne Reingold, Austen's sister, sat with Vidal as tears rolled down his cheeks. They would speak every couple of weeks, him telling her "I miss him, I miss Howard." "He lost half of himself after Howard died," says Burr Steers. "He couldn't really function, do the most basic things." Matt Tyrnauer says, "Howard's death ended the main chapter of Gore's existence pretty much. Gore was in perpetual mourning after Howard died." His drinking, says Tyrnauer, "became epic. He drank after he finished work, Macallan 12 [a single malt Scotch] usually. He didn't stop till he collapsed. After Howard died I spent a lot of time with him. He was in deep mourning and grieved very openly. He talked about how sweet Howard was, how much he missed him. He wore a ring of Howard's. He talked about how wonderful and talented he was. He'd listen to recordings of him singing on CD, which he'd listen to again and again."

Scotty Bowers would go over to Vidal's house for supper, then afterwards Vidal would put on the CDs; Claire Bloom also remembers this. Bowers, says, "He would sit there with tears in his eyes, and I would hold his hand, run through ten or twelve songs, then begin the CD again. Pretty soon it was four in the morning, and there were still tears in his eyes. He never said, 'I miss him,' says Bowers, but rather, 'Howard's great.' When he was sad he talked about happy things." Matt Tyrnauer says, "Howard never got adulation when he was alive but he did after he died, not unlike Jimmie Trimble. Presumably Gore never told Jimmie what he wanted to tell him, and he never told Howard what he wanted to tell him."

Tyrnauer thinks it "very unlikely that he told Howard he loved him. Sadly it's inconceivable. That's not what Gore Vidal did. He felt he couldn't. He didn't believe in romantic love and didn't want to frame that relationship as a love relationship. I think it might have been out of fear that if he did love Howard and expressed it, it might have ended because romantic love to him had an ephemeral quality. As long as he didn't say, 'I love you, Howard', Howard would continue to be there and love him. He said once that love doesn't exist and that when you say to someone, 'I love you,' you're saying 'I love you almost as much as I love myself.'"

"Gore was not interested in the end in romantic love," Tyrnauer continues. When in *Palimpsest* Vidal described that he briefly thought the dancer Harold Lang "was the new Jimmie," says Tyrnauer, "there is no higher compliment. If you're an ambitious, narcissistic, insecure person in a very competitive field, to have someone on an equal footing as you in a relationship, who you have to tend to, is not tenable. You don't have the time to worry if their socks are dry or if there's food in the refrigerator. That's not conceivable. I think Gore did want love but couldn't deal with the fact he couldn't. Because of his narcissism he couldn't return it and I think that hurt him deeply. Howard was as close as he was going to get, because that was unconditional in a certain way or close to it. As cruel as he was to him, Howard never went away. So it worked, he could have a kind of master/slave dynamic and Howard would not leave and he was amusing and he made the trains run on time. That was a form of love for him, but it wasn't romantic love."

Vidal was loving and capable of love, thinks Fabian Bouthillette, his former caregiver. "Would he take you by the hands and stare into your eyes? He did not. But he was a closet romantic. When it came down to it, he couldn't express it with the man he shared life-long intimacy with. Howard was the closest he came. Maybe he later realized he should have expressed that. If there was an uneasiness in Gore it was around romanticism, especially with Howard and Jimmie. Several times in the Beverly Hills Hotel, Gore would break down talking about Howard. I'm speculating but maybe he realized he had taken him for granted. I think he had come to realize that, and it was on his mind every day. Howard was the sweetest man he ever knew, he said. He talked about Howard had died singing and he had found Howard dead in Howard's room."

At the Beverly Hills Hotel he would tell Bouthillette, always at the same table he had beside the piano, how Howard "was the life of the party and how he would sing songs with the pianist. He regretted not telling Howard that he loved him, I think." Lucian Truscott IV, author of *Dress Gray*, which Vidal adapted for television, told Bouthillette that Vidal "was a closet romantic and that's true. He was a very emotional man, but like a typical man he didn't let that emotion out."

Claire Bloom says, "Gore was devastated by Howard's death." "Afterwards it was 'Howard this, Howard that,' says Michael Childers. "I have a photograph I'd taken in the late '70s of Howard, he and Rat. Gore was so moved by it." Edmund White thinks Vidal, despite his public disavowal of Austen's role in his life when he was alive, "probably had a very intimate relationship with him and was probably very devoted to him. He was a bit like Tennessee Williams, who fell apart after his man-friend [Frank Merlo] died. Both men were kept reasonable by their lovers and fell apart when they died." Nina Straight, says, "Only Howard could scream at Gore like a real fishwife. When Howard stopped drinking in the middle half of the '90s, then when he had emphysema and lung cancer, he'd force Gore to go to bed earlier."

After Austen died, Vidal told Scotty Bowers, "'I was really in love with Howard.' He'd cry. 'I didn't realize how much I loved Howard until now that he's gone,' he'd say. He'd sit there with tears in his eyes for ten to fifteen minutes. I sat there playing with his big yellow kitty. It didn't surprise me: many people don't realize until someone has gone how much they love or care about them…like having a little doggy who you love and don't realize until they're gone that you've taken them for granted." Vidal's friend Patty Dryden says, "I think it was a generational thing: men of his generation didn't declare love." Underneath all Vidal's bravado and wit, Jean Stein says, "there was his desperate loneliness. It got more severe after Howard's death." Vidal wrote to Judith Harris saying "he couldn't see how to go on," says Harris. "He was in despair."

Vidal received a thousand letters of condolence after Austen's death, he told Dryden. "It was a huge, huge loss when Howard died. He was emotional when he talked about Howard. He told me he had given Howard an allowance, which Howard had grown into a large sum when he died: Gore mentioned a figure of $3 million. When Howard died, it was the biggest disappointment of his life, and I just wanted to spoil and pamper him." Vidal was "terribly distraught" after Austen's death," says Barbara Howar. "He could make Gore laugh. There were like two old pals, very different. Howard was more social, but they were like comrades. Gore drank. He was sad and alone. But he didn't run around and wring his hands. The night Howard died, I went round there and the cook [Norberto Nierras] told me Gore had gone out for dinner."

John Rechy, having sent Vidal a condolence note, received a "very touching letter" in response that "life allowed certain things only to take them away." Jay Parini recalls that after Howard died "Gore completely fell apart, his mental capacity shrank, his delusional qualities increased. I took him back to Ravello three years ago. He was drinking so heavily. He could walk but preferred the wheelchair. He knew he was going to die soon, 'the sooner the better,' he said. He certainly fought to keep living when dying, but after Howard died he didn't want to live. He was lonely, he had lost the love of his life; it shows you marriage is about companionship just as much as sex."

Vidal's decline accelerated after Austen's death: gone was his gatekeeper, organizer, caregiver, moderator, partner, love. "These rehearsals for death take more and more out of one until at the end there is, I suspect, nothing at all left except Howard's old dressing gown hanging on the back of his bathroom door, a refuge for moths," Vidal wrote in 2006. He had sold La Rondinaia to a group of investors for around eighteen million dollars. In these later years, growing more isolated and unhappy, he employed handsome male assistants, like Muzius Dietzmann and Fabian Bouthillette. "He surrounded himself with young men: typically straight, handsome and strong. There was no sexual element at all," says Parini. Another friend adds: "Here was this guy in his eighties and he had these devoted adjutants. These weren't bunnies or Gore Vidal's two prostitutes. These guys were really devoted to Gore. It wasn't a matter of 'Stand in the background and look pretty.'"

"Muzius was very splendid, a first class guy, very, very heterosexual," says Parini. "He's married with children now. Fabi was a very smart ex-sailor." Other friends raise their eyebrows at the mention of both men's names, as if they cannot believe there wasn't something sexual going on between Vidal and these young men. Dietzmann worked for Vidal for over ten years. He called Muzius "my son," says Patty Dryden. "There was probably some wishful sexual thinking on Gore's part towards these young guys," says Nina Straight. "Maybe he'd ask them to take off their pants or something. He used to like to say, 'They're all boy'— i.e., they're all hetero macho men, they're all Jimmie Trimble." One of Vidal's friends told me Bouthillette "occasionally wore his uniform around the house and Gore called him 'my naval adjutant.' He treated him like a soldier fantasy."

Arianna Huffington, chair, president and editor-in-chief of the Huffington Post Media Group, called Dietzmann "perhaps the most beautiful man I've ever seen." Most pivotally, he became Austen's caregiver as he fought and then succumbed to cancer. "Muzius is a wonderful person," says Matt Tyrnauer. "He became like a son to Gore. Clearly he cared for him, although, as chilly as he was, Gore would never share that. I think he liked to imagine the great times Muzius was having as a sexual athlete, and he would discuss that. He was very proud of Muzius's conquests and made sure you knew." Dietzmann, who has two young daughters, mulled contributing to this book—"I am not sure to be ready for your project, to be able to avoid saying something stupid or even worse nothing interesting at all"—and then declined to speak.

Bouthillette had been a twenty-eight-year-old lieutenant in the Navy and part of the protest organization Iraq Veterans Against the War when he met Vidal in November 2008. "I was super-angry, trying to adapt to civilian life after the military in Los Angeles," he tells me. They were introduced by a mutual friend, Jean Stein. "I went to his place, drank Scotch and talked for, like, ten years," Bouthillette says. After that, for two months, they had dinner around three times a week, bonding over the memoirs of Ulysses S. Grant, politics, American and military history and veterans. "I became his assistant, but he introduced me as his naval attaché or 'Fabian, a lieutenant in the Navy who was head of the veterans' anti-war movement.' He wanted me to talk about military culture and why veterans were against the war. His public persona was snobby and 'aristocrat-y' and he liked fights, but to me he was one of the kindest people I have ever known. He really took me under his wing."

At Outpost Drive, Bouthillette wore T-shirts, shorts and walked around barefoot, watching "too much CNN and griping about the wars." At night he and Vidal would stay up till midnight or one o' clock, they would go to the Beverly Hills Hotel once or twice a week, Bouthillette says he managed Vidal's medication and spoke with his doctors. "Gore was kind of a dude in a way, his inner boy never went away," says Bouthillette. "He was very in tune with my character and could tell I was a little shy."

Some of Vidal's friends also raise eyebrows at that: they think the young man knew that Vidal sexually desired him and responded, or played up to, it in some way. One evening Jean Stein invited Vidal to dinner with a couple and their daughter, and Vidal was "obsessed with the idea of the young woman and Muzius making out together," Stein tells me. "My impression was that the girl didn't count and that Gore was not so secretly obsessing about Muzius. He had to have been attracted to Muzius. I remember years earlier staying with Gore and Howard at their house on Outpost, and there was rough trade coming round to see them. The bell would ring, I would retreat. In the last years there was a lot of weird, murky stuff going on. I hope Gore had fun at least."

Was there a sexual dynamic between Vidal and Bouthillette? "It wasn't anything overt," insists Bouthillette. "Yes, I was an attractive guy and he responded to that. He wanted someone with competence to take care of him and with the social grace to look good while doing it, and I guess I had that. He was in a wheelchair and needed someone to be with him wherever he went. I could do the job of personal assistant and wheelchair-pusher and look good doing it. Of course he appreciated that: Gore always got what he wanted."

Did they have any kind of sex? "We had a very intimate, non-sexual relationship," says Bouthillette. "I was the manifestation of a young, strapping guy to push him around, he was my manifestation of a role model to help me. He felt comfortable with me. I had to put my hands on him a lot and he trusted me and for that I loved him. I loved him in the real sense of that word love. Of course he liked to have beautiful young men around. I had people tell me Gore was smitten with me. I was completely taken with him too."

Vidal would argue strenuously against Bouthillette's hetero-sexuality. Bouthillette would reply, "I don't know what to tell you, Gore, I like to have sex with women." No," Vidal would tell him, "you're fooling yourself." But the author had no problem with Bouthillette and Dietzmann "hooking up with women" when they travelled together in Europe—indeed he would boast of his young staff's conquests. "He did tell me that he loved me, and that I was one of the only people he had loved," Bouthillette says. "I can't prove that and I know people could say I am an assistant seeking attention, but it's true." Bouthillette never saw any hustlers in Out-post Drive. "I think he would have liked to have been sexual in those last years, but there's no way he could have. He wasn't phys-ically able. I stumbled on his porn collection one day: it was mostly

Hispanic, and I'm half Puerto Rican so we joked about that. He would ask, 'Are you sure you're not into guys?' 'Gore, stop it,' I would say. I would leave porn on for him to watch when I left him at night. He enjoyed that."

Bouthillette indulged Vidal's smutty humor. After Vidal bought a Japanese bidet and Bouthillette, who had used them in the Navy, went to go to the toilet one day, Vidal said, "Number one or number two?" "Number two," replied Bouthillette. "Why don't you use my bidet?" Vidal suggested. Bouthillette did and Vidal asked if he had liked it. "It became an inside joke. 'How was the bidet?' he'd say. 'Oh, it was glorious,' I'd say. 'Do you feel nice and clean?' he'd say. 'Better than ever,' I'd say."

For Bouthillette, Vidal "was a hundred years ahead of his time" in how he viewed sexuality. "In a hundred years time we'll get to the point where love can be expressed whichever way. We would have long conversations about it. He would say, 'You understand love, but you only want to have sex with women?' 'Gore,' I'd say, 'I'm sorry, I don't know what to tell you. I can't get sexually interested in a man.' 'With guys,' he would say, 'it's all about developed quadriceps, which is what Lincoln would have liked.' Gore definitely preferred men to women."

Vidal was politically despondent and professionally unfulfilled, adds Bouthillette. "By the late 1990s he was in a very peaceful place, I think, but the election of Bush, invasion of Iraq, Howard's death, and his own deteriorating physical health just finished him. He thought America was in the shitter, which hurt him deeply. I'd say, 'Gore, you're the most famous American of the twentieth century, what else do you want?' 'Well, I want to be president,' he'd reply. Hell yeah, Gore Vidal would have been the best president America ever had," says Bouthillette, "but American society would never have elected him. I believe he was conscious of the fact that discussion of his sexuality would have prohibited him from taking political office."

In a note to Sean Strub on December 12, 2000, when the Supreme Court rubber-stamped George W. Bush as the winner of that year's presidential election over Al Gore, Vidal wrote, "I'm writing this on the day your Catholic Justices finally folded our Protestant republic—Jefferson & Adams foresaw this in their last years and deplored the decision to allow the Jesuits in. Well, it was a fair run. Now Authority will rule as the One God declaims."

Vidal observed presidential office-holders balefully, he told me in 2009. "The only one I knew well was Kennedy, but he didn't impress me as a good president. It's like asking, 'What do I think of my brother?' It's complicated. I liked him to the end, but he wrecked his chances with the Bay of Pigs and Suez crises, and because everyone was so keen to elect Bobby once Jack had gone, lies started to be told about him—that he was the greatest and the King of Camelot." He felt strongly that the right-wing had hijacked America, proclaiming the "War on Terror" an abstract, baseless concept, a bit like saying "the war on dandruff." The catastrophe of 9/11 had been used by the neo-conservative movement as "the basis for a *coup d'état*." Burr Steers told me that after his criticism of the US government became more voluble, post 9/11, Vidal was removed from planes, and even claimed his water and power supply were being "stolen" after he installed solar panels at home.

Religious mania had infected the political bloodstream and America had become corrosively isolationist, Vidal told me. "Ask an American what they know about Sweden and they'd say, 'They live well but they're all alcoholics.' In fact, a Scandinavian system could have benefited us many times over." Instead, America for him had "no intellectual class" and was "rotting away at a funereal pace. We'll have a military dictatorship fairly soon, on the basis that nobody else can hold everything together. Obama would have been better off focusing on educating the American people. His problem is being over-educated. He doesn't realize how dim-witted and ignorant his audience is. Benjamin Franklin said that the system would fail because of the corruption of the people and that happened under Bush." Vidal added, "Don't ever make the mistake with people like me thinking we are looking for heroes. There aren't any and if there were, they would be killed immediately. I'm never surprised by bad behavior. I expect it." Vidal's depression was personal and political: his life was wasting away and so, he felt, was his country.

In 2008, Vidal switched allegiance from Hillary Clinton to Barack Obama during the Democratic nomination process for president. In 2009, after Obama's presidential election victory, he told me when we met in London that he had changed his mind again. Obama was doing "dreadfully. I was hopeful. He was the most intelligent person we've had in that position for a long time. But he's inexperienced. He has a total inability to understand military matters. He's acting as if Afghanistan is the magic talisman: solve that and you solve terrorism."

Vidal's all-consuming disillusion struck me. Frail but angry, he was being physically assisted by Dietzmann and Bouthillette. America should leave Afghanistan, he told me. "We've failed in every other aspect of our effort of conquering the Middle East or whatever you want to call it." The "War on Terror" was "made up," Vidal said. "The whole thing was PR, just like 'weapons of mass destruction.' It has wrecked the airline business, which my father founded in the 1930s. He'd be cutting his wrists. Now when you fly you're both scared to death and bored to death, a most disagreeable combination. One thing I have hated all my life are LIARS, and I live in a nation of them. It was not always the case. I don't demand honor, that can be lies too. I don't say there was a golden age, but there was an age of general intelligence. We had a watchdog, the media."

Was the media too supine, I asked him. "Would that it was. They're busy preparing us for an Iranian war." He retained some optimism about Obama "because he doesn't lie. We know the fool from Arizona [as he calls John McCain] is a liar. We never got the real story of how McCain crashed his plane [in 1967 near Hanoi, North Vietnam] and was held captive."

Vidal originally became pro-Obama because he grew up in "a black city" (meaning Washington), as well as being impressed by Obama's intelligence. "But he believes the generals. Even Bush knew the way to win a general was to give him another star. Obama believes the Republican Party is a party when in fact it's a mindset, like Hitler Youth, based on hatred—religious hatred, racial hatred. When you foreigners hear the word 'conservative' you think of kindly old men hunting foxes. They're not, they're fascists."

Obama was "fucking up" healthcare reform, Vidal said. "I don't know how because the country wanted it. We'll never see it happen." Well, Vidal seems to have been wrong about that. As for Obama's wider vision, Vidal said, "Maybe he doesn't have one, not to imply he is a fraud. He loves quoting Lincoln and there's a great Lincoln quote from a letter he wrote to one of his generals in the South after the Civil War. 'I am President of the United States. I have full overall power and never forget it, because I will exercise it.' That's what Obama needs—a bit of Lincoln's *chill*." Had he met Obama? "No," he said quietly, "I've had my time with presidents." Vidal raised his fingers to signify a gun and muttered, "Bang bang." He was referring to the possibility of Obama being assassinated. "Just a mysterious lone gunman lurking in the shadows of the capital," he said in what I remember as a wry, dreamy way.

In 2009 Vidal believed, as he had originally, Hillary Clinton would be the better president. "Hillary knows more about the world and what to do with the generals," Vidal told me. "History has proven when the girls get involved, they're good at it. Elizabeth I knew Raleigh would be a good man to give a ship to." The Republicans would win the next election, Vidal believed; though for him there was little difference between the parties. "Remember the coup d'état of 2000 when the Supreme Court fixed the *selection*, not election, of the stupidest man in the country, Mr. Bush."

There was a period when Vidal "realized he was losing his mind then stopped realizing that," says Bouthillette. "It was very sad. The alcohol physically incapacitated him, it was long, drawn out. The world was collapsing around him." When Felice Picano moved to L.A., he reconnected with Don Bachardy, Christopher Isherwood's partner. "He often has celebrity-filled dinner parties as he seems to know everyone famous." At one with Jacqueline Bisset and Brian Bedford, just after Vidal had moved back to L.A. for Austen to die there, Picano said "something about Gore being here, figuring they must know each other. Dead silence greeted the remark and then Brian changed the subject. When I was walking Jackie to her car after, she said, 'Felice, you ought to know that Gore burned all of his bridges in this town.'"

If you visited Vidal at home, the vibe from him, says Matt Tyrnauer, was "I'm going to sit here and talk until I collapse and you are going to sit across from me and listen and engage." That's what Vidal needed after Austen's death, "when there was no one to fill that vacuum. Gore could be up for hours talking and you'd just listen. Howard would just have said, 'Gore, go fuck yourself, I'm going to my room.' Muzius really managed his life."

Was Vidal depressed, I asked his friends? "Yes, that's why he drank so much, although that made him morose," says Jay Parini. "He worked and travelled so he wouldn't get depressed or morose. I once asked him if he'd considered therapy. He told me, 'It would never work with me as I have no unconscious.' He thought everything he did was conscious. I think he was a clinical narcissist, not just an egotist—he was one of those too—but he was desperate for reflection. He needed to see himself in the mirror of other people. He needed endless reinforcement. He felt completely erased. He would say, 'The great eraser has struck again,' when something like a piece in the *New York Review of Books* about historical novels ran but didn't mention his. Warding off 'the great eraser' led to an amazing productivity; he really was Sisyphus rolling that stone up the hill." In 2000 Vidal said, "Part of my being erased, which goes on and on, is that nobody knows what it is I've done. One ends up with a famous name but nobody has any idea why." Many student theses had been "aborted" by professors who thought him a "queer, Communist, or anti-Semite."

Of course, as the many obituaries and commentaries after he died revealed, Vidal was far from "erased"; the problem was no glory was great enough for his supersized ego and omnipresent sense that he had been cheated out of greatness, out of being president. He wasn't appreciated or valued or prized enough, he felt; despite all the fabulous people and parties, despite his public standing and fame, despite the prizes and books with his name bigger than the titles themselves, he had not risen high enough. And at the root of this scratchy sense of erasure, of not reaching that ultimate White House peak, as Vidal sometimes alluded to and then brusquely brushed off, was his troublesome homosexuality and how he had expressed it so soon into his career and so tellingly in *The City and the Pillar*.

Vidal never reconciled the opposites that the novel's early notoriety brought him: it had made him and defined him and, contrarian as he was, he then made it a life mission never to be defined, captured, or contained. Instead, he would create his own self, no matter how awkwardly his left-wing radicalism sat alongside his patrician sense of entitlement, or his claim of bisexuality jarred alongside a lifetime of homosexuality, or what the implications were of calling his devoted partner his "friend." He was frustrated he wasn't loved enough and cherished enough, for his talents and brilliance. So damn all conventions, Vidal would do it his way.

Inevitably, Vidal had a whimsical sense of his mortality. Fifteen years before he died, he told Sean Strub, then suffering from Kaposi's sarcoma, "At seventy-one we do occupy the same boat, though I need not look for a lesion—only listen for a marble rolling loose and lost." He would say to his half-sister Nina that he would wake in the early hours "and in a great flash feel time's winged wastebasket and think, 'Oh dear, I better get a hustle on.'" Hubert de la Bouillerie, son of Elinor Pruder and friend of Vidal's, recalls Vidal and Mailer drinking later in life "and saying the publishing industry had turned its back on them, that they weren't getting the respect that they deserved." In 1994, Vidal reminisced with Allen Ginsberg about Kerouac, Buddhism, and Bowles. "We are all fading, at different speeds, to black…After a certain age—eighty? (free of the cruel and insane master, sex)—one is soon going to be free of the greatest tyrant of all, life itself."

Boaty Boatwright told Vidal she wished he'd sell the Outpost Drive house and stay at a bungalow in the Beverly Hills Hotel where he could sing a lot at the piano. Vidal told Boatwright he had invested a lot of money and after financial giant AIG collapsed in 2008 she called him, worried he had lost funds, but he told her he had been joking about investing large sums: "I'm not sure that he was," she says today.

After Austen's death Vidal still used hustlers, "though not in the last year," says Scotty Bowers. "He was in a wheelchair and not really able to move. But he still wanted to see people. I would go to the house and sit with him. Sometimes there would be guys there, in their thirties and handsome, he had met. Nothing happened. He thought he wanted someone in bed, but Gore just wanted company. We'd talk, have four, five, six drinks and soon Gore would fall asleep. In the last couple of years he was not in the position to have sex. One of the guys he thought was wonderful. Gore held his hand and talked to him about knowing me for so long, and then after a couple more drinks, halfway into a conversation, he'd fall asleep. He'd drink wine, Scotch, Portuguese port, and I'd sit there and think, 'He hasn't got up to take a piss.'"

Bowers was not the only pimp Vidal used in his later years. Bowers says he also employed the services of Dave Damon, who had a small statues and ceramics store in West Hollywood. (Damon died in 2005.) "Dave cruised for numerous people, and picked up people every day," says Bowers. "He was one of the best cruisers in world and such a nice guy. He was out picking people up all the fucking time. Gore always agreed with me that Dave was one of greatest picker-uppers there ever was. We were different in that the people I used I knew personally, Dave had no fucking idea who he was sending round to you, but Gore used Dave for years."

Vidal could still charm and humor. The painter Juan Bastos recalls his 2006 visit to Outpost Drive with great affection. "I was supposed to be there for ten minutes, to take some pictures for preparation to do the portrait. It was three in the afternoon and he said, 'What would you like to drink? Gin, whisky, vodka?' I said a glass of water would be fine." Bastos mentioned growing up in Bolivia without TV in 1969, and reading a lot, including Hermann Hesse. Vidal responded, "Hesse was popular here in the '50s...he's good, but I find him a bit sugary." Bastos said his favorite writer was Thomas Mann, that he hadn't been able to put Mann's 1924 landmark novel, *The Magic Mountain*, down and read it again after he had finished it. Vidal said he had done the same. But then Bastos committed two literary faux pas: he confused Faulkner with Saul Bellow and didn't know the name of Thomas Mann's last novel [*The Black Swan*, published in 1954, or the unfinished *Confessions of Felix Krull*]. Vidal said, "You should be doing some more reading, young man, rather than hanging out with old queens like me." Vidal describing himself as an "old queen": he was mellowing.

On the table was a picture of Jacqueline Kennedy at the White House, with a dedication to Vidal, says Bastos. "It read something like, 'Gore, it's impossible to keep this serious when one is with you, Jackie.'" Vidal said the picture had been in a drawer for years: "I don't like the woman, but Howard did. Howard said, 'Let's frame Jackie,' so we did. He's no longer with us, so the picture is there because it reminds me of him. I still don't like the woman." Vidal told Bastos: "When Onassis died, he left Jackie twenty eight million dollars and the yacht. Jackie grabbed the check before the ink was dry."

There was also a picture of Vidal, featuring a male model coming out of his swimming pool, with Vidal and his sour expression looking out at the viewer. Vidal told Bastos he had shown the picture to a straight friend who said the model had the best ass he had ever seen, which, said Vidal, showed that even straight men will appreciate a beautiful ass. "He liked Southern men, he told me that Southern men were the best in bed," says Bastos. "One day he was watching television and the person was saying 'Today in North Carolina…,' and Gore said, 'Beautiful boys in North Carolina, working class kids, very nice. South Carolina's pretty good too.'" (In a 1970 article Vidal recalled a guilt-ridden friend having sex with young cowhand in Wyoming who said to him about gay sex, "You know, you guys from the East do this because you're sick and we do it because we're horny.")

Bastos took some pictures of Vidal indoors and in the garden. I said, "Gore, you have such a great face." He held his cheekbones and said: "It's all here. If you don't have these, just forget it." One drink—for Vidal, whisky on the rocks—followed another. He would doze off, then awaken. There was a "big ego and vanity to him" and he "still saw himself as a sexual being," says Bastos. "When he saw my pastel portrait, he said, 'I didn't know I had these jowls.' 'Let me soften them up,' I said. 'I never thought I looked like my father—my father looked like a fox,' said Gore. I took a finished, enlarged portrait to him in a beautiful frame as a present. He showed it to Norberto [Nierras, Vidal's majordomo] and said, 'Put this picture next to my father, so there will be two foxes on the table.'"

Bastos certainly saw the best of late Vidal. Dennis Altman saw him grow more bitter, "and he was very, very unhappy after Howard died and in his last years was very miserable. He had a terrible fear of being forgotten and overlooked: he would have crawled over broken glass for a microphone. I've known a number of people like Gore: people who are extraordinarily generous and kind in private, when, as soon as a microphone hovers near, become monsters. The problem for Gore was that he believed in his golden age of the '50s and '60s, he never really engaged with the 'golden ages' or eras that followed. It's why I don't think you can criticize him for not talking about AIDS. It simply happened in a time he wasn't that engaged with. It wasn't a world he recognized."

His friend, later to become arch critic, Christopher Hitchens (who signed his letters "Hitchypoo") wrote to him in 1994 that "mighty and aloof monarch that you are, you may occasionally forget to remember that some of your adoring subjects actually do adore you." Hitchens referred to Vidal as the "Pope of Ravello," and that, says Matt Tyrnauer "very much described him: the appreciative would come and kiss the ring." He suffered scattered bouts of illness. Vidal wrote to "dear Poo" in 1996 that he was recovering from hemorrhage of the bowel due to removal of benign polyps "treated solely with vodka and aspirin." Vidal wrote to a friend in an undated letter that the "thermostat is jammed," adding he has "senile diabetes...After being on guard for all sorts of exotic cancers and virtual mysteries, I shall die the death of all four grandparents—a stroke within an age range of seventy to eighty-eight, or so the tarot cards hint."

For years, Vidal had anointed the left wing polemicist Hitchens as his "Dauphin," a younger writer he greatly admired who would take on his mantle. But Hitchens's and Vidal's relationship broke down after 9/11: Hitchens became a supporter of the war in Iraq, a betrayal in Vidal's eyes, while Hitchens wrote, a "crackpot strain...gradually asserted itself as dominant" within Vidal. There would be no need for a Dauphin, said Vidal: he wasn't planning on giving up the throne just yet. There is one awkward scene in Nicholas Wrathall's documentary, *Gore Vidal: The United States of Amnesia*, in which Hitchens tries to get Gore to sign a copy of a book at a Washington function, but is shooed away by Vidal's hostess, or handler. The younger man would die before the older: Hitchens died in 2011, aged sixty-two, from complications of cancer of the esophagus.

Vidal's drinking was already visibly damaging him when Richard Harrison approached him about it in the late 1980s. "He was so vain, handsome, brilliant. That's what gets me about the end, and why he let himself go to hell. In Ravello he would get up, read the papers in an old robe and write forty pages before lunch. The drinking started in the early afternoon until he went to bed. I decided to talk to him about it. He said the drinking 'doesn't bother me one bit.' I said, 'That's what all alcoholics say. Gore, you've got a great mind, you have to take care of it.' That hit a nerve with him and he was never really the same with me after that."

Other long-held friendships also suffered. Jason Epstein, Vidal's editor for forty years and husband (until their divorce in 1980) of Vidal's good friend Barbara Epstein, founder and co-editor of the *New York Review of Books*, was "very, very close to him, I admired him, I loved to be with him. It can be difficult to be someone's editor, but it never got in the way of anything till the end." That point came in the 1990s when Vidal started "trying to recapture the *Myra* moment" says Epstein, pursuing the idea of the sexual continuum, there was no such thing as gay and straight—that it was only in this puritanical, monotheistic world which he deplored that there were these categories." Epstein "agreed 100 percent with Vidal," but it began to infect the novels he was writing. *Live from Golgotha* was about some presumed love affair between St. Paul and St. Timothy, and *Duluth*, which I don't know what the hell was about."

The Book of the Month Club, "on which he depended," was dying and readers were deserting Vidal, says Epstein, who was writing out of character. Epstein let him know his feelings "and received a very angry, sharp letter of a kind you don't write to a very, very close friend: 'How dare you' was the tone of it. He was obviously frothing at the mouth. His politics had gone to the far, far left and become very silly. His career as a novelist was going downhill. The country wasn't responding to his defense of the sexual continuum. I thought the best thing to do was to maintain the friendship by not pursuing it."

Jason Epstein ceased being his editor. "I was relieved. It was a complicated relationship. I knew his career as going to go down and I was going to have to take some responsibility for that and I didn't look forward to dealing with those issues of decline." Epstein didn't contact Vidal after Austen's death. "I should have written to him but maybe I didn't want to resume that relationship. I didn't want to be hollered at. Gore behaved like Coriolanus: 'I banish you' was his attitude. 'You can't reject me, I reject you.' But in this case, I had rejected him." Boaty Boatwright doesn't recall Vidal's drinking affecting his work, but this longtime friend felt she'd lost him "years ago, it was too difficult to have a conversation with Gore. He wasn't himself. If you got angry with Gore, it didn't matter because he didn't care."

Jay Parini thinks that "early on" Vidal "put on this Gore Vidal mask, this supercilious grandee, and it kind of stuck. It was superglued on, He was suffering in it, it didn't have much air in it. I would see it 'off,' at three o' clock in the morning, drinking a bottle of whisky. He would talk about the novels he should have written, whether he had wasted time with his historical novels. There was a sense of him feeling he had never stuck with one thing: novels, TV, movies. He was a very lonely man, he was the loneliest man I've ever met in my life. Without Howard he would have had nothing."

Parini had met Vidal in Italy over thirty years before, talking on the phone once a week, "sometimes every day: I was one of the few friends who put in the time." Vidal "was a true pain in the ass" says Parini, cataloguing the repeated mentions of his grandfather

T.P. Gore, his congressional record, the family's move to Merrywood. "Socially he was very awkward. He had no social graces. In the last ten years in L.A. he was a completely sodden drunk: whisky and Scotch. I drank wine and too much when I was with him. He would collapse in front of you, fall asleep on the couch. He drank himself into oblivion, he was so fucking miserable. He was a sad man, he didn't connect with people. His conversation was laced with brilliant political and literary reflections; he had a good performing self, but his self grew thinner and thinner."

On airplanes, Vidal told Fred Kaplan, he was too scared to drink. "I do sleep. With age, something happens with your sense of time. You get up in the morning and suddenly you're getting back to bed again. And the day is over—all old people report this, *ad nauseam*. But no less true for that. So, a long boring flight isn't that long. You haven't even finished the book you've brought with you because you tend to stare straight ahead. Old age is like early youth. Idyll of woolgathering."

As Kaplan was writing his biography of Vidal, Vidal himself was working on the first slice of his memoirs. He had already engaged a biographer before Kaplan, Walter Clemons, who secured a $350,000 advance, engaging Kaplan after Clemons died before completing his biography. Clemons gave up after working on it for almost four years. "He couldn't pin the material down," says his good friend and beneficiary Bernie Woolf. "He would go to Italy and spend weekends and time with Gore, but the stories kept changing. Walter was a gentleman, truly one of kindest and smartest people I have ever known. He should never have taken on that job. He was about to retire and thought it might be something nice, but it just wasn't a meeting of minds."

The only power Vidal had was to look at and correct his own quotes, "but he kept wanting to see everything Walter was writing," says Woolf, who for the first time showed me what remained of Clemons's work. "Walter absolutely wouldn't let him see anything. It became a real drag for Walter, and I think he regretted ever taking it on."

Vidal sent a note to historian Jonathan Ned Katz in May 1991, claiming, "Walter Clemons will never get the book done—a nice man but diabetic, vague—four years of interviews (suspiciously, mostly with movie stars I have known) & still no text—He does not need a helper; he needs a ghost."

A diary entry of Clemons's from Friday March 11, 1994, records calling his editor to tell him, "I'm giving up on the Vidal." Clemons's therapist, he writes, "recommended that I go home and try to write a characterization of Vidal, to try to free myself from my reluctance to criticize him. 'You've let him make you crazy. He is a cruel bastard, everyone who's ever dealt with him knows that, and you've let him push you into a corner you've got to get out of.'" Clemons died, aged sixty-four, of diabetes on July 6, 1994. "Walter had been sick for six months before he gave up," says Woolf. "If he had been in better health he would have probably finished it." The last pages of Clemons's diary reveal, heartbreakingly for Woolf, his shame and embarrassment about not being able to manageably control his illness, which in fact he did as sensibly as possible, Woolf insists.

"Gore wasn't kind about Walter after his death," says Woolf. "He said he had been too ill to write the book and he hadn't written anything, which wasn't true, but he hadn't completed the book." Woolf inherited a box of tapes with notes and an outline of how the material was to be ordered. "Walter had lots of tapes of interviews, he had been everywhere and talked to everybody, and after Walter died Gore called me, wanting them. I told him, 'They're not yours and I think you've treated Walter so badly you can whistle Dixie for them. They're not yours, they're not mine to give and not yours to receive and that's the end of it.'"

Woolf and Vidal's friendship—which had begun in Rome many years earlier—ended and Woolf intended to give the tapes and what material Clemons had written to a library. But then Woolf became the caregiver for George Armstrong, his and Vidal's mutual friend who lost a lot of money on the stock market in the final years of his life. Woolf says Vidal sent Armstrong money when Armstrong "lost everything in 2008 after putting every last dime he had in hi-tech stocks. He passed away a couple of years later, and in the last two years Gore would send him four to five thousand dollars every four or five months which was a huge help. I took care of George, and I sent Gore a letter saying thank you for the help Gore had given him. Gore sent me a letter in which he said how much he appreciated George and what I did to help him."

This "meant a lot" to Woolf after he and Vidal had fallen out over the tapes Clemons had left and Vidal wanted. "Gore fell out with people: people came in and out of his life like a revolving door," remarks Woolf. "They were very close, then they disappeared." Sadly, Woolf's basement flooded and the tapes and most of what Clemons wrote were "ruined." Woolf gave me what remained to use in this book. When he heard Fred Kaplan had been commissioned to write the second attempt at Vidal's biography, Woolf felt like saying to him, "You've made the sorriest goddamn choice of your life." It perhaps didn't rank as that, but it was unpleasant. "Gore had a great brilliance for non-introspection; he was proud of it and it proved a great shield for him," Kaplan says. After Kaplan finished his biography "that was pretty much the end of our relationship," Kaplan recalls. "Gore claimed never to have read it. It was a comparatively minor break in the litany of breaks he had had from his mother, sister and literary contemporaries. I regretted that it ended without us able to achieve a friendship or continued association, but I could see it coming."

Fred Kaplan was editing a collection of Vidal's letters when Vidal asked to rewrite some he had sent to Vidal's cousin, Louis Auchincloss. "I told him he couldn't do that, 'You're rewriting history.' 'Well,' he said, 'I don't want to be on Page Six [the gossip page of the New York Post].' When I signed up to write the biography I didn't know he was also writing Palimpsest, which came out before the biography. Many reviewers said, 'Read what Gore Vidal says in his own words. It's much more entertaining than the biography.' He scooped me." Even though Vidal had been cooperative with Kaplan, the men fell out: "I felt sad when our friendship ended. I admired him but I didn't miss him. I'd had a great deal of Gore." Vidal phoned Kaplan in the last communication they had, and then affected not to have done. "I've dialed a wrong number," Vidal said before hanging up.

Vidal's final insult to Kaplan comes in the opening scene of Nicholas Wrathall's documentary, *Gore Vidal: The United States of Amnesia*. The eighty-nine minute film opens with Vidal surveying where his ashes will be interred alongside Austen at Rock Creek Cemetery in Washington D.C., noting that his biographer—Kaplan, who he doesn't name—begins his book at the cemetery, before going on to "get everything wrong," beginning with recording how much Vidal feared death. Why would someone who feared death take his biographer to his planned resting place, Vidal asks in the documentary, eliciting laughs from the audience. It's a typically withering Vidal jab, but an unfair one at Kaplan's expense: he doesn't write that Vidal fears death in his scene-setting introduction at the cemetery.

Vidal's once-barnstorming, scene-stealing TV performances were on the wane as his moods became more erratic and as he drank more. On a visit to Ravello at the time the United States was invading Afghanistan in October 2001, Steven Abbott recalls Vidal reading "Perpetual War for Perpetual Peace," his essay, aloud after dinner one night and the handing it around the room asking Abbott, his partner Jim Stephens and Rob Bregoff, a friend from San Francisco, each read part of it. The essay had been given a kill fee by *Vanity Fair* and rejected by *The Nation*, which "devastated" Vidal, says Abbott. "Gore said that he wanted witnesses to hear his essay that was being suppressed during the Cheney-Bush junta." A year later, the essay became the centerpiece of his last international bestseller, *Perpetual War for Perpetual Peace*.

Vidal was also extremely upset, says Abbott, by being cut off in a television news interview about Timothy McVeigh, who in 1995 killed 168 people and wounded more than 800 in a bombing attack on the Alfred P. Murrah Federal Building in Oklahoma. "There always used to be a film crew there, but that faucet was being turned off," says Abbott. Vidal corresponded with McVeigh and became a supporter of his. "It was a privilege to know Gore," says Bernie Woolf, "but I think some people stay on the stage too long. Gore was so important and immediate for so many years that when you saw his last appearances he is just repeating himself and seems less viable. It's time to absolutely retire when you're not up to standard and Gore wasn't at the end. It had all become a cliché and people were not taking him as seriously as they once did."

"Are any of us fulfilled?" asks Claire Bloom. "Gore would have liked political office: he was very suited to it, he was a wonderful orator and had a great mind. Too few politicians—Obama and Bill Clinton—have those qualities together." For Susan Sarandon, "One of his biggest heartbreaks was not winning public office, but being gay made it impossible at that time. He channeled that love of history into writing novels." And holding court: the last time Dennis Altman saw Vidal, in 2005 at a PEN event, he introduced him to novelist Ursula Le Guin. "I left them ruminating on their mutual fame together."

In his memoir *Lies: A Diary, 1986-1999*, Ned Rorem records in January 1994 seeing a late-era Vidal on television. "A generation ago, except for Paul Goodman, Gore Vidal was the only homosexual publicly versed in general politics, as distinct from specific gay-rights politics...He *has* an Achilles' heel, on which he stands above the fray: knowing the sole cures for our planet's ills, he leans back and smiles as we go to pot for not heeding him." His fiction and non-fiction "reflects an aloofness that keeps it from soaring, thrilling, inspiring, even repelling. But that's him: his faults conspire to define him, so perhaps they aren't faults at all but 'traits.'"

Lately, though, Vidal's complacency had grown smug, writes Rorem. "Seer in the broad-heterosexual-world of politics though he be, he demonstrates a leaning that can only be termed homosexual (it takes one to know one). Tonight on the *Charlie Rose* show he likened the tight smile of Inman [Bobby Ray, who withdrew from being then-President Clinton's then-nominee for Defense Secretary] to the tight smile of Chicago's Cardinal Bernardin, accused of molesting boys long ago. 'It is as though,' smirks Gore, proud of his wit, 'Bernardin had simply wiped the smile off his own face and lent it to Inman.' That's a bitchy remark—a remark one can't imagine from any heterosexual politico, no matter how sleazy. Straight men don't mention each other's looks."

Physically, Rorem adds, Vidal resembles "an all-knowing

Buddha in the body of a Lucian Freud portrait." But he retained a deep affection for Vidal, sending him letters reassuring him of love and support, wryly noting the physical fraying of ageing ("one more birthday and one less prostate"), and one plaintive, undated note following a report in a newspaper saying "that you are about to die—please do not."

A nadir in Vidal's TV appearances was reached the night Barack Obama was elected President in 2008 when Vidal appeared, slurring and disheveled during a needlessly testy interview with BBC presenter David Dimbleby. Vidal was speaking from a Los Angeles studio and began imperiously, "May I talk the facts of life to you?" He proceeded to loftily lecture Dimbleby, a veteran, much-respected broadcaster. "You think of the Republican party as a party like the British Conservative party, but it isn't. The Republican party is a mindset: they love war, they love money." He then told Dimbleby, "I don't know who you are." Dimbleby, puzzled like the viewer at the unprovoked onslaught, said mollifyingly, "Well, I know who you are Mr. Vidal." "Well, you're one up on me," Vidal shot back.

Dimbleby began a discussion about race. Vidal talked about growing up in Washington D.C., then "an all-black" city. "I know the territory, I'm surprised you even ask me, I know too much about the subject. You like to get people who don't know that much about the subject." There was a stunned silence from Dimbleby as he tried to navigate himself away from an unwanted fight on live television. "It's your turn," says Vidal. "Well, I think, as you might say, we'll quit while we're ahead Mr. Vidal," Dimbleby said, bringing the interview to a conclusion. "Thank you very much for joining us this evening." Dimbleby turned to his studio panel of experts. "Well, that was fun and unexpected," he said, a little stunned. His guests laughed; one reassured him *they* knew who he was.

After the incident with Dimbleby, Vidal asked his friend Patty Dryden how he had come across. "I told him he'd done himself a disservice," says Dryden. "I told him, 'I don't think that's how you want to see yourself.' He had apparently waited a long time in a cold room before going on air. I told him he hadn't made sense.

He asked Burr, who was diplomatic, then he asked Muzius, who said, 'I think you had one or two bowls of whiskey. He lashed out then at Muzius. But Muzius was right: Gore's inability to handle alcohol was his Achilles' heel."

As for Vidal's writing, in almost the last conversation Walter Clemons had with Vidal, he records in his diary that Vidal had told him he didn't think he'd write his previously discussed final novel in his American historical series, the one that was to have been called *The Golden Age*, meaning the period 1945-50, which Vidal described as the only peaceful era since World War II. "Instead, he's writing memoirs. He has as his reason for not writing any more novels that 'Updike and Roth's last novels sold seven thousand copies each. It's over.'" But Vidal did publish it, in 2000; *The Golden Age* would be his final novel.

Vidal indicated to Clemons he was planning another book of history, having realized he had left out the Mexican-American War of 1846-8 from his historical cycle, "a very dumb thing to do because then you get to the roots of the Civil War, and the Civil War gives you the roots to American empire and our conquest of the Philippines and other atrocious deeds which we have done. I'm lacking that piece, and I thought I should put it together and insert it in order to make the narrative more coherent." Vidal never wrote that book, but in the last ten years of his life he wrote non-fiction galvanized by his disillusion over George W. Bush's warmongering. A history book about America's founding fathers, *Inventing a Nation: Washington, Adams, Jefferson* (2003), was followed by *Imperial America: Reflections on the United States of Amnesia* (2004), a collection of essays and articles that again vocalized his frustration with the condition of the US under George W. Bush.

Advancing age didn't blunt Vidal's desire to feud and fight, and again—after Buckley and Mailer—his sexuality was at the heart of his last significant contretemps, with the novelist Edmund White who wrote the 2006 play *Terre Haute*, imagining an intimate relationship between Vidal (named "James" in the play) and Timothy McVeigh ("Harrison"). *Terre Haute* is the Indiana federal prison in which high-profile Death Row prisoners such as McVeigh are incarcerated. The huge loss of life, indeed McVeigh's act of mass murder, goes unmentioned by Vidal in the play. "He was a true patriot, a Constitution man," Vidal claimed of McVeigh to me in 2009. "And I was torn, my grandfather [the Democrat Senator Thomas Gore] had brought Oklahoma into the Union." McVeigh said he had carried out the bombing as a protest against tyrannical government.

White wrote the play for "T," a younger boyfriend for whom White was a sex slave. "I said, 'You know, you are my master and you could command me to write you a play.' He suggested I do something about McVeigh, whom he resembled." Initially Vidal, who admired McVeigh's anti-government beliefs, "didn't mind" White writing it, White says, but said he would never be interested in a 'piece of rough trade' from upstate New York." Vidal had corresponded with McVeigh for a long period of time. "I put into the roles the anguish I was feeling about the thirty-year age difference between T and me," White told me. "When he finished with me I felt wretched. T was a fan of my work, just as McVeigh was an admirer of Vidal's."

In real life Vidal never met McVeigh, though they did correspond and Vidal wrote several articles defending McVeigh. McVeigh invited Vidal to attend his execution in 2001. Sean Strub, who optioned and developed White's play, recalls that on the day McVeigh was originally scheduled to be executed, May 16, Vidal was planning on attending. "But at the last minute, there was a stay for two weeks, so Gore canceled his trip and, instead, took me to lunch at Sardi's. It was my birthday."

The play imagines four conversations between McVeigh and Vidal, interrogating the parallels between two men who believe passionately what they believe, what it means to be American and what that leads them to do in their lives. The play focuses on the men's evolving intimate relationship: in Harrison's cold dismissal of James and the latter's unmet sexual needs, White told me in 2006, "When you're old, if people like you, they see you as venerable; if they don't, you're invisible. Sexually and romantically, you're turned into a eunuch." At the end of the play Harrison/McVeigh asks James/Vidal what he would want if he could hypnotize him. "Just to see your torso," James replies.

The character of James in the play was not purely Vidal, White tells me. "I made him an amalgam of me and him. His own agent said, 'I don't know why Gore objects. Your character is much nicer than he is.' Gore felt I'd made my career out of being gay. He didn't like that label. He felt my play had muddied the waters. Since he admired McVeigh's actions, I was diluting the whole thing by making it into this crummy sexual thing. I felt I had represented the ideological positions faithfully."

If McVeigh was a hero to Vidal, he was a "bitter person unable to make it as a marine" for White. He gave Vidal a copy of the play and said the BBC wanted to produce it. "Gore predicted it would be a success. I said that I didn't think I'd ever had a big success. He said, 'Well, maybe because I'm in it, it will be a big success.'" But Vidal wasn't happy. "He was mad, he felt I hadn't represented his arguments fairly, he accused me of not reading his books. I was never a fan of his writing, I really hated his historical novels, which I thought were pure taxidermy: no life, no style. I read a few of them: they're all pretty horrible."

Vidal gave permission for the play to be produced by the BBC; then it was performed in Edinburgh and New York. White received word, not from Vidal directly, that Vidal was threatening legal action, after a producer mentioned her desire to make it into a Broadway production. "I was so tired of this," said White. "I really took the high ground. I sent him a very obsequious letter making him sound like a mentor, which he never was. I mentioned he'd already given permission for it to be produced by the BBC. I think that kind of shut him up. I never heard another word from him. He could see I was not going to squabble with him, and I pointed out that I was very poor, so it was pointless to sue me anyway."

Vidal later said of White to me: "He's a filthy, low writer. He likes to attack his betters, which means he has a big field to go after." Had he wanted to meet McVeigh? "I am not in the business of meeting people," Vidal said. "That play implies I am madly in love with McVeigh. I looked at his [White's] writing and all he writes about is being a fag and how it's the greatest thing on earth. He thinks I'm another queen and I'm not. I'm more interested in the Constitution and McVeigh than the loving tryst he saw. It was vulgar fag-ism." To Sean Strub, Vidal appeared to find White's sexual openness, both on the page and in life, "distasteful": a clash of gay-generational sexual mores. For Strub, the final draft of the play "depicted a more sexualized relationship between the characters and trivialized Gore into a panting old queen trying to get his rocks off with McVeigh. Gore was offended. If there is one thing Gore Vidal wasn't, it was one who longed for the unattainable boy across the room. I never saw him convey a lecherous persona."

Vidal's animosity towards White continued: over lunch with Jonathan Burnham, White's publisher at Chatto, he accidentally swigged what he thought was wine but was olive oil. "He spluttered it all out and claimed Jonathan deliberately hadn't stopped him. He said: 'You want me to die so your writer Edmund White will be King Fag!'" Vidal may not have liked to have been known as gay, but he didn't want to be deposed as "King Fag" clearly.

Maybe it's White's self-definition as gay, and his success as an author of gay-themed books, that angered the anti-category Vidal. In his interview with Donald Weise, Vidal, while not dismissive of White's work, was dismissive of his self-definition: "There are certainly people who call themselves 'gay novelists' like Edmund White. I think he's out of his mind. Why limit yourself any more than literature has limited you? In a world where people don't read, what are you going to make of a man who calls himself a 'gay novelist'? What's that supposed to mean, that he only go to write about cock? He's a quite good writer, but I didn't think he was that dumb to characterize himself."

How much of that scorn is internalized? Vidal had categorized himself when *The City and the Pillar* had been published, and his career and political ambitions were skewed after that, he felt. By 1999, in his interview with Weise, he claimed defiantly, "With my temperament I didn't give a damn. It didn't mean I didn't get irritated. I didn't care what people thought of me. I was too busy judging them. I just let it all go." Vidal said he had rejected his election to the National Institute of Arts and Letters in 1976 on the grounds he "already belonged to Diners Club. This is how I treated the literary world, with the same disdain as they have treated the fags over the years. They don't mind apologetic meek little fags passing with one point one children and a wife who drinks, and they don't mind the caricature fag like Capote, that's how fags are meant to be." Vidal said he was among the first of the "war novelists" who were "rather tough." Here Vidal is suddenly playing the proud gay freedom fighter, but on his own terms— never as a "fag."

For his part, White doesn't rate Vidal as a significant figure in gay-themed literature. "What's the young gay man of today going to read? *Myra Breckinridge*? It's fun but I don't think he's widely read like Alan Hollinghurst, or even Christopher Isherwood. To me, Isherwood was a great man and *A Single Man* the first really good gay novel." What did Isherwood find so warm in Vidal, I wonder aloud. "Intelligence and worldliness," says White. As for *Terre Haute*, White thinks "it's too complimentary as a portrait of Gore. James has a lot of my own pathos and sweetness. I don't think he had any of that."

In a friendly gesture, White called Vidal on one of his last New York visits. "You should come by and have some dinner. I'll invite some cute boys around," White told him. Vidal replied, "Oh, cute boys, that's the last thing in the world I want." Today, White says, "I don't know what that meant. Was he bidding a farewell to sex altogether, or he had enough cute boys around him anyway? I had the feeling he wasn't interested in sex at all: one more reason why he was so bitter perhaps. He was mainly into booze and revenge." Vidal's decline was only going to become more painful, for himself and those close to him.

Chapter Fourteen

The Door Marked "Exit"

Vidal opened his second memoir, *Point to Point Navigation*, writing that he hoped he was moving graciously "toward the door marked Exit...For the young, death is supremely unnatural. For the old, it is so natural that it is not worth thinking about." In 2007, he told a TV interviewer "One doesn't like death," quoting Gerard Manley Hopkins's poem "Spring and Fall": "It is the blight man was born for." Death was "unavoidable," Vidal said of Austen's passing. "One or the other is going to die, it's inevitable that both will be dead. I'm stoic."

But Vidal's physical decline in the last three years of his life was dramatic and painful and shocked his family and friends, as he continued to feud with some and excommunicate others. Scotty Bowers remembers him talking about being interred next to Austen. "His fucking feet and ankles swelled up. He couldn't move, he was drinking heavily and taking the pills he was supposed to, but so many pills I said 'Don't drink.' That fucking wheelchair: I remember how vibrant he was." His half-sister Nina Straight says it was the culmination of leading "a brutally disrespectful life when it came to his own well-being. Howard tried to control it. Ice water did not run in Gore Vidal's veins, as he said, buttermilk did and eventually it curdled. He died the same way as his mother did."

From 1995 onwards, Vidal "was sucking back heavy-duty alcohol," says Straight. At La Rondinaia, Vidal would drink two bottles of Scotch in a sitting, drinking a bottle "without saying boo." He would eye a guest's comparative sobriety with arch disapproval: "I *suppose* he drinks *wine*," was the disparaging remark aimed at someone Vidal felt was a lightweight. Why did he drink so much? Straight shrugs. "It released his imagination, allowed his passions to rage, and him to scream at the bathroom mirror and at the poor person sitting next to him. It allowed him to talk about anything, to fantasize and have a full fantasy life sitting by himself on the cliffs of Ravello." Once back in Los Angeles, the drinking became "insanity," Straight says. "He didn't have anything to live for but himself, and that's pretty boring. You couldn't talk to Gore rationally. One person said you couldn't debate him. In the middle of a discussion about policy he'd suddenly shout, 'Your mother was a Polack,' and suddenly you're emotionally down on the floor trying to strangle him."

Not everyone felt the same. Claire Bloom says, "Gore drank too much. I wish he hadn't, but he enjoyed it and it never interfered with his work. He drank after a day's work, he seemed able to take it. He loved it." For Susan Sarandon, too: "As much as he drank, he would be up at the crack of dawn writing."

Sarandon and Vidal returned to La Rondinaia after it had been sold. "That day there was a double rainbow," she recalls. "He couldn't get down the stairs because he was in a wheelchair, which I was quite glad about: the little room wasn't as he or I would remember it, every window was open and the wind was whipping through." Vidal told Sarandon that "everyone was dying," that "he was the only one left, he and Joanne [Woodward]. He told me, 'I think about death all the time. Who would have thought I'd be the last one standing?' But he never seemed morose. He was befuddled sometimes, but on certain subjects—and if he had to give a speech—he was as clear as a bell." Juan Bastos recalls before the 2009 presidential election, Vidal saying, "The country is almost over, so you hope for a pleasant requiem...I'm afraid Obama is going to get killed."

Vidal's decline and growing anger and bitterness made his friends—those he kept—sadder when they recalled how kind he could be. Steven Abbott last saw him in 2009 at the National Book Awards dinner in New York where Vidal, introduced by Joanne Woodward, was given the Medal for Distinguished Contribution to American Letters. "After the event, he greeted me, 'Ah, Brother Steven!', his *nom d'ami* for me for thirty-five years." It was their first meeting since Abbott's bibliography of Vidal's complete works had been published. "He inscribed my personal copy, only this time, signing not a book of his, but one of mine, 'Steven from Gore Vidal with thanks for a monumental task.'"

The next day, Vidal was holding court at the Ritz-Carlton hotel, wearing his Lifetime Achievement Medal. "It was a festive gathering," says Abbott. "Friends arrived and many stories were told, including Gore reminiscing about Hollywood's peccadilloes. When asked if he wanted to take off the heavy medal, he replied, "No, it impresses the stewards on the plane." Vidal was talking about moving to France, says Abbott. "He said he wasn't writing any more, but planned to write another historical novel about his family's history. I think he knew he was no longer the person capable of writing *Julian*, *Myra Breckinridge* or *Creation*. Abbott's voice breaks. "I didn't say what I wanted to, which was that I was concerned that Gore did not have a sustaining relationship with the people around him. Howard had died, I knew he pushed people away. I thought, 'He's going to push everyone away and in the end there'll be nobody with him. He always said, 'I'll outlive you all.'" In farewell, Abbott took Vidal's hand, "pecked him on the cheek, thanked him and gave him my love."

Abbott had tried, unsuccessfully, to get Vidal to consider leaving some money to AIDS Project Los Angeles, which Vidal's nephew Hugh Steers had been close to. Vidal told Abbott he had left "everything" to Howard and joked about his mortality, saying the Gores had lived long lives. His view of death, he told me in 2009, was, "Either you accept there is such a thing, or you're so dumb that you can't grasp it." I asked if he was in good health. "No, of course not. I'm diabetic. It's odd, I've never been fat and I don't like candy, which most Americans are hooked on."

In 2009 Vidal published his final book, a reflective, coffee-table photo book of his life called *Gore Vidal: Snapshots in History's Glare*. When David Schweizer visited Vidal the same year, Vidal said how strange it was "not to have Howard darting in and protecting him." Vidal told Schweizer, "I miss that protection," adding he missed Austen more than he ever realized he would. Vidal "just sitting there, growing fat, drinking, like Orson

Welles. Young men were running in and out refreshing the wine, two bottles of French white between the two of us. At first I was shocked at how infirm and lonely he seemed. He was vain, such a peacock about his body. To be wheeled around…"

Schweizer told Vidal he wanted to turn *Myra Breckinridge* into a grand opera. Vidal remembered the conversations of their afternoon teas in Rome in 1970 and "got excited" talking about the *Myra* project, which he wanted instead to be adapted into a Broadway musical. "That's just the thing it shouldn't be," Schewizer replied. "Why not?" said Vidal. "Let's make some money." Schweizer said he wasn't averse to that, but the "transgressive, prophetic" nature of the work in a commercial musical "would reduce it to the wrong kind of resonances." Vidal gave Schweizer the rights, "which weren't his to give," says Schweizer, but the company that had produced the much-lambasted 1970 movie which Vidal "hated," says Schweizer. Vidal laughed a lot during the meeting; Schweizer returned once more to discuss "some scenario ideas" before the project fizzled.

When I interviewed Vidal, I asked what he wanted to do next. He misheard me. "My usual answer to 'What am I proudest of?' is my novels, but really I am most proud that, despite enormous temptation, I have never killed anybody, and you don't know how tempted I have been." That wasn't my question, I said. "Well, given that I'm proudest that I haven't killed anybody, I might be saving something up for someone."

Vidal told me he was single. "I'm not into partnerships. I don't even know what it means." At the time he "couldn't care less" about gay marriage. "Does anyone care what Americans think? They're the worst-educated people in the First World. They don't have any thoughts, they have emotional responses, which good advertisers know how to provoke." You could have been the first gay president, I told him. "No, I would have married and had nine children," he replied quickly and seriously. "I don't believe in these exclusive terms."

In 2009 Vidal went on a barge holiday with Claire Bloom, accompanied by Muzius Dietzmann and Fabian Bouthillette, on the Canal du Midi in Southern France, which Bloom said was wonderful." However, looking after Vidal was demanding and de-moralizing. "He died horribly," says Bouthillette. "He was defi-nitely drinking too much, especially for an elderly diabetic. He was lonely. The last ten years bought the worst out in him. He just lost it. It was so hard taking care of him. Many days I felt like say-ing 'Gore, go fuck yourself,' but knew he was a sad, lonely man and you could see the true spirit of him. Gore and I got each other. I've never had a better relationship with man or woman. He cared deeply about the well-being of humanity. He would not have been labeled a spiritual person—he didn't read Deepak Chopra—but he had real equanimity. He was a bit humble in reality. In public he played the tough guy, the big bad boss guy, but he was a very good listener if you had something of use to say."

This is an especially fulsome tribute, as Vidal claimed Dietz-mann and Bouthillette had "kidnapped" him in France on an-other trip there in 2010. They had not, but it was a sign, for Burr Steers, of how quickly Vidal's mental deterioration was progress-ing: "The paranoia and drinking were becoming incredible." Be-fore they left for Europe, Bouthillette had lobbied against the trip. "I could see he was beginning to really lose it. Reason and rational thought started to go away, his memory took a turn for the worse. There was confabulation. He started filling gaps in his memory incorrectly. He wasn't lying, the details shifted. There was a time when I was literally the extension of him, whether that be physically or his memory, and he wouldn't mind if I cor-rected him. At dinner parties he would want me to push him to the most interesting conversations in the room that I had heard. There was a lot of intimate non-verbal communication between us. But then he started resenting the fact I had started correcting him. He became paranoid, certain that people around him were out to get him, and completely losing track of time."

Bouthillette knew the trip to Europe "was a disaster waiting to unfold," but knew he had to go to help Dietzmann take as good care of Vidal as possible. "All the driving, changing loca-tions, not having his blood sugar as closely monitored as it would have been in L.A. was disastrous." Vidal decided suddenly he wanted to return to L.A., but when Dietzmann and Bouthillette didn't sort out the tickets as quickly as he would have liked, he accused them of kidnapping him. Bouthillette says Vidal called Burr Steers to say what they had done, then accused him of colluding in it. When they returned to L.A., both young men left their jobs, moving out of Outpost Drive. One friend of Vidal's was outraged at how he treated the young men. "Gore, in his declining years, was impossible. You needed to be a professional nurse to put up with his shit. Muzius particularly had toiled for him for too long to be accused of that."

"Both Muzius and I were an emotional disaster afterwards," says Bouthillette. "We knew he was ill but we had worked so hard for him, particularly Muzius who had been with him for years. That was very hurtful. For me it reminded me of the trauma of leaving the military: the notion of giving yourself to something for a reason—I had joined the Navy because of the weapons of mass destruction propaganda—and then to have been lied to there and now I had committed to Gore with the same passion and belief and was being betrayed again."

Around the same time, Vidal fell out with Jean Stein, one of his oldest friends. The actress Fiona Shaw and she were dining with Vidal and a few of his friends at Musso and Frank restaurant. "He was turning against everyone at that point and I sadly didn't understand that his paranoia was due to dementia," says Stein. "I had gotten him a helper, but that relationship had gone bad. When I suggested we split the bill at the restaurant, he turned on me enraged. I got my courage up and told him I wasn't his mother or his sister and he had no right to treat me that way, and paid my share of the bill and left."

A few months later at a reception following a memorial service for their mutual friend, the art collector and philanthropist Max Palevsky, Vidal claimed their friendship split had been caused by Stein insulting the theatrical producer Michael Butler when they were both at dinner at his house. "I regret to say that Gore had fabricated this as an excuse for the way he treated me at Musso and Frank. When I was on my way out of Max's home, I passed by where Gore was seated in his wheelchair and I said softly, 'Bye-bye, blackbird,' and that was it."

Towards the end, Patty Dryden "could see the writing on the wall" for her friendship with Vidal. "Muzius is a dear person, and no one was closer to Gore or could do more for him. So when Gore accused him and Fabi of kidnapping him I stood my ground, asking what on earth he was talking about, which he didn't like. The alcohol got too much and ravaged his beautiful mind." Dryden asked why they would want to kidnap him. "Money," Vidal told her. She told him he was being ridiculous. "They didn't want his money. But there was no reasoning with him, he was paranoid. I saw him two weeks before he died. Gore wasn't talking much. He was physically there but not there. I held his hand and didn't feel bitter. I focused on the good, but was still angry with him. When Howard was alive and they were invited to someone's house for dinner, the next day Howard would have sent their thanks. After Howard died, forget it. Sue Mengers [Vidal's one-time agent and good friend, who died in 2011] called him and told him his manners were terrible. He told her to go fuck herself."

When his sister Nina saw him in the spring of 2011, "after he had gotten home from that farce in which he claimed he had been kidnapped," Vidal "ranted and raved about everybody who had, in fact, helped him. It was absurd and I just let Gore have it. 'You're drunken, out of your mind, none of these people are liars,' I told him. We really went at it hammer and tongs. He just kept repeating himself: that he had been betrayed and that everyone was against him. I kept grabbing his nose and pulling it, calling him Pinocchio. The third time I did that he grabbed my wrist and left a great black mark on it. I told him to get real. As I left he said, 'You're worse than your mother.'"

Boaty Boatwright would beseech him to "leave off the sauce. He'd just get furious and drink another martini. It wasn't worth fighting over, you weren't going to change Gore, his drinking had already taken its toll. Howard's death, the lack of social activity, people weren't fussing over him, getting older...Hollywood is a town for youth. People get bored when you're drunk, you stop being funny and charming. Thank god Gore never did drugs."

Still, as Juan Bastos had seen, there were flashes of a warmer Vidal. Arlyne Reingold, Austen's sister who spoke to him once a fortnight, said she wasn't aware of his dementia: his mind seemed sharp to her. Elinor Pruder visited him, and while being struck at how fat Vidal was, "we giggled. It was very nostalgic. He spoke of 'dear Howard.' It was such a deep relationship." Vidal was also always kind and generous to Norberto Nierras, his devoted personal chef and houseman for the last eleven years of his life.

The first time he interviewed Nierras for the job at the Beverly Hills Hotel Vidal had asked, "Do you know the name Gore Vidal?" Nierras told him he was sorry, he didn't have any idea who Gore Vidal was. "When I found out afterwards who he was, I was surprised he didn't take offense. He asked, 'Don't you read books?' I said, 'To be honest I get easily distracted reading books.' Afterwards I found out who he was and thought, 'Good-bye prospective employer.' When I got the job, I thought I'd start to read his books."

Vidal treated Nierras "like family. He was kind to me and I came to like him. After Mr. Austen passed away he entertained my conversations; he told me Imelda Marcos had once crashed one of his parties in Ravello." Vidal liked cheese soufflés and though he was diabetic would ask Nierras for chocolate ones too. He enjoyed beef broth, minestrone, and gumbo made from okra, green peppers, celery and onions. "In the first two years with him, when Mr. Austen was alive, I made them eleven ounce rib eye steaks. They enjoyed dinner with wine, a cocktail before. After-wards he would sit in one chair and Mr. Austen would sit opposite him. They were very close. I never heard them argue. After Mr. Austen passed away he didn't eat so much, he lost his appetite. I was worried about him and would say, "Mr. Vidal, I miss the time of the eleven ounce steak." "No, no, I can't anymore, since Howard has gone I stopped eating," Vidal told Nierras. "You should never stop eating," Nierras said. "I don't feel like eating, Norberto," Vidal would say. This saddened Nierras. "From then on I made small portions and soups, like Hungarian goulash, and the bowl was always finished. "In the last three years he didn't eat that much. I felt sad when he wasn't eating," says Nierras. Dinner always came with red wine, French, not American. Vidal loved cognac; he always had it with cheese after dinner.

"Mr. Vidal was jolly, but after Mr. Austen passed away he was sad," recalls Nierras. "He would sit at the table by himself and sometimes say, 'Sit down, Norberto, have some wine. You've been tiring yourself on your feet in the kitchen.' It delighted me, I was an employee...being a Filipino liked by Mr. Vidal, that is something." Nurses were hired to tend to him, but late at night if Vidal needed anything he would call for Nierras. "He asked me to play the music of Mr. Austen. He cried when he talked about him. I never heard him say 'I love, or loved, him' but he said he missed him."

Vidal's condition and state of mind deteriorated. He confused his half-sister for their mother; he accused his nephew Burr Steers of being a CIA imposter, "because the nephew in his head, the real Burr, was frozen at eighteen, needed a haircut and a grammar tutorial." Vidal would constantly try and stay up all night when he couldn't write any more, says Steers. "There was nothing to stop him drinking twenty-four-seven and that's pretty much what he did. He wouldn't just go through bottles. He was drinking as soon as he woke up."

Vidal's longtime doctor told Steers that "Gore was drinking himself to death and needed to cool it," so Steers "very gently suggested" that his uncle spend time at La Costa near San Diego, the spa he went to in previous years to lose weight before TV appearances. Somehow Steers's suggestion became scrambled in Vidal's mind that Steers too was organizing to kidnap him, and the two became estranged. Steers says Vidal instructed his lawyers to tell him he was no longer to make any arrangements for him. "I had to try and remember the person he was. In that state you lash out at the people closest to you, because you're afraid of being abandoned or just afraid. One of the most usual things that happens is that you turn against your children. I think if the young Gore had seen the old Gore he'd have taken a pillow to himself and ended it."

At the beginning of 2011, Vidal put Outpost Drive on the market for $3.495 million. Ernie Bernal, his nurse at the time, says his plan was to move back to Rome. "He wanted to sell up because he felt his house was dirty and people weren't visiting him." Vidal told Bernal the Italians were more cultured and the environment was better for him in Italy. But Vidal changed his mind when the house was repaired: he took it off the market.

Jay Parini says Vidal "was thinking of moving to an apartment in New York. He really hated L.A. and felt he had no social life out there. He wanted to be around literary people." With Nierras and Bernal he went on trips to Portugal and Bangkok, where Vidal took them to a bar Austen used to sing in. Bangkok was a favored sexual holiday destination for Vidal. In December 1993 the writer Jonathan Ned Katz took a call from him from there and in typed notes afterwards wrote: "Gore Vidal just called from Bangkok. When I asked, 'What are you doing there?' he answered, 'For the boys, who are marvelous in bed.' He had been to a Thai bar before he called and he sounded a bit drunk."

David Schweizer approached Vidal in 2011 to appear in a cameo in Tennessee Williams's last, and unfinished, play, *In Masks Outrageous and Austere*, which Schweizer mounted at New York's Culture Project in April 2012, by which time Vidal was in hospital. Vidal had worked on the manuscript with director Peter Bogdanovich years before, but nothing had come of it, says Schweizer. "Gore said to me, 'Tennessee had half a dozen useable lines and we're figuring something out.' But I saw it before and after he worked on it and nothing had been changed."

In November 2011 Michael Childers took a last photograph of Vidal for his book, *Author, Author: 100 Greatest American Writers*. He told Childers to come at ten o' clock in the morning: "I'm a morning person." "He was in bad shape and fading fast, in a wheelchair," recalls Childers. Vidal "was gussied up and had had his hair cut. Instead of drinking coffee for breakfast he was having red wine. I took some portraits. 'Ernie, I'd like a vodka,'

Gore said to his nurse. Ernie asked if he wanted that in a shot glass or on the rocks. 'No, just pour it into the red wine,' Gore told him."

Vidal opened up to Childers about how unhappy he was with the American political climate. "I hate living in this country," Vidal told Childers. "I want to die and have my ashes spread in Italy. I loathe America." Vidal was drunk, recalls Childers. He said how much he loved the terrace and patio of Outpost Drive. "It gives me such pleasure because the trees look like the pines of Rome," Vidal told Childers, so Childers photographed him out there. Vidal talked about *The Best Man* re-opening on Broadway, telling Childers, "I don't give a shit. I don't know why they're doing it. It was revived twenty years ago." Childers said gently that Vidal's name was in lights. "Yes…" Vidal said, clearly happy about that. He was getting ready to write another political essay, he told Childers, then softened a bit towards *The Best Man*. "I hear some of it's quite good, some of it works."

At the end of their meeting Vidal surprised Childers by reaching over and giving him a hug. "He wasn't usually demonstrative, he was a cool guy. When he pulled away there was a tear in his eye. He knew he was saying good-bye and would never see me again."

Bernal said his drinks were separated into "the brown drink" [Macallan 12 or 18] and "the red drink" [vodka with Angostura bitters]. Bernal tried to wean him off drinking "most of the day" by making sure the drinks were watered down. "I couldn't take alcohol away from him but I wanted to save his health," says Bernal, who organized small plays and recitals for Vidal in the evenings. Vidal "wanted to live life completely," says Bernal. He was "intensely energetic" and would sleep only four to five hours a night. From an Italian restaurant in the fashionable Los Angeles neighborhood of Silverlake, Bernal hired some tenors to sing some "sick-ass notes" at an impromptu concert in Vidal's living room to which Vidal invited his next door neighbor, the actress Charlize Theron.

Bernal says Vidal was angry at people for plagiarizing his

work and just as testy about confronting his mortality: while he loved listening to the CDs of Austen singing, there was one song he couldn't bear listening to, "On a Clear Day You Can See Forever," which to him signified death and which Austen sang without accompaniment. Bernal says he identified with Christopher Marlowe's hero Tamburlaine the Great, who like Vidal, was "fighting with god because death was coming to pick him up," says Bernal. "You could not tell Mr. Vidal what to do, I did my best for him." Vidal also liked to hang out at the Polo Lounge at the Beverly Hills Hotel and drink Gibson vodka martinis, and eat at Musso and Frank where he enjoyed the eggplant, spinach dip and Dungeness crab.

Vidal and Bernal flew to New York to watch rehearsals for the Broadway revival of *The Best Man*. Susan Sarandon saw him there. He told her, "You have to come and hear me sing." She asked what he meant. "Gore said he was singing at his hotel, where Ernie had set him up with a piano player in the lounge." On a trip to Italy in 2011, Vidal's friend Judith Harris, the morning after a talk he took part in in Pompeii, recalls him drunk at ten o'clock in the morning, shouting in the foyer of a hotel that "he was not the kind of man to be fucked by another man." Still then, towards the end of his life, Vidal was emphatic about the sex he wanted, the need to feel in control, to be "the man": Vidal's vision of his homosexuality, his homosexual sex, was forever fixed.

Vidal's last public appearance, on February 8, 2012, was at the launch party for Scotty Bowers's autobiography at Chateau Marmont, fresh off the plane from New York, where he made a short speech. Days later he was admitted to St. John's Hospital with pneumonia, where he stayed for around a month and a half. Then he went home and got "very sick again," says Bowers. Vidal was readmitted to the hospital: this time Cedars Sinai. "They got rid of his infection and he turned to me and said, 'You saved my life yet again,'" says Bernal. Bernal told him he was worried the hospital doctors were making mistakes and told Vidal he would do "anything to save your life."

The last time Diana Phipps Sternberg called Vidal he couldn't talk. "The phone was placed beside him in bed and I was talking on and on and at some point he just said, 'Yes.' He worked so hard, he had such a rapier wit. I was there when he said at a TV panel, 'I'm all for corporal punishment, but only between consenting adults.' I remember when we were both godparents to Kenneth Tynan's daughter, Gore saying: 'Always a godparent, never a god.'" Six months before Vidal died, Hubert de la Bouillerie had lunch with him. "He said he had given up alcohol and then finished half a bottle of Scotch. 'I don't drink any more, now just at lunch and dinner,' he said. He asked how my mother [Elinor Pruder] was. I said OK, but that she hated getting old. 'Tell her I hate getting old too,' he said."

Burr Steers feels Bernal did not discharge his duty of care properly. In the spring of 2012, "when the doctors finally did a brain scan, they found so little left they couldn't believe it was still functioning. It was horrible. It was exactly what happened with my grandmother, his mother. She, like Gore, had dementia and 'wet brain.'" The proper name for the syndrome is Wernicke-Korsakoff, a brain syndrome suffered by long-term alcoholics characterized by a number of symptoms, including confusion and hallucinations. When Vidal and Steers had taken Austen's ashes to be interred, Vidal had said "that he really didn't want that kind of long, drawn-out thing to happen to him, and yet it happened and in the worst way," says Steers. "It was a really horrible final act."

Nina Straight says her half-brother was "a physical coward but not scared of death." At his bedside she told him, "I'm here, I love you," focusing on the "wonderful" things he had done for her, like encourage her writing. Was Vidal capable of love, I ask her. "He adored his mother. In later life he would defend her to hilt," says Straight. I ask whether he loved her. "I haven't any idea. I think he loved me as the printed word crept out from me on the page towards him and he started to read me." She smiles. "I did love some of his lines, like when he described John Lindsay [former US congressman and New York Mayor] as "destiny's tart."

Norberto Nierras called Fabian Bouthillette in March 2012

and told him he should go to the hospital. "I brought the beginning of my book I'm writing about him with me. He was awake and had pneumonia. He'd lost a ton of weight. He told me to keep going with the book, and we talked about the Occupy Wall Street movement: he said it was 'chic.' I got teary and told him I loved him and that he had made me a man."

"I went to Cedars three times," recalls Scotty Bowers. "He was unconscious and looked like he was dead. I held his hand and kissed him, but he didn't know I was there. There was a tube in his stomach feeding him, poor baby." After two months in Cedars, Vidal went home. "I saw him there and he was totally unconscious," says Bowers. "I held his hand and said, 'Gore, you sweetheart, to think what a great on the ball guy you were, it's really sad to see you like this, poor baby.' Some people are dull in life, but for someone that sharp to end like that…" Bowers's voice clots and he tears up.

"I saw Gore in the hospital, then at home," recalls Matt Tyrnauer. "He had pneumonia and couldn't speak very well. He held my hand, which was very atypical, squeezed it. He said something I couldn't hear that sounded sarcastic, which was reassuring. I think I told him I loved him, which he wouldn't have liked. I didn't get an 'I love you' in return. But everything is relative. A faint squeeze of the hand was more than sufficient."

Near the end of his life when Vidal was in Cedars Sinai hospital, Jean Stein, by then estranged from him, sent him flowers. "I understand from Norberto that when he saw them he said, 'From my ex.' When I heard that, it made me smile and forgive him." Vidal's friend Barbara Howar says, "His legend mattered to him, not his longevity. If he cared about dying, he would have stayed sober. I saw him falter when Barbara Epstein died [in June 2006]. He squeezed my hand and said, 'You're my favorite Barbara now.' I don't think he was ever depressed. He drank because people bored him."

Susan Sarandon went to see Vidal in the hospital a few times. "He had lost so much weight. He had had his lungs drained and seemed a skeleton of himself. But Ernie had people coming in and chanting or playing the cello. One time I was there, there was an infomercial on TV about butt-firming. 'Oh, those butts are still there,' Gore said." Later she called him. "He was hoping to make the opening of *The Best Man* in New York [which he didn't manage to]. In other calls "he sometimes seemed confused" to Sarandon, although she relayed the news that *The Best Man* had been nominated for the Tony for Best Revival at the 2012 awards; the Tony was eventually won by *Death of a Salesman*.

Claire Bloom says that "Gore was wonderfully taken care of by Ernie, who deserves every credit for keeping him alive and getting him to the hospital." Jay Parini says Burr Steers, given all Vidal had put him through, was a "saint" as his uncle's condition deteriorated. Bloom and her daughter spent ten days in L.A. two months before he died. "We went to the hospital. It was a great shock, but he recognized Anna and me immediately and he occasionally spoke. There was a marvelous performer from the Beverly Hills Hotel, who after finishing performing for the night, would bring his keyboard to the hospital and play all the tunes Gore and Howard had loved. I didn't think it was possible that one could look as he did and survive that much longer, but we were assured that there was hope. But we both knew in our hearts we wouldn't see him again."

Amid the gathering gloom there were laughs. When Patty Dryden was at the house one day, Vidal's blanket fell off his knees and Dryden went to scoop it up, realizing her hands were suddenly covered in excrement. "Gore, I don't know if this is you or your cat," she said. He "just howled with laughter." "Mr. Vidal always slept with Baby Brown, the cat," Nierras said. Baby Brown died around six months before Vidal. "Mr. Vidal was very, very sad when he died. That night he was very quiet and very sad," recalls Nierras. When the cat died, "I don't think he felt there was much to carry on living for," says Dryden.

Burr Steers recalls that in his last months, Vidal "was all twisted up, his brain had gone. You heard him drowning from the inside. He had all this fluid that was filling up inside him. You heard his lungs. They'd drain him every day and there was tons of fluid coming out of him. He had congestive heart failure, so that was all leaking. It was really miserable. In the last couple of months he was gone. The only thing he reacted to was pain. He didn't like being touched or cleaned, so when they tried to do that he'd go, 'Oh nooooooo' then be out completely. His eyes were open but he was struggling to breathe. But his body didn't give up. The doctors said it was as strong as an ox, considering he was so sedentary. He was drinking in the hospital. He was in such a miserable state for such a long time. His eyes were open but there was no recognition. They would clean him, he'd go, "Argggh,' seem to focus, then drift off again. Pain was the only thing that brought him around."

The last conversation Norberto Nierras had with him was in the hospital. "After that he could only look at me. He would give me a little smile which made me feel really sad. He wanted to talk to me but couldn't. I'm a Catholic. In the last month, I said, 'Mr. Vidal, I will pray for you.'" Vidal "so wanted" to go home and he did, says Claire Bloom. "He was so vital, it's even harder to accept his death than that of someone less vital. He was much more a man than most men. If he had survived for longer than he did for any length of time I don't think he would have had any quality of life."

Steers bought his two young daughters, Katharine and Theodosia, the latter "named after the daughter of Aaron Burr," Steers says. "The only thing he ever pushed me for was to name her that, which I'll tell her when she curses me as a teenager. The girls seemed to calm him." Vidal cherished his family, says Steers. When Katharine was three months old, suffering from meningitis and hearing loss, her father took her to Ravello for the first time. "Gore was very attentive and doting and a grandfatherly figure to them. It made what happened to him in the last two years really tough. At the end I don't think it was him. Gore, in his right mind, and I were family. He was so instrumental and encouraging to me in my life. My sense is he regretted not achieving something politically: because of his grandfather, living up to his image, because of power, because of the Kennedys."

Jay Parini was with Vidal days before he died. "I held his

hand, he nodded, he seemed very vague. 'Well, you'll be pleased to know the *New York Times* is still the *New York Times*,' I said, about some silly story." On the last occasions he saw his uncle, as Vidal lay dying in the living room of Outpost Drive, Burr Steers held Vidal's hand and "forced myself to say what I needed to say to him, that everything I had done I had done to help him, that I loved him, that I had always admired him and how much he meant to me. I'd take his hand and he'd grip mine. There was a sweet and sad look on his face. His death didn't need to be as bad as it was."

When Vidal died, says Norberto Nierras, "his eyes were open and I asked the doctor if we could close them. His color changed right away: he was pale already and he went grayish." Just as Vidal planned, his ashes are interred at his joint plot with Austen's at Rock Creek Cemetery in Washington, equidistant between the final resting places of Jimmie Trimble and Henry Adams. In his Los Angeles home, for the first nine days after his death Norberto Nierras lit a candle next to a picture of Vidal, though he says he doesn't feel Vidal's presence at Outpost Drive.

Epilogue

Unfinished Business

At the time of writing, July 2013, nothing had progressed or been "anywhere near resolved" in Nina Straight's challenge to her brother's wish to leave his entire estate to Harvard University. "Things in my life take a long, rigorous amount of time," she told me drily. In 1974, Vidal told *Gay Sunshine* magazine his epitaph would be: "When I die, I'm going to take you all with me." He certainly left confusion and not a little bitterness. Why didn't Vidal leave anything to his family, I ask Straight. "Because he liked what he wasn't. He had contempt for some of us and on the other hand resentment." Did blood family mean anything to him? "Except for bragging rights?" She shakes her head and adds softly: "He was always very kind. If you had serious problems you could come and talk to him."

When I inquired with the university directly, Harvard was keen to emphasize it was not taking part in the unfolding legal proceedings. "The University has been provided with notice of an interest under Mr. Vidal's testamentary plan and is aware of ongoing proceedings related to it, but is not involved in those proceedings and awaits resolution of all issues," a university spokesman said. "The University can offer no further comment at this time."

There is an irony, as well as mystery, to Vidal's bequest. "He had an incredible insecurity about not having gone to university," says Jay Parini. "It half drove him mad on many levels. He was terrified of professors and academics, When he got an honorary degree from Brown he was thrilled. But he was such a good actor, he could go into a room and intimidate a group of academics." In 1974 Vidal told *Fag Rag* magazine that he was "supposed" to have gone to Harvard, but went into the army at seventeen and got out at twenty. "What was the point of going into another institution when I had already written my first novel?" He lectured at Harvard when his classmates from school were undergraduates there, "the greatest moment of my life," he said in 1974. "I mean, I really rubbed it in. It's all been downhill since." Perhaps leaving everything to Harvard was intended as the ultimate statement of his dominance.

As the will currently stands, Nina Straight says, Harvard not only receives all of Vidal's estate and fortune, but also profits from the continued sales of his books, as under the terms of Vidal's will the Gore Vidal copyright remains with them; Straight intends to ask Harvard if some arrangement could be reached where her son's daughters receive some monies. Through "bad handling" of the estate so far, she claims around seven million dollars has been "wasted." She is angry he was "allowed to die weighing only ninety pounds. It's a sad, pathetic situation, in sync with a Greek tragedy. He didn't want to admit he was dying, or given all the things he cared so much about—family structure, class—willing to say to his family, 'I give you the house, I'll leave something for the kids.'"

Vidal "didn't give a shit" about Harvard," says Boaty Boatwright over Vidal's bequest. "He didn't have any ties to Harvard. Why not fund a Gore Vidal School for Young Writers or a Foundation for Women? He was always championing feminism. He just got angry at the end and couldn't take it with him. I guess Harvard struck his fancy as a snobby intellectual academic Ivy League college. He was one of the few people not to have to go to university to be brilliantly educated." Perhaps, then, the bequest is an act of vengeful vindication: in *Gore Vidal: The United States of Amnesia*, Vidal says he had been accepted into Harvard as a young man, but had turned the offer down to write instead. The bequest shows his final mastery, the correctness of his choice to write, the rightness of his original snub not to study at the most blue-chip of Ivy League universities; a snub Harvard cannot return when it comes to housing the great Vidal's papers. Of course it wants them. Now he has imposed himself on them as a benefactor. Vidal wins.

One acquaintance says it is Vidal's lawyers who were behind Vidal's bequest—that they had lobbied Vidal and opened channels of communication with the university before the will was changed. Vidal's estate declined to co-operate with this book, or address any questions I sent them. A more prosaic explanation for Vidal's bequest is that it is the culmination of a late-in-life relationship with Harvard that Vidal had formed. Vidal already had a relationship with the university's Houghton Library since it took possession of his papers in 2002. His entire archive and all his printed works are housed there, alongside the papers of writers including Henry Adams, Sarah Orne Jewett, Louisa May Alcott and John Ashberry.

At the time, Harvard said the acquisition had been precipitated by "a recent chance meeting" between James Walsh, Houghton's retired keeper of printed books, and Vidal. "Walsh took a trip sponsored by the Boston Athenæum to Italy... Author and bibliophile spent the afternoon conversing and an idea was born. According to Vidal, he was already seriously considering Harvard as a repository for his papers as a result of conversations about the nature of his work with former Harvard professor and Lincoln scholar David Herbert Donald. Houghton Library has long been regarded as a major repository for 19th and 20th century literary papers, and Vidal felt it was an appropriate place for his collection."

Did Vidal see Harvard as the best place to safeguard his legacy? In his 1970 autobiographical novel *Two Sisters*, the narrator V writes ambiguously of a desire for legacy. "I shouldn't have thought that I was the sort who would want world fame at any price. Yet I suppose I do want something of me to last." To documentarian Nicholas Wrathall, Vidal said of the notion of a legacy, "I couldn't care less." Nina Straight tells me that Vidal himself had little sense of leaving a legacy. One night, after they had seen a Shakespeare production, she turned to him and said, "Wouldn't it be fabulous for Shakespeare to somehow see his works still being performed?" Vidal replied, "Do you think Shakespeare gives a shit, do you think Shakespeare gives a damn, up there tonight, saying 'Oh my, what a great revival.' It's the here and now, that's all there is." Her half-brother felt the same way about his own work: "No one's keeping score." So, he wouldn't have cared about a Foundation or library? "No, there was only the 'Gore Vidal' in his own mind and after that, nothing. His works? He didn't give a damn. He cared that his books carried on selling, but didn't live his life thinking about leaving a legacy."

It saddened many of Vidal's friends that he wasn't included in the "In Memoriam" section of the 2013 Oscars, given his Hollywood career. "But he was in good company, neither were Andy Griffith, Larry Hagman and Ben Gazzara," says Boaty Boatwright. In Ravello, Vidal's much-treasured La Rondinaia stands in disrepair. Its owners are struggling to unite on a plan to renovate the approximately nine thousand square meter property into a luxury rental. They may now sell. The pool, once the site of parties and suppers, is now filled with dead fish with bruised purple backs hovering beneath the dark green surface. Abandoned sun chairs lie by the side of the pool.

Inside, the house looks like a building site. The cavernous entrance-way with its wide stairwell is filled with bags of work materials. A tiled kitchen stands in disrepair. Wires and work tools are scattered throughout. The two men's bedrooms on the lower floor connect on either side to a now-empty studio, all with spectacular views of the coast. Vidal's room with its old yellow and brown tiles is stacked with small wooden furniture Vidal left behind. Other rooms contain old books and photos and odds and ends left when he returned to Los Angeles. Upstairs, much of his office remains intact, with rows of wooden book shelves still containing his literature and an old wooden desk and typewriter in the center facing the wall and not the ocean. Owner Vincenzo Palumbo intends to keep it this way. A picture of Jimmie Trimble still sits on Vidal's desk. "He said the only love of his life was a young person who died in the war," says Palumbo, who promised Vidal a room would be kept at La Rondinaia "as a museum to him"; this will most likely be this office.

There is a passage at the end of Vidal's novel *Burr*, in which Aaron Burr tells his son Charlie that he regrets not fulfilling his political ambitions, but he has led a fulfilled life and helped boys mature. For Fabian Bouthillette "that's the Gore I remember: a leader, a mentor. I was the last one he helped." Bouthillette's proudest moment was at the House of Commons in London where Vidal, having misplaced half a speech, asked him to address the audience of politicians instead as "head of one of the leading war veterans' associations in America." Bouthillette says, "I miss him. But I was relieved. He really was a warrior. He had that spirit and charm. He had the strongest mental constitution of anyone I know. I will stay loyal to him and his legacy forever."

Vidal's significance in gay-literary, cultural and political terms, his status as a radical, an icon, a key gay figure, remains vexed—not least because of his defiant opposition to being categorized as gay in the first place.

After his death, the novelist Bruce Benderson posted an appreciation of Vidal on Facebook that was both withering and celebratory, acute in its criticism of Vidal, while acknowledging the psychological complexity of the author. "Shut up, Gore Vidal, and rest in peace for once. I'm in awe that we've lived to see the demise of that energetic old whore, a Wife of Bath who lived as long as Methuselah and still coveted the limelight. A lousy novelist, because he refused to take second seat to his characters, as all novelists must do, and a provocative essayist, who put strategically sensationalist political commentary that he didn't really believe in at the service of his narcissism and grandiosity—to the great delight of all his readers, including me. 'Gore is a man without an unconscious,' his friend the Italian writer Italo Calvino once said. Mr. Vidal said of himself: 'I'm exactly as I appear. There is no warm, lovable person inside. Beneath my cold exterior, once you break the ice, you find cold water.' May you have the last laugh, you old curmudgeon, and finally get a little peace of mind."

However, Michelangelo Signorile, radio show host and editor-at-large of the *Huffington Post*'s Gay Voices section, said that Vidal's beliefs on homosexual "acts vs. orientation were pretty 19th-century, pre-Oscar Wilde." Reviewing Signorile's 1993 book, *Queer in America: Sex, The Media, and the Closets of Power*, Vidal rejected the notion of a gay movement organized around identity, while—Vidal's radical gay heartbeat asserting itself—agreeing with Signorile that "To be within the closet is to admit that to be a fag is the most evil thing that anyone can be."

Gays should balance Vidal's rejection of labels with the social (and for so many gay men of that era, personal) importance of *The City and the Pillar*, wrote Signorile, and Vidal's own openness around the sex he had with men as well as first-hand knowledge of a homophobic culture, when Buckley called him a "queer" on television. He rejected labels like "gay" and "transgender," but, writes Signorile, "interestingly, there's a whole new generation of gender-variant and queer people who don't use any of those labels, either. There are many trans people who don't want to label themselves 'male' or 'female,' and there are more and more young people who find 'gay', 'lesbian' or 'bisexual' too confining and limiting. So was Gore Vidal really a relic of the past, or was he way ahead of his time? We'll probably be talking about that for a long time to come."

Sean Strub says, "*The City and the Pillar* was powerful for us, and he was never a hypocrite, there wasn't an ounce of hypocrisy within him. He was intellectually fierce. I don't feel disappointed by him." The author and "It Gets Better" activist Dan Savage, asked by the *New York Times* in June 2013 which author he wanted to meet, dead or alive, replied that it would be Vidal. "I admire his range, his passion and the rate at which he cranked out work. Novels, essays, plays. My process is very, very slow, and I am in awe of writers like Vidal. I'm in awe of writers who write like it's what they, you know, actually do for a damn living. I don't think writing comes easy to anyone. Writing is a painful process. But some writers have a higher tolerance for pain. It makes me jealous. Also, *United States*, a collection of Vidal's essays (including "The Birds and the Bees," which I consider one of the best essays ever written about sex), was the first gift I gave to Terry after we started dating."

Christopher Bram lauds Vidal as a literary and social figure. When Capote died in 1984, Vidal famously quipped that it was "a good career move," Bram says. "He was right. Capote spent his last decade as a complete mess, which got in the way of his literary reputation. Only after he died could people see again that he was sometimes a wonderful writer. The last years of Vidal's life were not nearly as ugly as Capote's, but they come close. He became mean, predictable, and charmless. Now that he's gone, I hope we can rediscover Gore Vidal all over again: the good Gore, the glorious Gore. He wrote some of the best essays in the English language since Orwell. He created two wonderful, startlingly different novels in *Myra Breckinridge* and *Burr*. He spoke truth to power with wit, charm and honesty. He was like the loud, original, exhausting guest whom we don't fully appreciate until he's left the party. We will miss his energy and humor and electric point of view."

His friends are left with a range of emotions, from warmth to sadness, anger to confusion. Claire Bloom tells me, "He'd had a fantastic life. Nobody could have had a richer life, with his work, travel, friendships and Howard, the beautiful places he lived in." Susan Sarandon also observes that sweetness of him. "He was probably the most romantic, idealistic and sweetest man I ever met: scratch beneath the surface of the biggest cynic and you'll find a romantic underneath, and he so was about this country and the republic he wished it was. He was a puritan about that. I miss him, but the voice of what he said goes on. Who replaces that? It's a loss for everyone, I think."

Others remain in awe of Vidal's achievements. Steven Abbott says he wrote Vidal's bibliography "because of my decades-long appreciation of the work of and my personal relationship with this influential man. Vidal's contributions to twentieth-century literature, letters, and political thought as an author, prognosticator, actor, celebrity, and prescient political analyst since 1940 are awe inspiring." In writing the Bibliography, he "recorded and documented this extraordinary body of work and took a fascinating journey through almost seventy years of American and foreign literature, culture and publishing."

Arlyne Reingold would like Harvard to allow her access to

some of Austen's possessions: a ruby ring he wore, a belt buckle, some of the recordings of him singing, and pictures of her family, particularly a collage Austen made of their father's old driving licenses: "Why would they want that?" she asks.

Scotty Bowers's voice breaks when he talks about missing Vidal. "He was a wonderful guy, nice guy, a sweet guy, an all-American guy, he was pissed off a lot at the way the country was run. My thoughts of Gore will always be great. I think of him all the time, every day. He was a sweetheart, one hundred percent." Bowers is keeping alive the Vidal tradition of "no-labels" when it comes to enjoying sex. "The last time I had sex with a guy was a week ago, a ninety-five-year-old. I still have sex with several younger men too. Lois [his wife] is cool: I don't go into detail."

For a bruised and still-traumatized Burr Steers, "I need to get back into my life and things." The most hurtful omission in Vidal's will, his family and friends agree, regards Nierras. "Norberto is not getting anything and he was devoted to Gore," says Steers. "He could have left Gore several times but didn't, and now has to figure out how to move back to the Philippines on his pension because he didn't get anything. Also Gore wanted a foundation to fight against those who would diminish the Constitution. It doesn't look like that will happen." Nierras, solicitous and humble as he is, also hoped his long service and devotion might be acknowledged by Vidal: "I'm sixty six years old and had planned to stay with Mr. Vidal until I retired. I will have to go back to the Philippines, I cannot afford to stay in America. I didn't expect he'd leave me anything, other people are surprised he didn't. If Mr. Vidal did leave me something I would be very, very grateful as it would help with my retirement in the Philippines, as I have a small pension."

Patty Dryden says of Vidal's behavior, "I'm so angry with him, Norberto was the most loyal person in his life. There were people in his life, like Norberto, who he could have helped and he didn't." His former editor Jason Epstein sighs when I ask how it felt when he heard Vidal had died. "I wished I could summon up the appropriate feelings when he died, but I couldn't. I'm a little like Gore. Once something is done, I cut myself off from it to protect myself."

Vidal died as he had lived—trickily, complicatedly, stubbornly but with love around him despite his best efforts to ward it off. Even though he had once been estranged, Abbott, his bibliographer, reconnected with Vidal. During our interview, Abbott cried when talking about missing Vidal and what he meant. After our meeting, Abbott emails me: "I had this dream about Gore shortly after his death. I was staying with him and went out for a walk. When I came back to the house, there was an open door and through the door I saw Gore sitting in a room alone in a chair. He looked quite frail. I went in and asked how he was, and he said he was cold, so I asked him if he would like a blanket or some hot chocolate. He gave me that look that he often gave when you asked about him...both appreciative and wary. I went to make the hot chocolate.

"When I returned he was wearing a tweed overcoat, and he handed me a duplicate of his overcoat which was folded and very heavy, and strangely I remember worrying about my skin reaction to wool and wondered if the coat had been his or Howard's and why he was giving it to me. Gore then asked me to build a fire in another room which had a gigantic fireplace with a few embers left burning and handed me two pieces of wood. I stacked the wood, crinkled and added some newspapers, stoked the fire, and we sat watching the flames. As I woke up, I felt gratitude, loss, and sadness. I was missing him and crying. I took an early morning bike ride through Provincetown and then a walk through the dunes to the beach."

Was he happy, I asked Vidal when I interviewed him in 2009. "What a question," he sighed, then smiled mischievously. "I'll respond with a quote from Aeschylus: 'Call no man happy till he is dead.'" If that leaves Vidal in too warm and cuddly a resting place, imagine instead the icy contrarian who, upon alighting from a cab in New York with his friend Diana Phipps Sternberg responded to the cab driver's entreaty to "Have a nice day," with: "No thank you, I've made other plans."

Bibliography

BOOKS

By Dennis Altman:

Defying Gravity: a political life (Allen & Unwin, 1997)
Gore Vidal's America (Polity, 2005)

Full Service: My Adventures in Hollywood and the Secret Sex Lives of the Stars—Scotty Bowers (Grove Press, 2012)

Eminent Outlaws: The Gay Writers Who Changed America—Christopher Bram (Hachette, 2012)

Sleeping with Bad Boys—Alice Denham (Book Republic Press, an imprint of Cardozo Publishing, 2006)

Hollywood Gays—Boze Hadleigh (Barricade Books, 1996)

By Christopher Isherwood:

Lost Years: A Memoir, 1945-1951—ed. Katherine Bucknell (Chatto and Windus, 2000)
Diaries Volume One, 1939-1960—ed. Katherine Bucknell (Michael Di Capua Books/HarperCollins, 1997)
The Sixties, Diaries Volume Two, 1960-1969—ed. Katherine Bucknell (HarperCollins, 2010)
Liberation, Diaries Volume Three, 1970-1983—ed. Katherine Bucknell (HarperCollins, 2012)

Gore Vidal: A Biography—Fred Kaplan (Doubleday, 1999)

The Diaries of Kenneth Tynan—ed. John Lahr (Bloomsbury, 2001)
Original Story By: A Memoir of Broadway and Hollywood—
   Arthur Laurents (Knopf, 2000)

Kate: The Woman Who Was Hepburn—William J. Mann
   (Henry Holt & Company, 2006)

By Ned Rorem:

Knowing When to Stop: A Memoir (Simon and Schuster, 1994)
Lies: A Diary, 1986-1999 (Da Capo Press, 2002)

Body Counts: A Memoir of Politics, Sex, AIDS and Survival—
   Sean Strub (to be published by Scribner in January 2014)

By Gore Vidal:

The City and the Pillar (E.P. Dutton & Co., 1948; Vintage, 2003)
The Judgment of Paris (E.P. Dutton & Co., 1952; Da Capo Press,
   2007)
Myra Breckinridge (Little, Brown 1968; Penguin Twentieth
   Century Classics, 1997)
Two Sisters (William Heinemann, 1970)
Burr (Random House, 1973, Modern Library edition, 1998)
The Second American Revolution and Other Essays, 1976-1982
   (Vintage Books, 1983)
Palimpsest: a memoir (Random House, 1995)
Sexually Speaking: Collected Sex Writings, ed. Donald Weise
   (Cleis Press, 1999)
Point to Point Navigation: a memoir 1964-2006 (Vintage, 2006)

ARTICLES

"The Importance of Being Gore," Andrew Kopkind, *The Nation*,
   July 5, 1993

"I regret nothing," Gore Vidal interview, Robert Chalmers, the *Independent on Sunday*, May 25, 2008

"We'll have a dictatorship soon in the US," Gore Vidal interview, Tim Teeman, *The Times of London*, September 30, 2009

"Gore Vidal Dies at 86; Prolific, Elegant, Acerbic Writer," Charles McGrath, the *New York Times*, August 1, 2012

"Postscript: Gore Vidal," Hilton Als, *New Yorker*, August 2, 2012

"On his father's old nemesis, Gore Vidal," Christopher Buckley, *New Republic*, August 2, 2012

"My Lunch at the Dorchester with Gore Vidal," Adam Mars-Jones, *The Guardian*, August 3, 2012

"Gore Vidal: Certainly Not The Last Word on a Proud 'Fag,'" Michelangelo Signorile, *Huffington Post*, August 8, 2012

"Gore Vidal/Jonathan Ned Katz correspondence, April 28, 1982-2001," from outhistory.org, August 2012

"The Gore They Loved," Judy Balaban, *Vanity Fair*, February 2013

"On the Other Side of Eternity," N.A. Straight, vanityfair.com, February 6, 2013

A Café in Space: The Anaïs Nin Literary Journal, volume 10, February 6, 2013, Kim Krizan; via The Anaïs Nin Blog

"Dan Savage: By the Book," Sunday Book Review, *New York Times*, June 27, 2013

ARCHIVE MATERIAL

From Gore Vidal's archive at the Houghton Library, Harvard University: correspondence from Howard Austen, Susan Sarandon, Claire Bloom, Vidal Sassoon, Christopher Hitchens, Christopher Isherwood, Princess Margaret, Muriel Spark (and letters to her from Vidal), Paul Newman, Anaïs Nin, Hugh Steers, Tom Driberg, Tennessee Williams, Christine White via Val Holley and from activist groups, including the Mattachine Society and the Gay Activists Alliance. Letters to Jay Blotcher and Judy Halfpenny. Call numbers: MS Am 2350 (840, 842, 910, 915, 994, 995, 1301, 1367, 1368, 1369, 1370, 1431, 1434, 1440, 1469, 1499-1504, 1550, 1561, 1627, 1639, 1767, 1772-1775, 1915, 1938, 1939, 1961, 1992, 2008, 2009, 2226, 2239, 2240).

Also at the Houghton Library, from Tennessee Williams's papers, Series I: Compositions, 242.

Correspondence and papers from the Claire Bloom Collection, Howard Gotlieb Archival Research Center at Boston University; permission to use material kindly given by Claire Bloom.

From the National Film Information Service/Margaret Herrick Library at the Academy of Motion Picture Arts and Sciences in Los Angeles: *The Celluloid Closet*—interviews (Telling Pictures records); Curtis Harrington Papers: Journal, 1953-1961; and Mike Connolly collection, compiled by Val Holley.

About the Author

Tim Teeman is a journalist and broadcaster. For fourteen years he has worked as an editor, feature writer, and interviewer for *The Times of London*, most recently as their US Correspondent, in which he covered stories like Hurricane Sandy and profiled many celebrities and public figures including Woody Allen, George Clooney, and Liza Minnelli. He has also contributed to publications including *Elle*, *The New Statesman*, *The Guardian*, *The Independent*, *Independent on Sunday*, *Attitude*, and *Time Out*. *In Bed With Gore Vidal* is his first book. He lives in New York City.